LONGFORD:

A Village in Limbo

LONGFORD:

A Village in Limbo

Wendy Tibbitts

© Wendy Tibbitts, 2022

Published by Historio Publications

A CIP catalogue record for this book is available from the British Library.

ISBN 978-1-7390822-0-8

Disclaimer:
Every effort has been made to contact copyright holders; any omissions are inadvertent and will be corrected in future editions if notification of the amended credit is sent to the publisher in writing.

Book layout and cover design by Clare Brayshaw

Cover photo 197041857 © Denys Bilytskyi I Dreamstime.com

Prepared and printed by:

York Publishing Services Ltd
64 Hallfield Road
Layerthorpe
York YO31 7ZQ

Tel: 01904 431213

Website: www.yps-publishing.co.uk

Contents

Introduction

Longford is a strange village. There is no church, or school, and in the past no official governance in the form of a vicar or Lord of the Manor. To be accurate Longford is not really a village, but a hamlet of Harmondsworth whose parish centre is a mile away. Longford is the last Middlesex village on the western edge of Greater London; a rural settlement long before it gained its Saxon name. This village grew and prospered despite a population with contradictory values. The non-conformist farmers with high moral principles survived alongside rogues, highwaymen, lawbreakers, and drunks. This was not a village cut off from the wider world and existing in isolation. This was once a bustling community that saw humanity in all its forms pass in front of its windows along the only road through the village – the Great Bath Road. This well-known highway, to Windsor, Reading, Bath and Bristol, carried Kings and Queens and the British elite, as well as rogues, vagabonds and itinerants. Now, the future of Longford is under threat.

On the evening of 25 June 2018, Members of the British Parliament voted 415 to 119 to approve the expansion of Britain's main international airline hub at Heathrow. The following day Transport Secretary Chris Grayling formally approved the National Policy Statement, allowing the Heathrow airport authorities to begin the planning process.

The expansion plan included the demolition of most of the buildings in the parish of Harmondsworth and the loss of 783 homes.[1] The two local Members of Parliament had, as expected, both been vocal in their opposition to any Heathrow expansion. The constituency labour MP was John McDonnell, Labour Shadow Chancellor (2015-2020). The Member of Parliament for neighbouring Uxbridge and South Ruislip constituency,

[1] Airports Commission: Final Report https://www.gov.uk/government/publications/airports-commission-final-report

Boris Johnson, was then Foreign Secretary and later Prime Minister (2019-2022). Obviously, both these influential parliamentarians from the two main political parties had the interests of their constituents as their main concern, but the majority of Parliamentarians were voting on the wider interests of the nation.

The white area is the compulsory purchase zone.

However, for the village of Harmondsworth and its two hamlets, Longford and Sipson, the decision was more personal. Most families were going to lose their homes. Harmondsworth, mentioned in the Domesday Book, has 19 listed buildings, including a Norman church and a historic medieval barn. Over half of the village centre would be demolished although the new plans are careful to leave just these two relics of history untouched on the edge of the new runway. For the hamlet of Longford, with eleven listed buildings, the third runway would mean total demolition.

The day after the monumental vote in the House of Commons, Longford was in all the newspapers as the news media reported the new runway plans with the use of maps and statistics. Some sent reporters and photographers, and interviewed disgruntled residents. Some newspapers used library pictures of aircraft, on their approach to the runway, flying over the Longford rooftops with their undercarriages down. To the casual observer this might suggest Longford is a noisy blighted rural village of no importance, but that is not the full story. No enquirers seemed aware of the depth of history contained in this small village; a village that had a life and soul centuries before the building of a nearby military airport in 1944.

A recent photograph of an aircraft flying over Chapel cottages and the former Baptist Chapel at Longford. (photo credit: Press Association).

The story of the village, its inns, travellers, and inhabitants, illustrates a bygone age of rural life with its customary obligations and class-consciousness. Class and religion culturally divided the population. The farmers and employers were non-conformist gentlemen farmers, who expected their employees to follow their example, but who managed to live in harmony with the secular service providers of the hospitality trade. The farming methods and animal husbandry had remained the same for centuries, but as the agricultural market changed, the Longford farmers adapted to the demands of the market. Sheep and arable farming evolved into market gardening. Orchards were planted and in later years pig and poultry farming were adopted. For all of the cultural differences to our modern way of thinking, there were also similarities in individual characteristics. There were still chancers, opportunist thieves, dilettantes, and rogues.

Longford village evolved in its present form sometime after the Romans left Britain around AD 400 and the country was wide open to invasion. The Saxon invaders settled in the forests of south-east England and gave their settlements Saxon names, and the area came to be called 'Middle Saxon' which evolved into the name Middlesex. The forest was cleared and the farming community of Longford made good use of the River Colne and its tributaries by building a mill, which was listed in the Domesday Book of 1086. Recent extensive excavations in the immediate area, carried out before the building of Heathrow's Terminal 5, have traced settlements in the area back to 1500 BC.[2] This area, with its flat terrain and the easily cultivated fertile soil, has been continuously farmed since that time.

The village of Longford was also on the edge of Hounslow Heath, a large flat barren area of 4000 acres on the western edge of London, which needed to be crossed in order to travel westwards.[3]

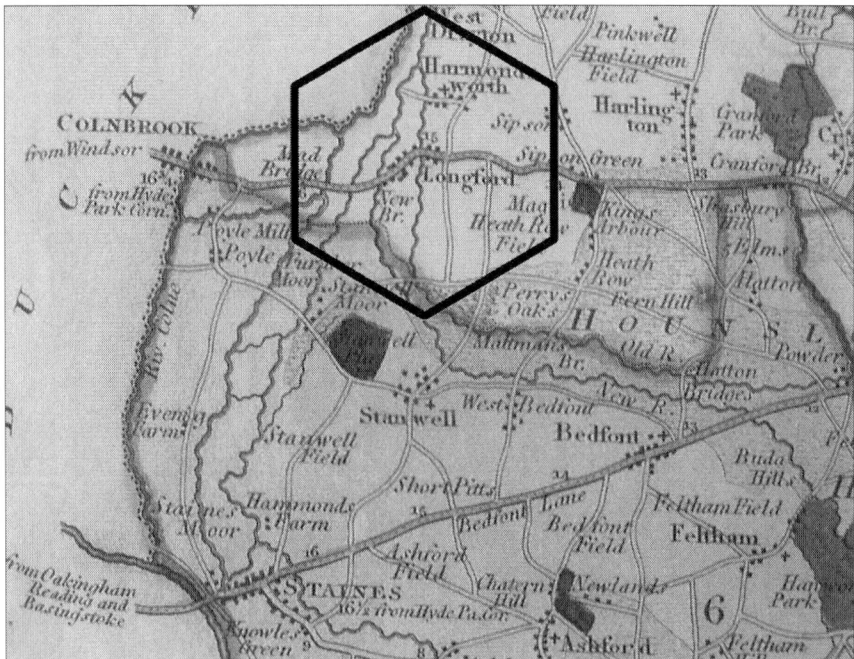

The area of the former heath. Teesdale's map of Middlesex 1829

2   Framework Archaeology unpublished report series. *wessexar1-10180.pdf (4 MB)*

3   Susan Reynolds (Editor). "Heston and Isleworth: Hounslow Heath." A History of the County of Middlesex: Volume 3: Shepperton, Staines, Stanwell, Sunbury, Teddington, Heston and Isleworth, Twickenham, Cowley, Cranford, West Drayton, Greenford, Hanwell, Harefield and Harlington (1962): 94-96. British History Online. Web. 03 August 2013. <http://www.british-history.ac.uk/report.aspx?compid=22271&strquery=1545>

When people began to travel more extensively in Tudor times, local roads between villages joined into one continuous route to Bath and Bristol, and by the mid-seventeenth century, it was a stagecoach route known as the Great Bath Road. This prompted the villages along the highway to provide hostelries in order to prosper from the coaching trade. Longford soon had four inns providing services to travellers.

In the days of horsepower, Longford, fifteen miles from London's Hyde Park Corner, was a convenient distance for riders and carriages to stop to change horses. Through the main street passed a kaleidoscope of vehicles and people; from the very rich to the very poor; from soldiers to cattle drovers; from farmers to villains. There were also local vehicles, among them carters taking produce to the London markets and returning with manure from the municipal stables. The Longford hostelries catered for the travellers' needs, whilst the highwaymen and footpads did their best to relieve them of their valuables.

Today, Longford is one of the few remaining villages in Middlesex that has avoided the tendrils of the outward-creeping suburbia of London. It has survived because it is part of the London Green Belt. This halo of verdant countryside around London was designated by law (Green Belt (London and Home Counties) Act 1938) to stop the spread of the London urban development by preserving a ring of nature around the capital – a smog-clearing natural antidote to the dust and grime of suburban living. In modern times, between the wars, there was a frenzy of house building in Middlesex. Large areas of the County's farms became housing estates. The London Green Belt protected Longford from the land grab, but any land that had a road frontage was prey to ribbon development. Alongside the Old Bath Road in Longford there are now a few twentieth century houses between the ancient listed buildings, but the core village, as it is today, would look familiar to the nineteenth century traveller. To preserve this village and its eleven Grade II listed structures and townscape, the London Borough of Hillingdon designated Longford village centre a Conservation Area in 1988. The main Bath Road no longer passes through the village and Longford has become a leafy hidden settlement on the western edge of the London airport complex, with only local traffic allowed to travel through the village.

Longford village 1910

Since the Second World War, with most of the farmland swallowed up by the land-greedy needs of the war-time airport in the hamlet of Heathrow, Longford has lost its agricultural roots and is more residential. Off the main road is a four-acre island surrounded by the river Colne on which was once a productive water mill. Now, on the island, there are uniquely designed cottages of architectural interest alongside the tranquil river.

The story of Longford is a fascinating account of a community of saints and sinners who co-existed in an extraordinary village. The experiences of the people of Longford highlight interesting, but little-known, historical events as well as giving us a glimpse into their homes and their lives. We learn how their lives became shaped by natural, national and international circumstances, and how these experiences brought drama, excitement and pathos to this once vibrant corner of England.

The timetable for the processing of planning applications for the third runway at Heathrow has now been delayed due to the pandemic. In the meantime the village of Longford is in limbo whilst awaiting a final decision on its future. Whether the Heathrow expansion happens or not, Longford has a story to tell which opens a fascinating window into rural life over the last three hundred years.

Longford Building

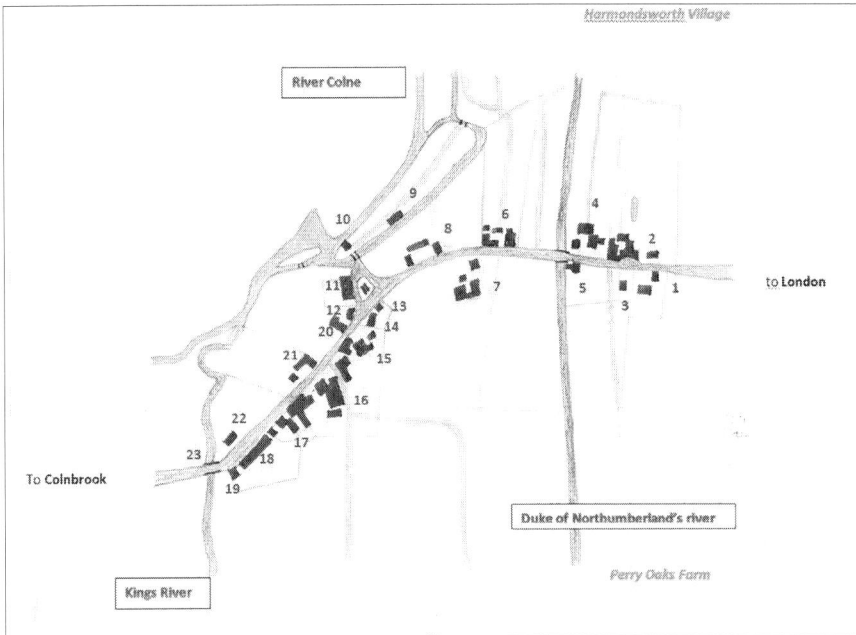

Key to Longford Buildings:

1. Mrs Neal's Sweetshop
2. The King's Head / Peggy Bedford
3. The Quaker Meeting House
4. Riverside farm
5. Riverside Cottage
6. Bays Farm
7. The Orchards / Orchard cottage
8. College Farm
9. The Mill / Colne Cottage
10. Island House
11. The Barracks
12. The White Horse
13. Springbank
14. Yeomans
15. The Forge
16. The Weekly House and The Farm
17. The Kings Arms
18. Wilds Cottages
19. The Shop and Post Office
20. Whites Farm
21. Heath Gardens
22. Zion Baptist Chapel
23. The Kings Bridge

Chapter 1

Out of the Flames (1676)

The journey had been hot and dusty. The cool spring of 1676 had given way to a warm June, which hardened the mud on the road surface. Carriages and carts then turned the mud into choking dust. Approaching the village of Longford, the road surface had been covered with gravel dug from the nearby fields, making 'the way mighty good'.[4] This road, known as the Great Bath Road, took London travellers westwards through the lush fields of Middlesex and, skirting the vast barren openness of Hounslow Heath, until it reached the country village of Longford.

The lone rider, travelling from London on horseback, surveyed the leafy hedges over which blossoming fruit trees decorated the orchards, and many thatched haystacks announced the abundance of the hay harvest. He noticed the grass verges, colourful with wildflowers, and watched as drovers, hay wagons, carriages and other riders, went about their business on this busy road. He was in no hurry. He relished the quietness of the countryside after the noise and bustle of London. He recognised the call of the cuckoo mixed with the sounds of the lapwing, wood-pigeon and crow. Sounds he had not heard since his childhood. He admired the acres of flat, productive, farmland stretching as far as he could see. A mile to the north he could see the cupola on top of the tower of the Norman church of St Mary's at Harmondsworth. To the south was the sharp projection of the spire of Stanwell church reaching towards the clouds; and in the hazy western distance the distinctive shape of Windsor Castle.

---

4   https://www.pepysdiary.com/diary/1668/06/17/ Samuel Pepys travelled through Longford on 17 June 1668 on his way from Bath to London.

The bucolic scene enchanted Thomas Weekly as he entered the village of Longford. It was haymaking time and there was much activity in the fields. Ladders were propped against haystacks as men passed each other sheaves to be stacked, and in the fields, men cutting the grass with the rhythmic swing of scythes and letting the fallen stems lie on the ground to dry. Others were turning the cut dried grass before piling it into carts. Chickens scratched and wandered from the farmyards as he passed and women bustled back and forth in their white aprons with arms full of washing, water or animal feed. This was a community whose whole existence was reliant on horse power and the smell of the horse-manure, left drying where it had fallen on the road, mixed with that of the farm dung-heaps, was more pungent in the summer heat, but unnoticed by country people who were used to this normal background aroma.

Horses were the engines of life. They were the only means of transport. Carthorses pulled the carts in the fields; whilst faster, high-stepping horses pulled the produce-wagons to market. On the highway, a traveller rode a well-shod horse and carriage horses powered their vehicles. Longford appreciated horses. The farrier in the forge, the ostler in the inns, the carters on the farms, all gave their charges the best of care for without them trade and travel would not exist.

Thomas was looking for somewhere to live. Somewhere he could build a home for his new wife and they could settle into a like-minded community to raise their children. He already had a house fifteen miles away in Tothill Street, Westminster, and was a successful merchant trading in sugar and other high-priced commodities from the West Indies, but on 26 May 1676, just a month after his marriage, a catastrophe had occurred. The winter and spring, although cold, brought no rain, and the same dry conditions that exacerbated the Great Fire of London, ten years earlier, were about to cause another disaster. A small fire at 3am in an oil and paint merchants shop in Borough High Street, Southwark, that Friday morning, would take hold and with timber-dry conditions and a brisk southerly wind the blaze spread though the wooden medieval buildings in the heart of Southwark. It burnt through houses, inns and waterfront warehouses. One of the warehouses belonged to Thomas. After destroying several streets and well-known inns there was panic. People fled their burning houses whilst sightseers poured across London Bridge from the north. The congestion on the streets slowed the arrival of the fire pumps. By the time the flames were licking the walls of St Thomas's Hospital, in the grounds of St. Mary Overy's church (now Southwark cathedral), the lessons learned during the conflagration of a decade earlier had been put in place. King Charles II and his brother the Duke of York supervised the blowing up of houses to make a fire break. After eighteen hours and the destruction of about 500 buildings, the fire was out.[5]

The fire was devastating for Thomas. His warehouse and goods were gone. It would take months to rebuild and replenish his stock from the West Indies. After the shock of losing his business overnight the twenty-five-year-old had to rethink his future.

Thomas was the son of a wealthy non-conformist landowner in Irthlingborough in Northamptonshire and a descendant of John Wycliffe, the Reformer. As a younger son, with no hope of inheriting his father's land, he had been apprenticed to his uncle, a mercer (grocer) in London. The family belonged to the Baptist church which had emerged early in the seventeenth century, and both Thomas and his wife, Ann, were ensconced in church life. After thinking through his predicament, he came to the conclusion that the Southwark fire was a sign from God that he should take another path in life.

Thomas had already spent some of his profits on land in Middlesex where he had installed a tenant. West Middlesex land, so close to London, was an excellent place to grow many crops, which found a ready market in the streets of London. The level terrain and the fast-draining brick earth, known to geologists as the Taplow Terrace Gravel Formation, was described as 'a magnificent soil – easily worked, adequately watered, of very high natural fertility and capable of taking and holding manure. It is a soil fit to be ranked with the world's very

> **John Wycliffe**
>
> **(1320-1384)**
>
> English theologian, biblical translator, reformer, priest, and a seminary professor at the University of Oxford. He became an influential dissident within the Roman Catholic priesthood during the 14th century and is considered an important predecessor to Protestantism.
>
> Wycliffe advocated translation of the Bible into English.
>
> https://en.wikipedia.org/wiki/John_Wycliffe

---

5   L'Strange, Roger. A Faithful accout of the late dreadful fire in Southwark. London: Thomas Pierce, 1676. Early English Books Online Text Creation Partnership, 2011, http:// https://quod.lib.umich.edu/e/eebo2/A85063.0001.001?rgn=main;view=fulltext (accessed 14 February 2022.]

best – a high-class market gardening and orchard soil, also growing fine grass and ordinary farm crops.[6] Thomas was now looking for more land where he could become a farmer and a maltster.

Thomas rode his horse slowly through the village on that sunny June day. In this post-Civil War period, with the restoration of Charles II, there was a new optimism. People were travelling more and Longford was servicing this new trade. Thomas saw a few buildings now under construction with their timber frames infilled with small, locally made, bricks. The labourers' cottages, he noticed, faced the Bath Road with small gardens separating them from the dusty road. The more substantial farmsteads were built gable-end-on the road so that their front doors faced into a yard which housed the stables, outbuildings, and water well. On the busy main road, local traffic mixed with eight carriers a week taking people and goods to and from Windsor and London, as well making space for the long-distance stagecoaches.

The former King's Head. © David Hawgood – geograph.org.uk/p/137591.

As Thomas passed the King's Head inn, built in Tudor times, but already too small for the growing number of travellers needing to change horses and buy refreshments, he saw the ostler barking orders to the stable hands

---

6   Stamp, L.Dudley, 'Land Classification and Agriculture', in Abercrombie (ed.), Greater London Plan 1944. (London, 1945),p.87

and escorting the customers to and from their carriages. Opposite the inn, and laid back from the road, workmen were just finishing the building of a brick and timber Meeting House for the Society of Friends. Longford, with no established church or resident clergy, had been a quiet place for non-conformists to hold clandestine meetings. Members of dissenting groups that emerged after the civil war faced persecution for their beliefs, but now meetings were taking place openly. Initially the plot of land opposite the King's Head was used by the Quakers (or Society of Friends as they preferred to be known) as a burial ground, but now enough money had been raised to build a Meeting House – the first in Middlesex.[7]

The former Friends Meeting House in mid-twentieth century.

It was built in an earlier vernacular style to match the Tudor building opposite. Longford residents and those from around the area were taking full advantage of the new religious freedom. The village was becoming an attractive haven for Quakers and Baptists alike. The villagers, free from interference from the Established church at the Harmondsworth parish centre, could indulge in their non-conformist's beliefs. Most of the farming

7   Beck, W. and Ball, T.F. **London Friends' Meetings**, (1869), p.282, p291.

families were Baptists and just over a mile away in Colnbrook, a parish on the Buckinghamshire side of the River Colne, there was a group of 200 Baptists observing the Strict doctrine of the faith in which Thomas was born. He made his decision there and then to settle in Longford, where he would raise his family,

While Thomas was appraising the village, the people were appraising him. They could see by the way he dressed and the well-bred horse he rode that he was a man of means. His hat, with its high crown and floppy brim adorned with a large bright plume, protected him from the mid-summer sun, and the long braided collarless coat covered by a cloak was deliberately left open to show his lavish lace cravat. The rich embroidery of his garments together with the frilly lace of his cuffs and long leather riding boots marked him as a gentleman. He had the air of authority, but also a quiet demeanor.

Unaware of this scrutiny Thomas felt at home in Longford immediately. The village was vibrant with productivity, and yet a quiet calmness among the inhabitants attracted his attention. He did not know then that there were also hazards associated with living on the edge of the wide-open plains of Hounslow Heath, hazards both natural and man-made, but on his first house-hunting visit his mind was firmly set on his business and family interests.

Chapter 2

Monarchy and Religion (1688-1703)

The sounds of horses, harnesses, and gravel-crunching carriage wheels, travelling along the Great Bath Road were the normal accompaniment to everyday life for the villagers of Longford. However, the sounds they heard on 18 December 1688 went beyond anything they had experienced before. There was a crescendo of noise coming from the town of Colnbrook in the west and getting louder as it neared Longford. The earthy road through the village was frozen hard in the harsh winter weather so the drumming sound of marching feet, soon brought the people from their homes, barns and stables. Mingled with the noise were people's voices, shouting and cheering in jubilation. Soon they saw Dutch soldiers and cavalry coming towards them, and with them English supporters walking by the side of the troops as they proceeded through the village. Along with the horses and soldiers were wagons and carriages, some carrying supplies and others with distinguished-looking people. One carriage contained Prince William of Orange on his way to London to be crowned King of England.

William and his army of 11000 men and 4000 cavalry had landed at Brixham, Devon, on 5 November after being driven back several times by the winter storms. He was travelling to England at the invitation of several government figures who were unhappy with the unpopular Catholic King James II who had succeeded his brother, Charles II. As William of Orange marched towards London, he gathered protestant supporters along the way. Meanwhile, the incumbent King James II was keen to restore the Catholic faith to Britain in opposition to his government's wishes. When King James heard that William of Orange was marching towards the capital he gathered an army of Irish Catholics who were now camped on Hounslow Heath. James ordered his army to stop William's progress towards London and the two armies engaged in the Battle of Reading on 9 December. With the help of the citizens of Reading, who rallied on the side of the invaders, James' army was defeated, and eventually James II fled to France leaving William to make a triumphal journey along the Bath Road through Longford and into London.

* * *

Longford Quaker Meeting House

The grounds had been bought by the local group of The Society of Friends in 1672 as a burial ground and a meeting house was erected in 1676. About 120 people are buried in the grounds which have now been levelled to be used as a private car park.

Now Grade II Listed. Timber-framed cottage of C16 appearance. Gable end to road with added chimney; and another at south end. Tiled roof. Nogging of old narrow bricks. Tiny, gabled west extension. Main east front of 2 storeys, 4 small bays. Stout timbers, swell-head posts, big braces. 1st floor modern casements. Modern porch.

https://britishlistedbuildings.co.uk/england/heathrow-villages-ward-hillingdon

For the non-conformist people of Longford it was a day of rejoicing. The new King William brought hope that there would be complete freedom of worship and the following year, six weeks after his joint coronation with his wife Mary on 11 April, King William III granted the Act of Toleration which allowed dissenters' meeting houses to be legally licensed for worship.

As Thomas Weekly saw, on his first visit to Longford, the Society of Friends (Quakers) had already built a permanent Meeting House in Longford. In 1681, to great excitement, George Fox, the leader of the Society of Friends, visited Longford. George Fox travelled a great deal preaching and meeting Quakers and he remembered the meeting at Longford on 8 September 1681 as 'a large precious meeting where the Lord's presence was preciously felt amongst us.'[8] There were about ten local families attending the Meeting House and many more from other areas of Middlesex. The Quaker and Baptist families lived harmoniously in Longford and the

---

8   Fox, George, Harvey, Thomas Edmund Harvey, *The Short Journals and Itinerary Journals of George Fox: In Commemoration of the Tercentenary of His Birth (1624-1924)*, (Cambridge, 2010)

incumbent of the Rectory in Harmondsworth parish centre, accepted the Christian fellowship of the non-conformists in his parish. Weddings and funerals of Quakers and Baptists alike took place in the Parish Church, but nationally the Established Church still fought hard against the increasing popularity of the Quakers, accusing them of blasphemy and enticing people from the true religion. An anti-Quaker polemic, published in 1702, told of an incident which happened at the Longford Meeting House.[9]

An ironmonger from Abingdon, Berkshire, Mr Whitchurch sat confidently astride his horse as he rode through Longford at noon on a Sunday. He was on his way to London. His wife was not with him. She was a Catholic and spent Sundays worshipping according to her beliefs.

Longford was quiet. It was a day of rest for the labourers, but a group of people leaving the Society of Friends Meeting House aroused Whitchurch's curiosity. As he idly glanced at the people, he saw someone he recognised. A man dressed in the normal plain, unadorned, clothes adopted by Quakers. This man he knew well. He was a catholic priest who visited Whitchurch's wife frequently to administer the sacrament. Halting his horse, he stared for a moment in astonishment not actually believing what he saw. He jumped down from his horse as his anger grew. Pushing his way through the group of Quakers he accosted the man, 'Sir, I beg an explanation. What are you doing here and why are you dressed this way?' The man was dumb-founded. He was many miles from home and thought his secret safe, but now he had been found out. He could give no explanation nor would he exchange angry words, he had seen the light and pacifism was now his creed. Receiving no reply only made Whitchurch angrier. He berated the man for posing as a catholic priest when he had secretly become a member of the Society of Friends. After getting no response from his opponent, Whitchurch gave up questioning the man. He picked up the reins of his horse, walked across the road and pushed through the throng of curious spectators who had emerged from the King's Head Inn at the sound of the angry confrontation.

---

9   This a dramatisation of the story told in: Leslie, Charles, *A Reply to a book [by J. Wyeth] entitul'd, Anguis Flagellatus, or, a Switch for the Snake, the Opus palmare of the Quakers. Being a Second defence, or, the third and last part of the Snake in the Grass.Shewing, that the Quakers are ... self-condemn'd in this their last answer, etc* (C. Brome, 1702).

After handing his reins to the ostler Whitchurch entered the inn and walked up to the spacious bar where he ordered a tankard of ale and some bread and cheese. His hands were shaking with emotion. He had to get over his astonishment and calm his anger before he continued his journey.

* * *

The King's Head early 20th Century.

The King's Head's original Tudor building with its low ceilings, exposed beams and stone floors lay a little way back from the highway. It had been used by travellers for decades, but now it had a new roadside frontage built in 1691 in front of the old structure. Guarding the entrance to the inn until well into the twentieth century were two huge elm trees, reputed to have been planted by Elizabeth I.

The extra accommodation both in the inn and in the stable yard made the hostelry an important staging post for travellers. It had four acres of ornamental gardens, a kitchen garden, stables for sixty horses, cart sheds, and an orchard. As well as the main bar there were other private rooms to be hired, and on the right of the entrance a large, lofty, newly built extensive wood-panelled room with a large fireplace and elaborate china cupboards in each side alcove. The room was known as the Queen Anne room and was sumptuously furnished for the reception of special visitors many of whom were royalty on their way to Windsor. As the Bath Road was the main route to Windsor, Royal carriages and military escorts were a regular sight to the villagers when the incumbent Monarch favoured the Castle as their country retreat. A fresh set of royal horses were stabled at the King's Head ready for the royal carriage. Pulling a heavy carriage was tiring for the horses so every seven miles the team would be changed. Longford, at fifteen miles from Hyde Park corner was the second stage, after Hounslow. Although a common sight, the appearance of a Royal entourage in Longford, with the liveried coachmen, and the cavalry escort, would cause a flurry of excitement in the street. Woman curtsied and men doffed their caps and bowed as a mark of respect as the carriage passed by.

* * *

Queen Anne was a familiar sight in Longford on her way to Windsor to use the State Apartments restored by Charles II, although more frequently she stayed at her more intimate and newly-built Queen's Garden House in the castle grounds.[10]

As Princess Anne she and her husband, Prince George of Denmark, had lived their whole married life in England. Their marriage produced seventeen children who all died through illness, stillbirth or miscarriage. As she got older, with her health failing and her weight increasing, she would visit Bath to take the medicinal water, stopping as usual at Longford to change horses. The journey from London to Bath took three days, but once there the fashionable society would enjoy the social events for months.

Queen Anne had inherited the throne after her widower brother-in-law, King William III, had died with no heirs. After her coronation in 1702 Queen Anne and her husband passed through Longford on their way to Bath and stopped at the King's Head to take refreshment while her horses were changed. The Queen, now aged 37, and overweight, was suffering from gout and could not walk unaided. She stayed in her carriage whilst food and drink were brought to her on a tray, and so the sumptuous new lounge, in her name, at the King's Head remained unseen. When she arrived in Bath, on her first visit as Queen, the Mayor, the Corporation, and a guard of honour of Grenadiers together with 200 dancers greeted her ceremoniously at the West Gate. Queen Anne was a popular monarch and

---

10 The Royal Collection Trust. https://www.rct.uk/visit/windsor-castle/who-lived-at-windsor-castle#/

society wanted to follow her example and visit Bath. This made the road to Bath a busy highway and increased the travelling trade in Longford.

Not only was Queen Anne herself stopping at the King's Head whilst the horses on her carriage were changed, but the new stage-coach services were also making their halts there. This gave plenty of employment for Longford villagers whilst those who were not in service in the inns and stables, were labouring on the farms.

* * *

The farmers and their labourers worked all available daylight hours. There were always jobs to be done. Sundays and Christmas Day were their only respite, but extreme weather would also stop them working in the fields. When the rain or snow prevented ploughing, the labourers would be given jobs like cleaning out barns, stables, or pigeon houses; repairing equipment or oiling the harness. September 1703 was a very wet month and very little fieldwork was done, but by November 1703 the heavy rain had gone and was replaced by a strong wind. By the 24th of the month, squally rain and strong gusts of wind were dislodging chimney pots and roof tiles. The extreme weather continued for another day and night by which time people hoped it had reached its peak and would soon blow itself out. Unfortunately, that was not the case.

On the night of 27 November 1703, people went to bed thinking that the storm had abated and they could get some sleep after the strong winds on previous nights in which they had laid awake fearing for their roofs. The wind picked up and by the early hours most were shaken awake by the wind buffeting their homes. In London people could hear bricks and tiles falling from houses and decided it was better to stay indoors even if the house might collapse than risk injury from flying debris outdoors.

The great storm, thought to have been a level two hurricane, raged across southern England and Wales. Buildings in London were badly damaged as were ships on the Thames. Queen Anne took shelter in the cellar of St James's Palace after the lead roof of Westminster Abbey blew off.

For Longford the storm was severe. The flat open plains of the farmland had no natural features to impede the path of the wind, and the previous month's rain had already brought flooding to this low-lying village.

The roar of the wind was terrifying. The storm was at its damaging height between 5am and 6.30am, but no one dare leave their refuge as the wind would blow them off their feet. There was no moon and the blackness of the night added to the terror. No one knew to what he or she would wake to find. As the early light brightened the sky, and the winds dropped, people began venturing out to survey the damage. The street was littered with debris from buildings and trees. Roofs and chimneys had disappeared. Whole hedges had been ripped up. Barns and stables had been damaged and the horses were as terrified as the humans were. With shocked faces people went from door to door to check on their neighbours. The wind did not die away for another few days, but it didn't return to its fury of the night of the 27th.[11] The wind had raised the height of the tide causing the Thames, into which the river Colne flows, to be higher than usual. This together with the rains from September caused flooding in Longford and gave the farmers another set of problems.

Daniel Defoe in his book *The Storm* (1704) described, in detail, the tremendous damage done around the nation. He describes the havoc done to buildings in London and the costs involved in rebuilding, but he also describes the multiple deaths from chimney, walls and steeples falling. At sea, twelve naval ships were lost and many more damaged. Lighthouses fell down. It was thought more than 10,000 people may have died. Some people saw it as a message from God on the sins of the nation and a national fast day was ordered for 19 January 1704. The non-conformists of Longford cannot have been immune to the idea that the storm was spiritual retribution.

The damage done to the individual farms of Longford is unrecorded, but by then Thomas Weekly had built up a productive farm, and settled into his new house, where he was raising a family that would have a major influence on life in Longford for the next three hundred years.

---

11 7 December in today's Gregorian calendar.

Chapter 3

Lords of the Manor without a Manor
(1679-1738)

There were several farmsteads fronting the Bath Road in Longford at the end of the seventeenth century, with their farmland radiating out behind them. There were also two Tudor inns. The King's Head catered for the coaching trade and housed the replacement horses for Royal carriages travelling to or from Windsor Castle, but there was another ancient inn. The sixteenth century timber-framed White Horse Inn in the centre of the village, later to be clad in whitewashed brick. Its low ceilings and small rooms gave it a hospitable ambiance, but without the facilities of its larger rival at the far end of the village it attracted the single rider rather than the carriage trade.

Just beyond the White Horse on the opposite side of the road was the farm which Thomas Weekly bought after his first visit to Longford. The House reflected his status. It had the gable side facing the road and the front facing into the yard where there were stables and cart-houses. The house was two storeys high with two attic rooms. It was built of red-brick with a high pitched tiled roof. The walls were thick and the large sash windows had internal wooden shutters.

The house was completed in 1679 and a weather-boarded malting barn was built alongside soon after. A substantial brick wall with sloped and rounded coping on the top edge fronted the road. The house, barn and wall are now Grade II listed structures.

For Thomas and Ann Weekly moving into their new home, (now always referred to as the Weekly House), was the beginning of their family life. In

The White Horse early 20th Century.
The Weekly House is the tallest building on the left-hand-side.

The Weekly House 1950.

1683 the longed-for heir arrived and they named him Richard. Two years later another son named Henry was born. Ann was not very well through her third pregnancy, but the arrival of a girl, Mary, on 23 September 1687 was welcomed by the whole family. It was to be their last child.

When Thomas first rode through Longford eleven years earlier he foresaw his future as a farmer, maltster, and family man stretching ahead of him. His dreams had been fulfilled. He had a substantial family home, the business was doing well and he lived in a supportive Baptist community, but tragedy was ahead.

The first years of a baby's life were critical. Child mortality was 30% but young Mary was growing stronger and the older she got the less the concern for her survival. Her mother, though, was not thriving. Ann never fully recovered from the birth. Thomas called in the best doctors, but she weakened and when she died, a year after the birth of her daughter the whole community mourned at her funeral in Harmondsworth Churchyard. She was only 36. She did not see her children, then aged 5, 3 and 1 grow up, nor did she know that the house built as her family home would still be resplendent well into the twenty-first century.

The death of his wife was devastating for Thomas. His faith gave him strength. He threw himself into his work. He was expected to remarry quickly in order to have domestic support whilst he ran his business. The culture at the time ensured a strong division of labour between the sexes. The husband was the bread-winner and the wife the bread-baker. She looked after the children and ran the home. When a spouse died, a widow needed a wage-earner to support herself and her children, and a widower needed a house-keeper, cook and child-minder. It was common for people in these circumstances to make an expedient early remarriage to resolve the division of labour in a household. Thomas, although only 36, could not bring himself to replace Ann. He never remarried. He hired a house-keeper and a nurse-maid and brought up the children himself. The children received a good education and grew up in the Baptist faith.

* * *

There was excitement at the Weekly house on the 14 April 1708, Thomas Weekly, now 57, climbed into his carriage thinking how proud he was of his three children as they joined him. His second son, Henry, a fine young man of 23, was learning the trade of a mercer in London; his daughter

Mary, at 21 the image of her mother, and strapping Richard, 25, who was now about to make a serious commitment to their church. It was a cold morning as they rode the short distance from the Weekly house, along the Bath Road, across two small rivers, which lie in the flat farmland of Longford Moor, to the River Colne at Colnbrook. Getting out of their carriage they joined a group of people walking down to the River Colne where it forked just below the Mill. It was a solemn and auspicious occasion for the eldest son, Richard. He was joining seven other men and four women who would be the first Baptists in the area being baptised in the River Colne by total immersion and who would become the first full members of the new Colnbrook Particular Baptist Church. Seven well-known Baptist Ministers from London and surrounding areas had gathered for the occasion. Three of the men baptised, including Richard Weekly were yeoman farmers from Harmondsworth.

> **Particular Baptists**
>
> Particular or Strict Baptists had formed out of the separatist's movements which emerged after the scriptures were written in English. Although attempts were made by the authorities to suppress dissenters the Particular Baptist emerged as a Movement around 1633 and had relatively few restrictions during and after the English Civil War but with the restoration of Charles II religious dissenters were persecuted and it was not until the 'Declaration of Indulgence' of 1672 that the Particular Baptists could meet openly.
>
> They called themselves "Strict" or "Particular" Baptists. Strict Baptists believed that the Bible was the fundamental authority for all Christian beliefs.
>
> Britannica https://www.britannica.com/topic/Baptist/History#ref466518

The whole family were an integral part of the Baptist community in the area where there was a tight network of like-minded farming families. The farmers and artisans also traded between themselves in an unofficial co-operative sharing purchasing, marketing, and selling of goods and services. It led to greater prosperity for the farmers and the church, with which they shared their income. The yeomen of the Baptist community took their responsibilities in leading the community seriously whilst the women looked after the welfare of their own families and those of their labourers.

For the Weekly family their strong beliefs affected every part of the way they led their lives. The children were expected to marry within the sect and this reduced their choice of spouses. Finding a partner who was of the right class and who shared their beliefs meant that the Weekly descendants married later in life or not at all. Those that did find partners married within other local Baptist families many of whose names appear on the chapel's foundation stone. This endogamy created a harmonious and unbreakable welfare, financial and trading structure which increased the success and wealth of the parish for centuries.

Young Richard Weekly had been courting Mary Tillyer, a farmer's daughter. She was four years younger than him and the daughter of another dynastic Baptist family from the parish centre in Harmondsworth. They were married in 1712 and moved into the Weekly House with widowed Thomas. Thomas was not well and Richard had assumed responsibility for the farm and malting business in Longford. His sister Mary had married, and brother Henry was a cloth merchant and living in the Tothill Street house in London.

Thomas Weekly, the founder of the Weekly's dominance in Longford, died just two years after Richard and Mary's marriage and was buried in Harmondsworth churchyard on 24 July 1714. Just a week later Queen Anne died aged 49 at Kensington Palace and the reign of the House of Stuart ended.

Queen Anne had reigned alone since her husband, Prince George of Denmark, died in 1708. The Act of Settlement 1701 proclaimed that only Protestants could inherit the throne. Anne had no heirs and as the closest legal claimants were Catholic, the Government had declared Sofia, Electress of Hanover, to be next in line for the British throne. Although the Electress was thirty-five years older than Queen Anne, she was in good health and remained so until a walk in the gardens of her palace. A sudden rain shower interrupted her usual walk and as she rushed for shelter she collapsed, died, and missed being Queen of the United Kingdom by two months. Her son, 54 year-old George, once considered a suitable husband for Anne, became George I of Great Britain.

* * *

A new generation was now in charge both in the Weekly House and in the United Kingdom. George I was in Germany when he became King on 1 August 1714. He travelled to England with his son, George, and his mistress, and arrived on 18 September. His marriage to Sophia Dorothea of Celle had been dissolved in 1694. A month after his arrival in England the King's coronation took place on Wednesday 20 October behind the closed doors of Westminster Abbey. The King could speak little English and the ceremony had to be conducted mainly in Latin.[12] Only the clergy, Government Ministers, and a few members of the Royal Court were present in the Abbey, other members of the nobility paid for a seat on the terraced scaffolds erected just outside the Abbey on the processional route. One seating scaffold was erected on Broad Sanctuary at the end of Tothill Street where Henry Weekly and his wife, Jane, lived. When King George I emerged from the Abbey and climbed into the carriage for a grand procession the crowds in the bank of hastily built seating surged forward to get a better view which was too much for the temporary scaffolds. As the procession passed, two of them collapsed killing and injuring many of the wealthy families who had paid for the privilege.[13] Among the dead was a lady from Tothill Street, a neighbour of the Weeklys. Henry's wife, Jane, was seven months pregnant with their first child and was deeply affected by the tragedy on their doorstep. When the King heard of the disaster, he offered his own physicians and surgeons to help with the wounded.

The newly crowned King George I was a rare sight in Longford. Unlike Queen Anne, King George disliked Windsor Castle and did not use it or maintain it, nor did his son George II when he became King.

* * *

At the Weekly House the farming routine continued as normal. In Thomas Weekly's will he divided his land and property between his three children. Eldest son, Richard, who had taken over the family's malting and farming business, inherited the Longford land. His brother Henry inherited a farm at Hatton (where Heathrow Terminal Four now stands). His daughter Mary inherited houses in Lambeth which had been part of her mother's inheritance. The two brothers shared the residue of Thomas's estate.

Not only was Richard farming his own land in Longford but he was leasing additional land and increasing his cropping capacity. His young wife Mary gave birth to a daughter, also called Mary, on 2 December 1715 who would grow up to marry into another leading Baptist farming family, the Wilds, thus uniting and strengthening two dynasties that intermarried through several generations, and between them farmed the majority of the agricultural land in the area.

---

12 https://www.westminster-abbey.org/abbey-commemorations/royals/george-i
13 Stamford Mercury – Thursday 28 October 1714

Richard's devotion to the Baptist faith resulted in him becoming one of the first two Deacons appointed at the Colnbrook Baptist chapel in 1719. The Baptists' meetings took place in a room above a Colnbrook shop, but Richard was working towards raising funds to build a permanent Baptist chapel in the town. Two years later, on 16 June, their son Thomas was born. Richard was a busy man running his farms, malting business and overseeing the administration of the Baptist Community. He was also head of the family and as such lent his support to his brother Henry who was experiencing a lot of sadness in his life.

Henry, and his wife Jane, had a son in 1714 but he was not a strong child and Jane was also unwell. Henry's business was prospering and he had property in Tottenham High Cross as well as his farm in Hatton. When his son died aged eight in 1723 the young lad was buried in St Mary's churchyard at Harmondsworth. Both parents were distraught at their loss, but Jane never recovered from her distress and eventually retired to the Hatton farm with a nurse to look after her. Henry continued to live in Westminster, running his business as best he could, but neither he nor the business thrived from then on.

As Henry's health deteriorated, he came back to the Weekly house to be cared for. He died in 1738. After his death Richard had difficulty in finding Henry's will, but eventually discovered it in the drawer of a desk in the Westminster House. The document was full of erasures and alterations. For it to be legal two people who knew Henry's handwriting had to swear before a judge that it was his handwriting and the will was declared valid. The will had been written three years before his death, and although the will made provision for a nurse for his wife, who he described as 'not sensible', he also, ever hopeful, made provision for any heirs. When he died he was buried with his parents and only child in St Mary's graveyard in Harmondsworth. His brother Richard, to whom he left the Tothill Street house in Westminster as well as the farm in Hatton, Howton Hall in Wood Green and other property at Tottenham High Cross, was the sole executor. but there were many debts. Richard, was still paying these off when he died twenty-four years later.

The Weekly House represented the citadel of the pious patriarchal Weekly family, who became the largest employers and the dominant influential authority in the village for decades. They were the Lords of the Manor in all but name.

This family and their descendants would see the village grow and change as society changed. They would witness crime, tragedy and spectacular events. They would see technology improve farming and transport. They would see good times and bad, but all the while maintaining their faith through the generations, and in the twenty-first century, although the farms had gone, the building that Thomas Weekly built still stands in a village that would be as recognisable to him as the day he first rode into Longford.

However, Longford was not always as peaceful as its pious citizens would wish. Travellers who had to cross the barren wastes of Hounslow Heath on the Great Bath Road did so in trepidation. There were many highwaymen lurking on the Heath ready to relieve the wealthy travellers of their valuables, and sometimes their lives.

Roques Map 1754 Showing Longford between two open stretches of the Bath Road'

Where once there were familiar faces in the taverns and the occasional traveller stopping for refreshments whilst changing horses, now there were more strangers to be seen in the village. The travelling public ranged from royalty and nobility down to itinerants and the villainous. The increasing popularity of Bath, and the new coaching routes that were opening up travel for ordinary citizens, attracted the attention of the less desirable types. These criminals were not just impoverished petty opportunists. They could be well dressed and well mounted, armed, and the robberies meticulously planned. If caught the law was unforgiving and highway robbery always carried the death penalty, but that was not going to stop them.

Chapter 4

Robbers and Thief-takers (1722-1729)

John Hawkins, was a large overweight man, born in Staines (five miles from Longford) in 1694, whose father had wanted him to learn the trade of a plasterer, but he could not settle to a regular job. He became butler to Sir Dennis Dutry, a wealthy London merchant and a Director of the East India Company, but Hawkins' addiction to eating, drinking and gambling became a problem, and he was asked to leave. Having learned about trading from his master he went to France and started trading in wines and brandy. His brother had a ship with which they imported the goods on which they paid the duty due, but they were not making any money. He left that business and started trading in the South Sea Company shares, and for a while made some good money until the share price collapsed in 1720. After this he and a friend, Ralph Wilson, went on a robbing spree. They were joined by George Simpson, a failed publican from Lincoln, who had recently been a footman to Lord Castlemaine.

The three of them plotted to rob the Bristol mail on 16 April 1722. They hired horses in Southwark, stopped for a meal at Brentford and then hung around on Hounslow Heath until going into The George at Colnbrook where they learned that the post boy would be passing by between 1am and 2am. They lay in wait. What they had not expected was that the post boy, Thomas Green, would collect a travelling companion at Slough. The two were strangers travelling together towards London. The conspirators followed the duo along the Bath Road, through Colnbrook and then to Longford. On the other side of Longford they pounced. Hawkins hung back because his obesity made him too recognizable. Wilson and Simpson put handkerchiefs around their faces and pulled down their wigs and hats as they rode up to the pair, grabbed their bridles and at the point of a pistol ordered them to dismount. They set the companion's horse loose after cutting the bridle and took the post boy's black gelding. Both victims were tied back to back to a tree beside the lane to Harmondsworth. After the robbers had left, the two managed to free themselves from the tree, but remained tied back-to-back as they made their way to the King's Head at Longford. The ostler freed them and walked back with them to the scene. They found the gelding loose beside the road and the bags cut open. The post boy had been carrying ten bags of post, some from Bath and Bristol as well as from the Kings household at Windsor. The robbers were selective in their choices believing the Bath and

The robbery of the Bristol Mail
From: HALF-HOURS WITH THE HIGHWAYMEN by Charles G.Harper
https://www.gutenberg.org/cache/epub/53111/pg53111-images.html#CHAPTER_XII

Bristol bags had more lucrative contents.[14] The other bags they scattered over Hounslow Heath as they made their get-away.

A week later Wilson was sitting in the Moorgate Coffee House in London listening to the other customers gossiping when he overheard a conversation about the robbery of the Bristol Mail on Hounslow Heath and the Royal Mail's determination to catch the robbers. Now seriously alarmed Wilson decided on a sea voyage to Newcastle to escape the hue and cry, but before he could board the ship one of the stolen notes was traced to him and he was arrested.[15] He was taken to the Post Office and interviewed by the Post-Master General himself and denied all knowledge of the robbery. He was kept overnight, by which time Hawkins and Simpson had been arrested and put in a separate room. The wait was on to see who would confess

---

14 *Old Bailey Proceedings Online* (www.oldbaileyonline.org, version 8.0, 16 April 2020), May 1722, trial of John Hawkins George Simpson (t17220510-3).

15 Harper, Charles G. *Half-hours with the Highwaymen,* London 1908) https://www.gutenberg.org/cache/epub/53111/pg53111-images.html#CHAPTER_XII

first to save his own neck and to convict his comrades. Wilson eventually cracked and gave evidence against Hawkins and Simpson. After a six-hour trial at which they protested their innocence and brought character witnesses in their defence the judge sentenced Hawkins and Simpson to be hanged. In the condemned cell, a priest interviewed them before giving communion and saying prayers. The priest described Hawkins during his trial as conducting himself in a civilized manner and who even addressed the Court about perceived irregularities in its proceedings. He delivered his complaints in a charming way that made an impression on the court, and when he eventually got taken to the condemned cell his sensibilities were appalled at the dark, dank, filthy place and the people he was incarcerated with who used lewd and profane speech. The priest said Hawkins was very bitter that his friend and accuser had given evidence against him and believed he would not have been caught otherwise. However, before his execution he became resigned to his fate and calmly declared that he did not feel ill-will towards anyone, although he added that he would rather have died than to have betrayed a friend. He expressed forgiveness and an acceptance of his fate and received the sacrament. However, his composure weakened as the time for the execution approached. He became agitated and shed a few tears during the prayers and his usually placid expression appeared to turn to terror which the priest concluded 'shewed he had a true Sense of his Condition, that Death is not only the Pain of Dying, but the appearing before God, with the Eternal Seal set upon our Actions, for happiness or Reprobation.'[16] They were executed on 21 May 1722, and afterwards their bodies were taken back to the scene of the crime and hung in chains at the Bath Road end of the lane between Longford and Harmondsworth, now called Hatch Lane.

* * *

At the Weekly House in Longford in January 1729 Richard and Mary Weekly's second daughter, Ann, was born. While Mary was still recovering from the birth there was a noisy altercation in one of the cottages on the Bath Road. On 2 February 1729 Ann Franklin was busy in her cottage in Longford when there was a sudden loud hammering of a fist on her door. She opened it to see William Jones, from the village, standing there. He

---

16 *Old Bailey Proceedings Online* (www.oldbaileyonline.org, version 8.0, 16 April 2020), May 1722, trial of John Hawkins George Simpson (t17220510-3).

carried a pistol and a short sword. He wanted to see her husband William Franklin who was not at home.

'I have a warrant for the arrest of your husband on charges of carrying out some robberies on the highway', said Jones. Ann protested she knew nothing about such a crime.

'Then I will take away some of his ill-gotten gains.' He violently manhandled Ann up the stairs and into the bedroom.

'Where is your husband's money?' The terrified Ann felt she had no alternative but to comply. She opened a drawer and took out six guineas, which he grabbed.

'I will return with the Constable and take other goods.'

Jones returned with some accomplices and the Harmondsworth Constable. They ransacked the house taking various items including furniture and clothes and two horses, all of considerable value, and said they were recovering them on behalf of the Lord of the Manor who had instructed them to take them to him in London. The Constable insisted on accompanying the men to London in order to ensure that the goods were delivered, but being 'a country man ignorant of such affairs', on reaching London was curtly told by the men that he had no jurisdiction in London only in his own Parish and they sped off. William Jones was eventually caught and was tried at the Old Bailey, for robbery. He did produce some warrants in his defence, but they were for William Franklin himself and not for his goods.[17] William Jones was found guilty of robbery and sentenced to transportation and in December 1729, he was taken on the convict ship *Patapsco* to Annapolis in Maryland in colonial North America.

This incident was not unusual. Other than the military, or the local militia, and the volunteer parish Constable, there was no formal police force who could hunt and arrest criminals, and so enterprising individuals, colloquially called 'thief-takers', would be hired by victims to search for criminals or stolen goods. The victim would obtain a warrant from a magistrate giving him authority to seize the person or goods. Sometimes the 'thief-taker' would negotiate the return of stolen goods for a fee, or receive a bounty for an arrest if it was on offer. They purported to be against lawlessness, but were often brutal and verging on criminality themselves.

---

17 *Old Bailey Proceedings Online* (www.oldbaileyonline.org, version 8.0, 16 April 2020), July 1729, trial of William Jones (t17290709-14).

William Jones was such a man, but this time he had overstepped the mark and became the criminal. There are no records to explain what William Franklin had done to deserve an arrest warrant.

We will never know if Ann Franklin's husband, William, was a highwayman, but the menace of the highwaymen was getting worse. Coaches could travel faster on the improved road conditions, but were vulnerable when they had to slow down to cross the narrow bridges in the open countryside between Longford and Colnbrook. The people of Longford felt secure as long as they kept to their own business. Things that were seen and heard by the villagers remained with the observer and in return, those that preyed on the travelling public did not trouble them, however the secret life of one of their own farmers was about to be revealed.

Chapter 5

The Longford Highwayman (1769-1795)

The frost was thick on the ground as the shadowy figure of a man, with his tricorne hat pulled down over his face and his cloak pulled tight around him, left the noise and bustle of the King's Head inn to make his stumbling way home on foot. He had drunk too much. It was a dark misty moonless night, but when his eyes adjusted to the dimness and with the light from the flickering oil lamps of passing carriages, there was enough light for him to find his way back to his farmhouse. Still drunk and full of fight and anger, he was looking for someone to take it out on. It was nearly midnight, but he took his horse out of the stable, saddled it, put his kerchief round his face and rode out onto Hounslow Heath.

It was only a week until Christmas and John Tillier was feeling particularly wretched. His young wife had died four months earlier after less than two years of marriage. He had already been a widower when they married and now once more he was alone. He was not a poor man, he had land, but his heart was no longer in farming, the farm was not making money and his only consolation was in drink. His Baptist family and the rest of the Baptist community had tried to help him, but he could not be consoled. He wanted his revenge on the world.

The Bath Road, as it crossed the nearly two miles of Hounslow Heath between Longford and Colnbrook was particularly dangerous for travellers. The low-lying road was traversed by several rivers that had to be forded or crossed on rickety wooden bridges. Carriages travelling at night moved at speed to avoid being stopped by robbers, but inevitably had to slow down at river crossings, and with the mist swirling off the water this was the ideal spot for highwaymen and footpads to mount an attack. On the road Robert

Jones, in his post chaise pulled by four horses was travelling to Fonman Castle, his home in Glamorganshire, with his Gentlemen friends, William Thomas and the Rev. Mr. Bruce.

Chaise and four.

As they approached the relative safety of the village of Longford the shadowy figure of a man on horseback rode out from a hedge and aimed a blow at Mr Jones's footman who was riding alongside the carriage. The servant, stunned, slowed down, and the assailant struck at a second servant, but the blow missed and hit the coach, and the travellers inside realised they were under attack. Another blow to the servant caught him over the eye but did not dislodge him from his mount and he was able to ride to the side of the carriage to warn the gentlemen about the attacker. Mr Jones told his servant to warn off the villain, but ignoring the threats that the coach passengers were armed the robber rode up to the side of the still moving carriage. Mr Jones saw the horse's head beside the door and fired his weapon. There was a shout, 'You have missed me by God' from the man and he rode off at speed.[18] One of the servants on horseback rode after him. Mr Jones and his passengers were worried that there might be an accomplice, but having descended from the carriage cautiously they walked on into the darkness. Two hundred yards along the road they found the robber lying on the ground wounded. They put him in the coach and took him to the King's Head at Longford, where he was recognised immediately as the farmer who had left the premises earlier that evening. The local customers were not surprised. It was an unspoken secret that when drunk John Tillier, with the bravado of alcohol, rode out as a highwayman with no more lethal weapon than a rough-headed stick which from a distance looked like a gun.

18 Derby Mercury – Friday 05 January 1770

The ball from Mr Jones's pistol had hit John Tillier in the chest. The surgeon could do nothing for him. The ball had done too much damage to vital organs. On 26 December 1769, Tillier dictated his will to William Wild, a leading local Baptist. He signed it in a shaky hand. William Wild was the witness and Mary Watts made her mark as the second witness.

Tillier died a few days later and was buried on 3rd January 1770 in St Mary's churchyard in Harmondsworth village centre. In his will, he left substantial legacies to a great many people in the village, and land and property to two of the biggest landowners in the parish. These strongly principled Baptist landowners, now executors to the will of a highwayman, would not have seen him as a criminal, but as a man clearly disturbed and distraught after the death of his young wife, but how much had they known about his nocturnal exploits?

The amateur highwayman had not chosen his victim well. It was particularly unfortunate for him that the owner of the carriage he was trying to rob was Robert Jones, a libertarian who championed the cause of freedom, and he was not going to become the victim of highway robbery. He was armed and well-guarded by servants. Jones was a Welsh squire and a a founder member, of the Bill of Rights Society formed in February 1769. This Society was formed to uphold the Bill of Rights Act after George III had put pressure on the House of Commons to overturn the election of John Wilkes as the MP for Middlesex. Robert Jones was a campaigner for moral justice and was determined to use force on anyone who threatened his right to travel in safety. John Tillier's fate was sealed as soon as he approached the carriage.

Bill of Rights Act 1689

This act established the rights of Parliament to decide its own affairs. The Bill effectively removed the Monarch from having any power over Parliament,

The Bill of Rights Society

In 1769 John Wilkes was expelled from Parliament where he held the seat for Middlesex. He was an early advocate of Parliamentary reform, and a vocal critic of the King. It was thought that the Kings supporters were behind his expulsion. John Wilkes' supporters formed the Bill of Rights Society to campaign on his behalf.

http://www.historyhome.co.uk/c-eight/18reform/ssbr.htm

* * *

One of John Tillier's executors was Thomas Weekly, a fellow Baptist and farmer. It is easy to imagine that he must have regretted the ignominious end of a member of his church, and the fact that their supportive Baptist community had failed to save Tillier from his own demons.

Copyhold

Copyhold tenure was a form of customary tenure of land common in England from the Middle Ages. The land was held according to the custom of the manor, and the mode of landholding took its name from the fact that the "title deed" received by the tenant was a copy of the relevant entry in the manorial court roll. (Wikipedia)

Yeomans

Grade II listed building. Sixteenth century building with central range and gabled crosswings. Two storeys apart from an attic room on the left. Tiled roofs. Exposed timber framing, fairly close set but not very stout, with brick filling. Irregular windows, mostly small modern casements, but one seventeenth-century cross casement to left of door in central range.

British Listed Buildings. https:// britishlistedbuildings.co.uk/ england/heathrow-villages-ward-hillingdon

---

Thomas Weekly, the grandson of the builder of the Weekly House in which he now lived was the dominant farmer in Longford, and now farmed in Harmondsworth, Longford and Hatton. He had also inherited the family house in Tothill Street, London (opposite Westminster Abbey). He did not marry until he was 32 years of age, when he married the daughter of Thomas Streating who lived just down the road in a large Elizabethan house, now called Yeomans. He and twenty-three year old Elizabeth Streating had both grown up in Longford. They married in 1753 and within nine years the marriage had produced five daughters. Farmers need sons to inherit the farm and to their delight their sixth child, Thomas, was born in 1763, but their happiness was not to last. The family was devastated when four-year-old Sarah died on 29 May 1766 and three-year-old Thomas died two days later.

Thomas Weekly, now 45 years old, was worried about the succession of his land, but his prayers were answered when the next two children were boys. The first named Thomas in honour of his father and dead brother, and the second was called Richard.

Soon after Richard's birth Thomas Streating died and was buried on 26 December 1773. The Elizabethan house was inherited by his daughter Elizabeth

Weekly and was converted into three dwellings for the families of farm labourers. It is still home to three families today.

When Thomas Weekly died in 1783 aged 62 his two surviving sons were 14 and 11 respectively, and classed as minors. At a special manorial court hearing they were allowed to take over their father's copyhold land. The court had no jurisdiction over their freehold land. Their mother lived for a further 30 years and so with her help and the support of their relatives they were able to continue farming their land.

* * *

"The Barracks" now two dwellings called Willow Tree Cottage and Queens River Cottage.

Willow Tree Cottage and Queens River Cottage.

("The Barracks")

Grade II listed. 1739. Two storeys and attic, four and five windows. Tiled roof with two and three gabled dormers. Rendered walls. Sash windows with glazing bars, some replaced, in box frames under segmental arches. Blocked central carriageway under oak beam. One window on left extension, with casement, under half hipped tiled roof. Modern doors and hoods.

https://britishlistedbuildings.co.uk/england/heathrow-villages-ward-hillingdon

The menace of the highwaymen was getting worse. The perpetrators were too often able to get away with their crime and the only way of catching them was to call in the military. Some regiments, when not engaged in wars abroad or protecting the Sovereign, were asked to mount horse patrols on Hounslow Heath. There was no civilian law enforcement body. Each parish had a Constable who had the power of arrest. He would put offenders of minor offences in the Parish lock-up. Those accused of more serious crimes went before a Magistrate who could send them before a Judge and Jury.

When the number of Highway robberies on Hounslow Heath proliferated, it became necessary to use local militia to patrol Hounslow Heath and a barracks was built at Longford to house them.

The jurisdiction between the two law-enforcing powers, civil and military, was unclear and inevitably led to clashes. Both the militia and the Parish Constable thought they had precedence over the other. The matter came to a head on 17 September 1790 in the King's Head.

Two soldiers from the Prince of Wales's own regiment of dragoons were at the King's Head. One of the soldiers was quartered there and the other was quartered down the road in the Barracks, but both kept their horses stabled at the King's Head

It was a cool September afternoon as William Stevens, the waiter at the King's Head, came out of the inn by the back door into the yard. He was on his way to the beer cellar to fetch a barrel, but he stood still when he noticed a man by the window of the wine cellar. He recognised the man as Joseph Marriott the soldier lodging at the inn. Marriott had not seen the waiter across the yard. Stevens watched Marriott put his arm into the open door and pick up a bottle of wine and put it under his jacket. He then climbed up to his bedroom via a ladder that was near the cellar. Turning round, Stevens immediately went to tell Mrs Bedford, the landlord's wife, who came out just in time to see Marriott take the bottle of wine to his room. John Simpson, his fellow soldier, was nearby waiting for his horse. Marriott joined him and they went out on patrol.

They were gone some hours, but Mr Bedford had already sent for the Constable. When the men returned the Constable and Mr Bedford went to Marriott's bedroom. Both soldiers were in the room, and as the Constable looked around the room he saw a locked box. The Constable said to Marriott, 'What have you got in that box?'

'Nothing'.

'Unlock the box'

'No I won't. You have no authority over me. I am a member of His Majesty's forces.'

'If you don't open it I will smash it open'

Simpson, the other soldier, had been standing back from the conversation. When asked, he admitted that he had the key, and reluctantly unlocked it. In the box were two bottles, one full of Lisbon wine.[19] Under the bed, the Constable found some empty bottles covered with a cloth. When asked

---

19 Wine was shipped in casks and then bottles would be filled from the cask before being brought to the table. https://vintageportsite.com/about-vintage-port/history-of-port

why the bottles were under the bed both Simpson and Marriott said they were the bottles they made water in. The full bottle of wine had a chalk mark on the cork, which Mrs Bedford identified as the mark she made when she bottled and corked it. The soldiers were arrested for stealing a quart of wine, value eighteen pence, and seven glass quart bottles, value two shillings. The soldiers argued that the Constable had no authority to arrest them, but nevertheless they were taken before a magistrate and sent to Court.

When the case came before the Judge at the Old Bailey in London, Marriott offered an explanation. In his defence he said had been helping in the cellars that day where they had been bottling a lot of wine, saw a bottle of wine in a manger, and joked about whether it contained wine or water but took it anyway.[20] Two officers from the Regiment stood up in Court and vouched for the soldiers good character and conduct, but the jury thought otherwise and found Marriott guilty and Simpson not guilty. The judge, whether intimidated by the official military presence, or just sympathetic to their authority, fined Marriott just one shilling and discharged him, a paltry amount considering a labourer, driving a cart whilst asleep, received a minimum fine of ten shillings (half his weekly wage).

* * *

The low lying land between Longford and Colnbrook was essentially a flood plain for the River Colne. It flooded frequently, and occasionally extreme weather caused problems for the Bath Road traffic. In February 1795 the heavy rain continued to raise the height of the River Thames until on Thursday morning, the 12 February, the water rose nine inches above where it was the night before and caused flooding at Staines and Maidenhead. The water level in the River Colne, which fed into the Thames, also rose. The Colne had several Mills along its banks which restricted the flow of the river until it built up into a flood. Between Colnbrook and Longford the water on the flooded plain was flowing so strongly that four carriages overturned, including a wagon, a chaise, the Gloucester coach from Charing Cross and the Windsor coach from Lad Lane in the City of London.[21]

* * *

---

20 *Old Bailey Proceedings Online* (www.oldbaileyonline.org, version 8.0, 28 October 2020), October 1790, trial of JOSEPH MARRIOTT JOHN SIMPSON (t17901027-45).

21 Hereford Journal – Wednesday 18 February 1795

Milestone

Bath Road Milestones

In 1741 the Colnbrook Trust erected mile stones along the seven miles of Bath Road under their administration. The stones were commissioned from Mr Woodruff of Windsor and cost £2 8s each. They were recut in the 1820s. The thirteenth, fourteenth, fifteenth and sixteenth miles stones are still in place today. They show the distance between towns as well as the total distance from Hyde Park Corner. They were erected for the convenience of the coach drivers and travellers, but also came to be start/finish markers for sporting events along the Bath Road

The danger of being accosted by Highwaymen on the Bath Road was an ever present problem. When they were caught the robbers knew there was only one punishment – death. To avoid the risk of being identified the highwaymen wore scarfs across their faces. They especially wanted to avoid anyone who might know them. In 1773 the Landlord of the King's Head in Longford, John Bedford, was riding along the Bath Road when he saw the Bath stagecoach stationary by the 15th mile stone near the inn.

As he got nearer, he saw that a lone highwayman on horseback was alongside the coach looking into it with a weapon in his hand. He was in the process of robbing the passengers and had taken about £5 from two men passengers when he heard the sound of a horse approaching. Glancing up he saw that the rider was the Landlord of an inn he knew well, and not wanting to be recognised quickly galloped off towards London leaving two other passengers with all their possessions. They described the man as having a light coloured frock coat and that he 'behaved with great civility'.[22] Whether John Bedford recognised the man or not he was discrete enough to keep it to himself. His customers treated him with respect and he would do the same – whatever their profession.

---

22 Stamford Mercury – Thursday 09 September 1773

John Bedford was the licensee of the King's Head during the last quarter of the eighteenth century. He was a genial host, a fair master to his servants and a respected member of the Parish Church. As the inn grew busier with the growing number of travellers, it expanded. The stables were enlarged, and the standard of accommodation improved to attract the more discerning customer. At 38 years old John was a widower when he married local girl Mary Dean on 6 December 1778 at the parish church of St. Mary's in Harmondsworth where he was a churchwarden. She was his help-mate and mother of their six subsequent children.

When he died in 1794, aged 54, his widow, Mary, left with five young surviving children, took over the running of the business. She posted an advertisement in the newspaper to confirm her decision and promised that the customers would be 'unremittingly attended too and gratefully acknowledged.'[23] Her two oldest children, Joseph and Peggy, were fourteen and thirteen and at an age when children were expected to work. They would spend the rest of their lives at the Inn and would make the King's Head a legend that would continue for two hundred years.

> **King's Head Inn, Longford, Middlesex.**
> MARY BEDFORD, Widow of the late John Bedford, deceased, begs leave to inform her late husband's customers, and the public in general, that she proposes carrying on the business of the above house, for the benefit of herself and five young children, and hopes for a continuance of their favours, which will be unremittingly attended to and gratefully acknowledged.
> LONGFORD, May 20, 1794.

Citation: British Library Newspapers. https://www.britishnewspaperarchive.co.uk

* * *

---

23 Reading Mercury – Monday 2 June 1794.

The danger of crossing Hounslow Heath was no deterrent to travellers and Longford was getting busier than ever. With the increased trade came prosperity and a population increase. The village, now only two hours drive from London, became attractive to prosperous Londoners who wanted a rural retreat. One London man who took up residence was Thomas Willing, a Quaker businessman, who moved into Island House and whose business and family interests would connect Longford with Africa, Colonial America and the dubious slave trade.

Chapter 6

The Secrets of the Island (1742-1773)

Thomas Willing looked out of his big bay window on to the tranquil waters of the river Colne as they flowed passed his house on the island. He loved watching the river on these bright summer days with the sun dappling through the branches of the weeping willows onto the dragonflies hovering over the clear bright streams flowing each side of Island House. The serenity was the reason he had chosen to live here. The house, hidden away in the centre of Longford on an island in the Colne river, was close to the Longford Friends Meeting House where he could follow his Quaker faith. It was a rural retreat for this businessman who had an apartment just a few hours ride away in the City of London at 4 Inner Temple.

As he watched the butterflies flit among the delicate pink flowers of the ragged robin peeping shyly from the tall rushes, he could hear the gentle burbling of the water as it continued its journey towards the Thames. The sound evoked the memory of his crossing of the Atlantic to the New World thirty years earlier, in company with his brother, Charles, for whom it was a familiar journey.

Thomas endured the six-week voyage, the ferocious seas and the seasickness by staying in his narrow, dark, first-class cabin and avoiding mixing with the immigrants who had to suffer the crossing in poor, unhealthy accommodation where hunger and disease often resulted in death. Eventually they reached land and in the relative calmness of the Delaware River they sailed towards Philadelphia, passing near Willings Town (now called Wilmington) which had been founded by an uncle earlier in the century.[24] It was with enormous relief that Thomas alighted from the

---

24 Balch, Thomas Willing, *Willing letters and papers : edited with a biographical essay of Thomas Willing of Philadelphia (1631-1821).* (Philadelphia, 1922) https://archive.org/details/willingletterspa00will/page/118

The tip of the island on the river Colne with watercress beds in the foreground and on the right a glimpse of the Island House. Early 20th Century.

The Island House, Longford, by Archibald Robertson 1792.

vessel when it docked at a jetty on the Delaware River in Philadelphia. From there it was a short carriage ride to Third Street where on the corner of Willings' Alley Charles had built a magnificent house for his family. His brother's wife, Anne, and children welcomed him into their home. Thomas remembered how the children danced around their father when they arrived and later when he sat sipping tea with Charles and his wife, the two eldest, Anne, aged nine, and Dorothy, seven, sat at his feet. Two more children were in the nursery with their nurse, and the oldest child, his namesake, was at school in England.

'Tell us about Tom', asked young Anne.

'He does very well. He is studying hard at his school. His grandmother in Bristol is giving him her best care and attention. I think he is very happy.'

'Will he be home soon?' asked Dorothy, who could barely remember her elder brother leaving home aged eight to travel to school in England two years earlier.

'He still has a few more years at school and then I will arrange for him to study law in London. He sends his love to you all.'

Charles and Thomas' father, also called Thomas, came from a long line of successful Quaker merchants in Bristol, and had decided to exploit the trading opportunities in Colonial America. Thomas senior had gone to Philadelphia in middle-age and formed a merchant house in the City. His ships carried grain to American ports and traded sugar, molasses, flour and wood to Europe. Some of the ships also carried a few slaves that had been purchased in Africa and taken to the Bahamas. Later his Grandson transported slaves from Barbados for clients in Philadelphia.[25] After Charles, in Bristol, turned eighteen-years-old his father took him to Philadelphia and installed him in the business. Charles took over the Philadelphia Merchant House and settled in the City. By 1731 he had married Anne, the daughter of Abigail and Joseph Shippen and they eventually had eleven children. This advantageous marriage established them as one of the most prominent families in Philadelphia. Charles was able to expand his trading interests whilst establishing an influential dynasty dedicated to public service that shaped the future United States.

Thomas from Longford, now staying with his brother's family in Philadelphia, worked with Charles in the fast-growing business and made

---

25 https://www.slavevoyages.org/american/database

Royal African Company

The Royal African Company was founded in 1660 by the Duke of York, later King James II. The company had a monopoly on trade to and from the West Coast of Africa, setting up ports and trading posts along the coast to trade initially in gold and other commodities, but later in African slaves, which were taken to the West Indies and America in a triangular trading route between Britain, Africa and the New World. For a while, the directors of this company, mainly members of the English aristocracy, found it was very lucrative, although by 1708 it had lost its monopoly on the African trade and when it became insolvent the British government took over the company's assets. A new non-profit company was formed by an Act of Parliament in 1750 which appointed nine Committee members who were responsible to the government for the administration of the organisation. The new company was called the African Company of Merchants. Shipowners and Merchants paid a fee to the African Company to use their ports and facilities. There was no control over what was traded and although gold was still one of the chief commodities, with which the British Government manufactured coins, so also was ivory and slaves.

many useful contacts among other merchants. Philadelphia was expanding rapidly and the 13,000 population was growing rich on the shipping trade, but Thomas found the climate abhorrent.[26] He could not get used to the very hot summers and very cold winters. There was the constant risk of malaria, and frequent outbreaks of contagious diseases, brought in by the trading ships as they travelled from port to port. He could see the business opportunities it offered, but he was home sick. Thomas Willing stayed in Pennsylvania for three years, but in 1745 he returned to England to continue helping his father with his Bristol and London business interests. When his father died in 1760 Thomas inherited the business and his directorships. He had associations with the Worshipful Company of Mercers, The Bank of England, and the notorious African Company. He also worked closely with his brother, Charles, in Philadelphia.

When Thomas arrived back in England, he arranged for his American-born nephew, already studying in England, to be admitted to the Inner Temple in London to study law. At the end of his education nephew Thomas returned to Pennsylvania to help in the family business. During his time in England young Thomas had developed a great fondness for 'Nunk', as he called him. He later described Nunk as a "man of abilities, sound understanding, and fair character".[27]

---

26 Watson, John F., *Annals of Philadelphia and Pennsylvania*, (Philadelphia, 1844)

27 Willing, Thomas, Balch, Thomas Willing, *Willing letters and papers: edited with a biographical essay of Thomas Willing of Philadelphia (1631-1821)*, (Philadelphia, 1922)

Five years after completing his education and returning to Philadelphia, young Thomas wrote to his uncle for advice when his father, Charles, the sitting Mayor of Philadelphia, died suddenly of typhoid at the early age of 44. Thomas, then 23, now had the huge task of being the joint executor of his father's will; running his father's enterprise; and supporting his mother and ten younger siblings aged from 22 to 2. In a letter to Nunk Thomas said, 'Every moment I am more and more sensible of my unhappy situation and that of so large a family. God knows what may become of them bereft of their protector and direction. My Father's affairs are widely scattered abroad and it will require much time and assiduity to collect and settle them. If I have life and health I may be able to do it.'[28] One of his problems was that his father's will had been written in 1750 prior to a voyage to England. He did not update it on his return and two more children had been born since then for which there was no provision in the will.

With Nunk's encouragement, young Thomas Willing in Philadelphia overcame all his original apprehensions. He was so busy with his business and family affairs that he did not marry until he was 32 and as well as raising a large family became deeply involved in public life. He would go on to become Mayor of Philadelphia, a judge on the Supreme Court, President of the Bank of North America, and a member of the Continental Congress. This made him an important figure in the legislation of the newly independent United States twenty-five years later.

But all was not well with his relationship with his English relatives. A feud was about to develop that would take ten years to resolve.

---

28 Maxey, David W. *A Portrait of Elizabeth Willing Powel (1743-1830)*, Transactions of jthe American Philosophical Society. New Series, Vol 96, No. 4 (2006) pp i-v, vii, ix, xi, xiii, 1, 3-5, 7-11, 13, 15-33, 35-49, 51-61, 63-65, 67-85, 87, 89-91 (90 pages)

Chapter 7

All Change on the Island (1773-1800)

In the Island House Thomas Willing was reflecting on his life as he sat by the big bay window of the first floor drawing room in the warm August sunshine of 1773. He knew he was coming to the end of his life and he was glad he was at peace in this well-equipped comfortable house of three floors with six bedrooms. Downstairs his housekeeper, Elizabeth Harris, the daughter of some friends from Bristol, prepared his meals in a 'modern' kitchen that had a dresser, a range, and a pantry. In the scullery was a sink and copper for heating water and in the middle of the floor a dip well that collected water directly from the river Colne.

Years earlier, after his parents died, Thomas had taken a lease on the four-acre island at Longford from its owner, the King. The mill, mentioned in the Domesday Book, had long since fallen into disrepair, but the impressive Island House made an ideal country retreat from his London apartment.

Thomas had acquired a lot of wealth in his lifetime. He was satisfied that he had led a respectable life, which was honoured two years earlier by election to the Inner Temple in London. This accolade, usually given to members of the legal profession, was occasionally offered to notable people. Throughout his life he believed he had done his duty to his family; kept true to his faith, and was non-judgemental over morality differences. He knew his father, brother and nephew had traded in African slaves, in fact, in his will his brother Charles had distributed his slaves individually to members of his family. Thomas himself had once had a covenant (contracted) black servant called, Charles Gombo, who was born on the coast of Guinea, but who died aged 28 in Longford in 1761. He was buried in the burial ground of St Mary's Church, Harmondsworth. In 1769 nephew, Thomas, in Philadelphia, had listed on his tax return '3 negros, 3 horses, 2 cows'.[29] By this time the Philadelphian Quakers were feeling uncomfortable about slavery and finally in 1774 decided to disown members who bought, sold, or transferred slaves, and those that still owned them had to prepare them for their freedom 'with religious and secular education'.[30] Connections with the slave trade were not abolished in Britain until 1807.

Thomas Willing had not found a wife among the Society of Friends, preferring business to domestic life, but he had a sister in Bristol and another in Lichfield. His most frequent visitor was his niece Dorothy who he had first met as an eight-year-old in Philadelphia.

When she was eighteen Dorothy had scandalised her family by eloping with a British Royal Naval Officer called Walter Stirling, later to become Admiral Sir Walter Stirling, and they married in secret. The shock caused her father, Charles, to collapse, but they were reconciled shortly before his death a year later.

Dorothy (known as Dolly), returned to England with her new husband, and they settled in Hackney, London. During her husband's long absences at sea she had the support of Nunk, her only relative in England.

Now, in his twilight years, Thomas's health was weakening. Dolly and her children were visiting him regularly, as were some of his friends. One day, Dolly left Nunk's side and went through the front porch into the stable yard to greet Peter Warren, Thomas's close friend.

'How does he do?', Peter Warren asked as they walked towards the house.

'He is full of cheer, but I fear he is weakening.'

'Has he mentioned if he has written a will? He has so many business interests I am worried there will be a lot of complications if he does not write one soon.'

'I do not know. He has not said anything to me'

'You are the one closest to him. Can you find a way of asking him?'

---

29 Ancestry.co.uk. https://www.ancestry.co.uk/imageviewer/collections/2451/images/40524_277039-00201?treeid=&personid=&hintid=&usePUB=true&usePUBJs=true&_ga=2.87086110.769457777.1601279749-1618364450.1601279749&pId=16212962

30 Levy, Barry, *Quakers and the American Family*, (Oxford, 1988)

'Oh dear. How can I ask that question without it seeming that we are waiting for him to die to see how much we will benefit. I am only concerned with his health now, not what will happen in the future. It is too awkward to contemplate. In any case I have great respect for his ability to transact his own affairs.'

'Please do what you can. We need to know what his wishes are.'

Dolly dismissed the conversation whilst Peter Warren was visiting, but sometime later she realised the wisdom of his request. On an occasion when Dolly was sitting with Nunk reading to him from the newspaper the question of a will presented itself. With a pounding heart and mustering all her diplomacy skills, Dolly said, 'Nunk, have you thought about writing a will?'

Memorial in St. Mary's Church, Harmondsworth

'Sacred to the memory of Thomas Willing, Esq., of Longford in this Parish, whom departed this life on 29 August 1773 aged 50 years.'

In the same vault lies interred Sir Walter Stirling of Faskine in Scotland who died 24 November 1786 aged 69.'

Photo: Bob Speel (speel.me.uk)

'Do not worry, my dear, I am well aware of my duties in that regard.'

In fact Thomas Willing had written his will the previous October soon after Dolly's husband, Walter Stirling returned from the West Indies as Captain of HMS Portland, whom he made one of his four executors.

Thomas died on 29 August 1773. His funeral was a grand affair with gentry attending from all over England, who reflected his wide range of business interests. As well as his niece Dolly and her husband Captain Walter Stirling and their sons, there was his sister Dorothy with her husband George Hand, a lawyer from Litchfield, with some of their seven children, and his other sister Ann Willing from Bristol. Among his friends were an insurance broker from London, Peter Warren, who had underwritten all of the ships commissioned by Philadelphian Thomas, and John Vernon, of Lincoln's Inn, a lawyer and owner of a plantation in Antigua. A Bristol friend was John Vaughan a merchant who was later involved in the creation of the Bristol theatre and from London, John Nightingale a Banker from Lombard Street, London. In addition, there was

Dr William Cadogan, a governor of the Foundling Hospital and pioneer of paediatric medicine; also the widow of a notable political and religious essayist who was Thomas Willing's boyhood school-teacher. Other people from the village accompanied the coffin as it was borne on strong shoulders along the Bath Road, past the King's Head Inn and the Friends Meeting House until, just before the fifteenth milestone, the party turned left onto a footpath that led northwards for half a mile and entered the village centre of Harmondsworth.

> ### The Island, Longford
>
> There had been a mill on the island since the Domesday book. The fast-flowing river Colne provided excellent power to drive the water-wheel for a variety of industries. In 1788 a new Mill was built and leased to a series of calico printers. The mill had a spacious yard and a range of workshops and buildings. The fine clear water was also used for silk printing. The bow-fronted impressive residence of Island House was surrounded by pleasure gardens with an orchard and stabling. It had a view of Windsor Castle (now obliterated by the M25). The island was one of the last remnants of Crown property in Harmondsworth, having been in the gift of the incumbent monarch since William the Conquerer's reign.

Thomas Willing was buried in St Mary's parish church, and later a memorial plaque was placed inside the church on the east wall of the chancel. After the service the melancholy group went back to the Island House for refreshments and to hear the will read.

Nearly everyone at the funeral benefitted. There were annuities for some, lump sums of money for his nephews and nieces. Business friends, although wealthy in their own right, received generous lump sums. Dolly inherited the lease on Island House and land and the will had stated 'it is my desire that she will reside there'. He had left her his Inner Temple chambers 'to reside in when she is in Town', but half a year before he died he had added a codicil giving the Inner Temple chambers and all its books and furniture to his nephew George Hand. He compensated Dolly by giving her an extra £560.[31] He also left sums of money to Dolly's two sons. The residue of his estate was bequeathed to nephew Thomas in Philadelphia. By this time young Thomas had been building on the legacy of the £6000 left to him by his father and was one of the richest men in Philadelphia.

Dolly and her family settled happily into the Island House, but soon after they heard grumblings from America. Thomas in Philadelphia had forgiven his sister for the scandal and shame she had bought on the family

31 The National Archives, PROB 11/991/67

by eloping, but now he was aggrieved over his beloved Nunk's will. Thomas Willing, the younger, having already been Mayor of Philadelphia twice, and now serving on a subversive Committee organising a shadow government against the British, had a busy life. It seems surprising, therefore, that he had time to initiate a prolonged correspondence with Dolly accusing her of manipulating Nunk into changing his will shortly before his death, and thereby reducing the residue that was Thomas's inheritance. Probably the perceived betrayal upset him rather than the size of his inheritance for he was already an extremely wealthy man.

In the spring of 1774 Thomas in Philadelphia questioned the legitimacy of the will with one of the Executors, Peter Warren, who replied furiously that he should not question the integrity of himself or his sister. He went on to say that Thomas in Longford had been worried that his self-written will might not be regarded as legitimate, but his handwriting had been verified and it passed probate. So bitter were the letters from Thomas in Philadelphia, that Warren deliberately did not show them to his fellow Executor, Walter Stirling, Dolly's husband, for fear of deepening the family rift. Walter Stirling wrote to Thomas Willing in Philadelphia to explain the will, 'his whole estate real and personal will be somewhere about £16000 [£2.5million today], you are the residuary legatee and I am afraid will not get £5000 [£770,000 today]. I always thought it would be double that sum.'[32] Walter Stirling assured him that he would do everything to protect his interests. Whatever the underlying reason for Thomas's display of discontent it simmered on for ten years before he was reconciled with his sister.

When Dolly Stirling moved into the Island House at Longford her children were 15, 13 and 11. She felt it was better that they could now grow up in rural Middlesex away from the smoke and the grime of London. Her husband's family had Scottish estates where they spent time when he was on leave. From 1773-1775 the Royal Navy had no wars to fight and Captain Stirling was made head of the Impress Service in the Tower of London.

Walter Stirling returned to sea in 1780 by which time his children were adults. Their daughter Anna had married her cousin, Andrew Stirling, and was living in Scotland. Their eldest son, Walter, was in business in London, and second son Charles was in the Navy. Admiral Stirling returned from the

---

32 W. Stirling to T. Willing, September 2, 1774, TW Papers, Historical Society of Pennsylvania

> ### Impressment
>
> The Impress Service (colloquially called the "press-gang") was formed to force sailors to serve on naval vessels. There was no concept of "joining the navy" as a fixed career-path for non-officers at the time, since seamen remained attached to a ship only for the duration of its commission. The Royal Navy impressed many merchant sailors, as well as some sailors from other, mostly European, nations. People liable to impressment were "eligible men of seafaring habits between the ages of 18 and 55 years". During the period 1773-1775 18,540 men were recruited for the Royal Navy and 50,903 for the Merchant Navy by this service.
>
> Fischer, Lewis R.; Nordvik, Helge W. Shipping and Trade, 1750-1950: Essays in International Maritime Economic History 1990, p. 25.

West Indies in February of the following year with despatches announcing the capture of St Eustatius from the Dutch, a small, strategically important, Caribbean island used by the American rebels to get arms into the continent to fuel the war of Independence. On his return he received a knighthood. Admiral Sir Walter Stirling returned to the West Indies, but was not very well and gave up his command to return to England.

Dolly nursed him back to health, and when she felt he had recovered, journeyed to Scotland to visit her married daughter. She was taken ill, died, and was buried there in 1782 aged 47. From her scandalous teenage elopement, she had developed into a society lady and produced a banker son, an admiral son and a grandson who would became an Admiral and first Governor of Western Australia.

After her death, her husband was appointed Commander-in-Chief, The Nore, a command based at Chatham that saw him responsible for all naval bases in the Southeast of England. When George III inspected his fleet in 1783 he was so impressed that he offered Stirling a Baronetcy (heredity title), which he declined. Walter Stirling died in his London House in Red Lion Square on 24 November 1786. His remains were bought back to Harmondsworth where he was buried. On the east wall of the chancel, in St Mary's Church, next to the monument for Thomas Willing, there is a memorial to Sir Walter Stirling of Faskine, Scotland, 1786.[33]

In her will Dolly left the Island House to her eldest son, Walter Stirling junior, now Sir Walter, who had persuaded Pitt to give him the baronetcy that his father had declined. After an education at Harrow School, he went into the City of London and became a partner in the Banking Company

---

33 Lysons, Daniel, *An Historical Account of Those parishes in the County of Middlesex which are not described in the Environs of London* (London, 1800), p.137.

of Hodsoll & Stirling. He also became an MP in 1799, Fellow of the Royal Society in 1801, and was appointed High Sheriff of Kent for 1804-05. He married Susanna, the heiress daughter of George Trenchard Goodenough of Kent and the Isle of Wight, and she bore him a son and four daughters. Their comfortable life was shattered in 1806 when, after complications from the birth of their youngest daughter Susanna Maria, she died aged 36.[34] Her daughter, who had lived for a week and died the day before her mother was placed in the same coffin and a sad little funeral procession consisting of a hearse, mourning coaches and the carriages of a number of friends made their way along the Bath Road to Harmondsworth church for interment in the Stirling family grave.[35] A memorial plaque to Lady Stirling was placed on the North Wall of St Mary's Church, which together with details of her lineage and the date of her death describes her as 'gentle modest amiable and with manners the most unassuming in virtue and accomplishments unequalled. Her loss can only be assinged [sic] by meeting hereafter in the Regions of Immortality where all tears shall be wiped away.' Her husband was now left with four children under 10 years of age including a son, Walter George Stirling, who later inherited the baronetcy.

By 1824 Sir Walter and his son were directors of The Royal National Bath Company in London, a new company formed to build public baths all over London.[36] Not only was he Chairman, but the company's bankers were Hodsoll & Stirling. A month later he was on the Management Committee of the Thames Water Company, committed to getting clean and constant water to Londoners. His bank was also the company bankers.[37]

It was a time of peace and people had felt confident in investing in safe company stocks and bonds. It was an opportunity for banks to capitalize on this economic optimism. In January 1825 Stirling's bank, together with a similar bank headed by Sir John Perring, launched an investment bank, and investors were invited to buy shares of £50 each, which included life insurance.[38] They could not have set up the bank at a worst time. In April 1825 the Bank of England had adopted the Gold Standard to ensure all

34 https://www.clanmacfarlanegenealogy.info/genealogy/TNGWebsite/getperson
    php?personID=I10019&tree=CC

35 Sterling, Albert Mack, *The Stirling Genealogy*, (New York, 1909). Ancestry.co.uk. North America, Family Histories, 1500-2000

36 The Times (London, England), Saturday, October 2, 1824, Issue 12459, p.1.

37 The Times (London, England), Saturday, November 6, 1824, Issue 12491, p.2.

38 The Times (London, England), Wednesday, January 12, 1825, Issue 12548, p.2.

currency was matched against its gold reserves. This followed some poor decisions that resulted in the amount of money in circulation being more than its reserves. The Bank of England therefore started withdrawing some of the notes in general circulation and calling in loans. A few days later, with spectacular bad timing the newly formed investment bank of Perring and Stirling went ahead with an advertisement announcing that it was ready to receive tenders for "advances of money".[39] Neither baronet realised that a storm was brewing.

With the Bank of England calling in loans and reducing the circulation of bank notes people tried to sell their stocks and suffered losses when they found the market had dropped. Many turned to small banks to withdraw their cash and by December, with newspapers reporting the crisis, panic set in and there was a run on the banks.[40]

Suddenly Sir Walter Stirling found himself in trouble. His original bank had run out of liquidity and although the Government stepped in to try and slow the crisis it was too late for Hodsoll & Stirling, at 345 The Strand. It was too small to survive. The run on the main London banks had ceased and confidence had been restored, but smaller banks had suffered. Sir Walter was in deep trouble as his debts mounted. The honourable way out was to sell all his personal assets and on 12 July 1826, his Pall Mall mansion and all its contents went up for auction with no reserve. So large was the mansion and its contents that the sale went on for six days. It included antique furniture, Italian bronzes, valuable paintings and prints, nine thousand ounces of plated articles, china, a library of books, and a cellar of fine old wines 'selected with considerable judgement and at very great expense.'[41] King George IV bought the house and by December that year the King had moved his private library and personal items 'of great value' into it from his home at Carlton House, prior to its demolition. He lived there whilst waiting for the completion of the work to convert Buckingham House into Buckingham Palace.[42]

---

39 The Times (London, England), Monday, April 25, 1825, Issue 12636, p.4.

40 Dick, Alexander J., "On the Financial Crisis, 1825-26" https://www.branchcollective.org/?ps_articles=alexander-j-dick-on-the-financial-crisis-1825-26

41 Sun (London) – Tuesday 27 June 1826

42 The Times (London, England), Tuesday, December 12, 1826, Issue 13147, p.2.

The sale of all Sir Walter Stirling's assets allowed him to pay off a substantial part of his debt. By March 1827 he had paid off fifteen shillings in the pound and was about to make payment on the rest.[43] This restored his good name and he appeared at King William IV's first levee (formal reception) on 21 July 1830 at St James's Palace where he presented his son, Walter George Stirling, to the King.[44]

When Sir Walter died on 25 August 1832 at 2 Albany buildings, Piccadilly, aged 74, a newspaper described him as having the 'most courteous and conciliating disposition, much esteemed by all who knew him.'[45] It mentioned that when his bank failed he not only fully discharged its debts in a short time, but paid interest to the creditors. In his will of 1829 he regretted that 'now that my situation is much altered in point of wealth' he could not give his daughters more than he gave them on their marriage, but that did not mean he loved them less than his son. To his son he left assets that included shares in the Drury Lane and Covent Garden theatres.[46] Most of the remaining assets, however, had to be sold so that he could reimburse his father-in-law, George Trenchard Goodenough, the £300 a year allowance he had been paying him. He was buried in St Mary's church, Harmondsworth, and a memorial plaque on the wall, underneath that of his father, states: 'To the Memory of Sir Walter Stirling of Faskine, Lanarkshire, and of Shoreham, Kent, Baronet, F.R.S. & A.S. (son of the above) whose remains lie deposited beneath this chancel. He was elected representative for Gatton in 1798: and sat subsequently in three succeeding parliaments from 1806 to 1820 for St Ives in Cornwall. High Sheriff for Kent in 1804 and a deputy Lieutenant for that County. He was a man of the highest honor [sic] and most amiable character. He was born in June 26th 1756, and died much esteemed and respected August 25th 1832.'

The sale of Island House did not end the Stirling family's connection to Harmondsworth because less than eighteen months later, Sir Walter Stirling's younger brother, Vice-Admiral Charles Stirling, died at his home at Weybridge on 7 November 1833. As his funeral procession passed through the town of Chertsey all the shops closed and the principal tradesmen joined the procession, along with fourteen carriages carrying the

43 The Times (London, England), Wednesday, March 14, 1827, Issue 13226, p.4.

44 The Times, Thursday, July 22, 1830, Issue 14285, p.2.

45 Morning Advertiser – Thursday 30 August 1832

46 The National Archives, PROB-11-1806-29

gentry of the neighbourhood who wished to attend the funeral of this well-respected local hero. The procession was on its way to St Mary's Church, Harmondsworth, where widower Charles Stirling was interred next to his wife in the family vault and fittingly passed through Longford and past his childhood home on the Island before continuing into Harmondsworth village. [47]

This mournful event ended the connection with the Willing/Stirling family of Longford who had resided at Island House for sixty years. New tenants (the Island was Crown property) moved into the house and the ancient paper mill, which had ceased operating at the beginning of the eighteenth century, was replaced by a new Mill and leased to a calico printer.

* * *

At the dawn of the nineteenth century agriculture was the primary occupation in Britain and farming practices were changing to make the industry more efficient.[48] There had been a succession of poor harvests, and farmers were worried about how they would find the means to pay the myriad of taxes being forced on them by the war-mongering Government. They needed to grow more crops and for that they needed more land. In the Weekly House both surviving sons of Thomas Weekly and Elizabeth Streating, were now grown up and married into the same dynastic Baptist families as their forebears. Young Thomas Weekly, like his grandfather married into the Tillyer family in 1788 and farmed Manor Farm in Harmondsworth village, owned by absentee landlord Arthur Annesley Powell of Quex House, Kent.

Richard Weekly inherited the Weekly house and its freehold 66-acre Longford farm, and by 1800 was also the tenant of a 300 acre neighbouring farm called Perry Oaks. His absentee landlord was Thomas Wood of Littleton. The landlords earned revenue on their land by leasing it to the resident Baptist farmers who passed the land down through the generations. If more land was available they could increase their income. The absentee landowners were hatching a plan to make this happen.

---

47 Windsor and Eton Express – Saturday 23 November 1833
48 https://www.geog.cam.ac.uk/research/projects/occupations/britain19c/papers/paper3.pdf

Chapter 8

Land Redistribution (1805-1819)

As the nineteenth century began, a change was creeping across the English countryside. Where there was once a terrain of woods and common land with vast open cultivated fields there was now a patchwork of individual fields separated by hedges. Cottagers, who for centuries had been allowed a strip of land to grow crops to feed their family in return for doing work, or supplying produce for the Lord of the Manor, were losing their customary rights to pannage on common land where they also gathered firewood and foraged for nuts and berries. Enclosing land into separate fields increased the efficiency and productivity of the land for the owners, but deprived the lower classes of their common rights.

Richard Weekly's landlord, Thomas Wood had arranged a secret meeting in Longford with the other absentee landlords, and now these gentlemen were comfortably seated in the private parlour at the King's Head. There was only one item on the agenda and that was to decide whether to invest money in hiring commissioners to survey the parish and apply to Parliament for an Act to enclose land within Harmondsworth Parish. Most of the cultivated land in Harmondsworth (1404 acres) was open arable fields, in addition there were 295 acres of meadow and pasture alongside the rivers. The prize for the landowners was the distribution of uncultivated parish land, which was the wasteland of Hounslow Heath. The Heath came within the boundaries of several parishes but Harmondsworth had the largest proportion at that time.[49] If the parish abolished manorial and vicarial tithes they could hand out portions of land in compensation to

---

49 Lysons, Daniel, *An Historical Account of Those Parishes in the County of Middlesex*, (London, 1800) p. 137.

the Lord of the Manor and the Vicar. This would increase their landholdings and any spare land could be sold off to pay for some of the cost of preparing the Parliamentary Act. At the meeting the landowners all committed to start the legal procedure.

To begin the process of enclosure the leading landowners had to appoint and fund commissioners who would examine evidence of individual land claims, draw up a map of ownership, and submit a proposal to Parliament. Only if the plan received the approval of Parliament did the proposed changes become legal. It took time for the commissioners to get landowners and parish representatives to agree on how the common land was to be distributed, but although there were many disputes it only needed three-quarters of the landowners of the most valuable parish land to agree and the dispute was settled, the smaller landowners being left with no voice. Harmondsworth Inclosure Act (which included the hamlets of Longford, Heathrow and Sipson) proposed to enclose and cultivate the 1176 acres of common parish land on Hounslow Heath, but it had to be allocated fairly.[50] In some parts of the country there was resistance to the loss of commons, but in Harmondsworth with no resident Lord of the Manor and most villagers employed by the farmers there was little change in the villagers' summary rights to protest about.

The Harmondsworth Commissioners began work in 1805. They held their periodic meetings at the King's Head in Longford where they took evidence of ownership from interested parties.[51] The Commissioners were John Trumper of Harefield, Middlesex, Thomas Chapman of Richmond, Surrey, and Abraham Purshouse Driver of the Kent Road, Surrey. Agreement was finally reached after a long-drawn out process where arguments from both the gainers and losers were discussed. Roads and footpaths were straightened and widened and those that lost privileges in the new arrangement received additional land elsewhere as compensation. The Act not only specified land allocation, but where drains (ditches) were to be built or maintained, as well as footpaths, bridges, tunnels and fences. Some of the reclaimed land was sold to pay the Commissioners expenses, and some landowners agreed to swap land between themselves if it resulted in a consolidation of their land holdings. At the end of the process a map

---

50 Inclosure was the official spelling at that time, although we now use the word Enclosure.

51 Sherwood, P.T., Harmondsworth Agriculture, West Drayton & District Local History Society, 1973.

detailing each land allocation and the names of the owners was produced. The final plan and agreement for Harmondsworth was completed in 1816, but inconveniently one Commissioner, John Trumper, died before it was submitted to Parliament. The Harmondsworth Inclosure Act was finally passed in 1819.

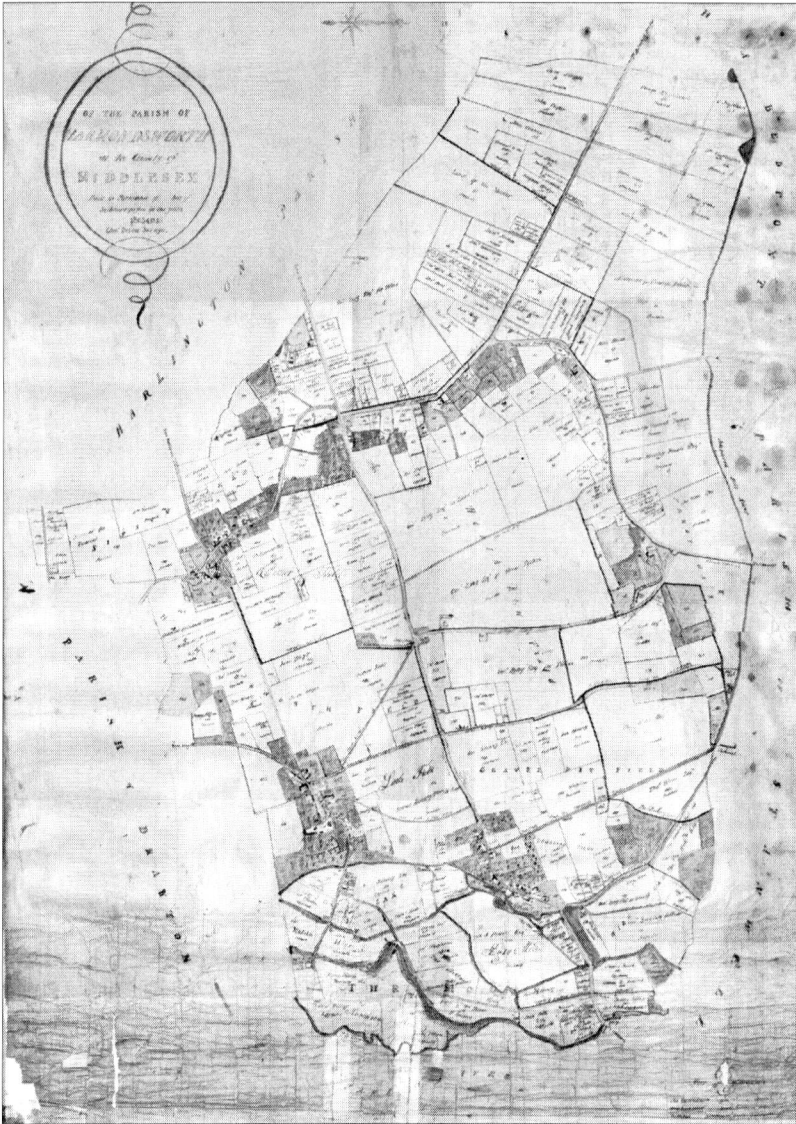

Original 1816 Harmondsworth Enclosure Map. Orientated east/west. Longford is at the bottom and at the top the reclaimed land from Hounslow Heath. The straight road is a new road through the new allocations of land.

* * *

King George III, took a great interest in agriculture and was keen to adopt new, scientific, farming methods on his own farms. It earned him the nickname 'Farmer George'. On a cold damp winter's day in January 1805, George III was returning to Windsor from attending, what turned out to be, his last Opening of Parliament.[52] He had been on the throne for forty years and now spent most of his time at Windsor Castle. The castle had been little used by the Monarchy after Charles II had repaired and restored it following the ravages of the civil war, but now George III was renovating and furnishing the castle to his taste.

Longford was to see a lot of George III during his reign, but only when passing through the village. He did not stop to change his horses at the King's Head like his predecessors. He disliked meeting the public, and had his own brick buildings with a red pantiled roof built along the route where he could change his horses in private.

On this January day the King sat snugly in his carriage wrapped in fur rugs whilst the carriage and his military escort stopped at a low modest building known locally as the Soldiers Shed on the Great Bath Road near the 14th milestone.

Here, the carriage horses and military escort from London handed over the escort duty to another troop. Only this day it was different.

Unfortunately, due to bad communication, two military parties turned up to escort the King to Windsor, the Light Dragoons and the Oxford Blues. After changing the horses, the carriage continued its journey towards Longford, with the Light Dragoons as the escort. The Oxford Blues, were not allowing this and insisted it was their duty to escort the King. A scuffle ensued and both parties defended themselves with swords drawn whilst His Majesty's carriage was still going on at the usual pace with each party trying to keep position as escort. After some distance, the Light Dragoons gave up and the Blues continued.[53] The elderly King, now nearly blind, was unaware of the skirmish, but out in the fields alongside the Bath Road, the labourers were highly entertained by the spectacle of mounted troops fighting each other. As usual, at the sight of the King's procession,

---

52 Belsham, William, Memoirs of the Reign of George III.: From the Treaty of Amiens, A. D. 1802, to the Termination of the Regency, A. D. 1820 : in Two Volumes, Volume 1, (Hurst, Robinson, 1824 – Great Britain) p.80

53 Evening Mail – Monday 21 January 1805

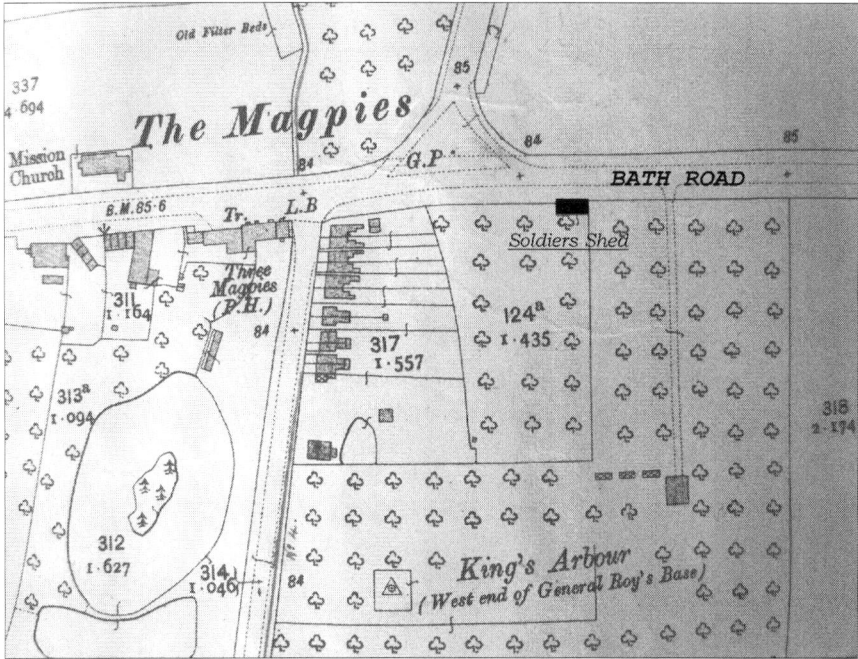

Position of Soldiers Shed. 1895 Map

King George III travelling along the Bath Road by R. B. Davis
From: Bath Road by Charles G. Harper.
http://www.gutenberg.org/files/37921/37921-h/37921-h.htm

they politely doffed their caps at the passing carriage, puffed on their clay tobacco pipes and returned to their toil.

Soon after this the King's mental illness confined him to Windsor for the rest of his life and one of his last journeys along the Bath Road was recorded by artist R.B. Davis in a painting. (page 59)

No longer required, the soldiers shed, and the one and a quarter acres around it, fell into disuse, but stayed in the possession of the Crown Estates until 1859, when Queen Victoria's Commissioners of Her Majesty's Woods Forests and Land Revenues sold it to local landowner, William Philp for £60.[54] The decrepit building was still there in 1910. It is now demolished and the site is an office car park.

* * *

Although after 1806, when George III went into retreat at Windsor, Longford no longer saw their Monarch, they did participate in a mournful royal event on 4th December 1818 when the funeral procession of Queen Charlotte, wife of George III, stopped at Longford on its way from Kew to Windsor for the burial service. The whole of London had come to a halt for the funeral. Churches of all denominations were open for worship and hung with black. Their bells tolled mournfully throughout the day. The procession left Kew Palace at ten in the morning with a military escort of the brigade of Guards wearing black crepe scarfs and sashes. The hearse was followed by seven private carriages each pulled by six horses. The 16th Lancers followed the procession as it slowly moved along the roads which had been cleared of traffic. There was a problem, though, when the procession reached Kew Bridge and the toll-keeper, after letting a few carriages through, decided to shut the gate as people were streaming through too fast for him to collect the toll and he was swamped by the masses.[55] In spite of the poor weather an estimated 5000 people followed the cortege from Kew in coaches, stages and carriages as well as on foot. Some carried bundles of provisions for the long journey. The procession reached Longford at 2pm and at the King's Head all the Ladies, Noblemen and Gentlemen of the Queen's household, as well as representatives of the royal family and government, entered the inn for refreshments. After a long slow bumpy ride in a carriage they were all pleased to have an hour's rest at the inn before continuing on to the funeral at Windsor.

54 London Metropolitan Archives. Acc2305/PH/17/1[?]
55 Northampton Mercury – Saturday 5 December 1818

The whole of the King's Head had been cleared of customers and put at the disposal of the mourners.[56] Longford had not seen such a spectacle for many years. By now the London crowds following the cortege had thinned out, but as the procession approached Windsor it was joined by carriages containing the Prince Regent and other family members. By the time the procession reached Windsor it was dark. The traffic in the town halted, to allow it to pass freely through to St George's chapel and the streets of Windsor were lined with Grenadier Guards every sixth one carrying a flambeau (flaming torch). Unfortunately, the procession did not have the precision timing of today's royal events and arrived at the chapel an hour early. This resulted in some of the members of the chapel procession, including the Chancellor of the Exchequer, arriving too late to take part in the funeral. Queen Charlotte's husband, George III, was too ill to have any understanding that she had died, and did not attend the funeral. It would be another thirteen months before he too, died and his body was interred in St George's Chapel.

* * *

By 1800 Richard Weekly had added to the 66 acres of his Longford farm by taking the tenancy of a 300 acre estate adjoining his property called Perry Oaks, a substantial freehold property once a sub-Manor of Harmondsworth. It was owned by Thomas Wood of Littleton, whose home is now the site of Shepperton Film Studios. Richard Weekly was 33 when he married Mary Wild in 1805 and brought his bride home to the impressive Tudor farmhouse at Perry Oaks (where Heathrow's Terminal Five now stands) leaving his

> ### Perry Oaks Farm
>
> House: built late 16th century, remodelled in 18th century with additions made at north end and the west side heightened. East side has three gables. Three doors of 17th and early 18th century. The barn: north-west of house is timber framed and probably 16th century. It has seven bays with queen-post trusses and a porch. The barn west of the house has been incorporated in a larger building. Pigeon House: 17th century.
>
> Royal Commission on Historical Monuments England. 1937

mother living in the Weekly House with some servants and farm manager, William Hester, at the Longford farm. Richard Weekly was a busy man, not only did he have a large acreage to farm, with a workforce of 17 men and eight women, he was very involved in the administration of the Colnbrook

---

56 Worcester Journal – Thursday 10 December 1818

Perry Oaks farm. Built late 16th century. Remodelled 18th century. Demolished 1939.
Photo credit A.S Peacock 1939

Baptist church, becoming a Deacon in 1827. The year after their marriage their first child arrived, a daughter called Mary. Their eldest surviving son, Richard, was born in 1814.

* * *

A year later nearly the whole world suffered from a devastating summer resulting from an enormous volcanic eruption on 10 April 1815 when Mount Tambora, a volcano in the Dutch East Indies (now Indonesia), sent an ash cloud into the atmosphere that caused a world-wide volcanic winter. It was the largest eruption for 1,300 years and had been preceded by a series of other eruptions which together built up a layer of dust in the atmosphere that caused havoc with the climate. The following year, 1816, universally known as the year without a summer, the temperature remained very low, the crops failed, there was torrential rain and flooding in some countries, and many people starved to death around the world. Middlesex crops suffered from the extreme cold. By May the ground was only just warm enough for seeds to germinate. The grass was so poor that sheep and lambs were having to be fed on winter storage.[57] On the fine fertile soil of Harmondsworth the wheat was managing to produce a sparse crop after the late frosts in May. In August, the normal time for harvesting corn, most farms were still gathering hay of poor quality, but turnips, potatoes, and cabbages were surviving in the cold and wet. The torrential rain laid most of the wheat crop flat. By 14 August in Middlesex most wheat was still green and although some of the ears of corn were beginning to brown, the kernals within them were still milky. Oats were in the same condition.[58] The general lack of sun and warmth was affecting all crops. Harmondsworth had the advantage of good soil where some germination had taken place, but in other areas whole crops failed. In Scotland and Northern England the harvest had still not began by 1 October. Peas and beans everywhere were not maturing, and wheat seed, for the next season's crop, was in short supply. In Southern England the corn harvest was beginning to recover with the late fine weather (a full year and half after the explosive eruption of Mount Tambora), and was still being harvested up to the middle of October although of poor quality.[59] It was a very worrying time for the Longford farmers.

* * *

It was not long, though, before the farmers discovered a new market. The fast-expanding population of London required feeding and Longford farmers now began growing market garden produce.

Even before the Piazza at Covent Garden was built in 1635 traders had set up stalls against the wall of Bedford House to sell fresh produce.[60] After the Great Fire of London, Charles II granted William, Earl of Bedford, a Royal Charter to hold a market for fruit and vegetables at Covent Garden in 1670. Covent Garden customers, only fifteen miles from Longford, appreciated the supply of fresh vegetables that now arrived daily from West Middlesex.

The farmers of Longford were now adapting to the market demand by changing the type of crops they grew. As well as growing peas, beans and cabbages, fruit was being grown in the orchards and some glass

---

57 Monthly Agricultural Report. Morning Chronicle – Wednesday 01 May 1816
58 Monthly Agricultural Report. Morning Post – Monday 02 September 1816
59 Monthly Agricultural Report. Kentish Gazette – Tuesday 05 November 1816
60 Webber, Ronald, *Covent Garden: Mud-salad market*, (London, 1969) p.16.

constructions were being erected to grow more delicate produce. In October 1803, there was such a heavy thunderstorm with rain and hailstones that they pierced the leaves of the cabbages and other plants, damaged fruit and broke glass-frames in the Longford area.[61] In spite of this the farms were prospering. So too were the inns as the coaching trade continued to increase. The fear of being robbed by highwaymen had declined after Hounslow Heath was enclosed and cultivated, and now travel felt safer, but for some there was less optimism.

61 Hampshire Telegraph – Monday 02 May 1803

Chapter 9

The Bath Road (1807-1827)

The King's Head inn was busier than ever. The large Queen Anne room hosted the Inclosure Commissioner's meetings, as well as inquests, and auction sales. The Bath Road, now widened through Longford, saw fifty-five coach services a week plying the fifty-mile route to Reading – a journey that could now be accomplished in one day. As well as the coach services, there were also thirty goods carriers a week on the same route and dozens of private carriages. All these travellers required refreshments and fresh horses.

Widowed Mary Bedford, the licensee of the King's Head, died in 1807. The alcohol licence then passed jointly to her daughter Peggy and son Joseph.[62] When Joseph died in 1833 aged 52, Peggy became the sole proprietor of the inn for the next 26 years. She was so well-known by travellers that the inn's original name was forgotten and was always referred to as the Peggy Bedford. She never married, but references to her being Dick Turpin's mistress became part of her legend. Hounslow Heath was not one of Dick Turpin's haunts so it was unlikely that they knew each other, although that does not exclude the possibility that she was involved with other infamous highwaymen. Whatever the facts there would have been a conspiracy of silence, among the villagers, around any illegal nocturnal activity for fear of being the next victim.

* * *

---

62 Required since 1736. 9 Geo. 2, c.23. *An Act for laying a Duty upon the Retailers of Spirituous Liquors, and for licensing the Retailers thereof.*

Miss Peggy Bedford

The Bath Road provided a pageant of unexpected events for the villagers of Longford. In May 1826, just as the first light of dawn was showing in the east over London, people heard a strange noise. It was the sound of many marching feet. The Third Regiment of Foot Guards was marching through Longford on its way from Windsor to London. It was a spectacle not to be missed by the farmworkers who ran out of the yards to see the troops in their red jackets and high black hats. [63] The carters returning from delivering to the London markets pulled their carts to a halt at the side of the road to let the soldiers pass and to wish them well. The Guards were on their way to Portugal. Although Britain was in a period of peace after the Napoleonic wars, British troops were being sent to help its ally Portugal restore order after unrest caused by a war of succession between the children of the late King John VI. The King's son, Pedro, was already Emperor of Brazil and briefly King of Portugal, but when the waring siblings reached an agreement, he handed over the Portuguese throne to his sister, Maria. Ironically, when her descendant, Manuel II, the last King of Portugal, was deposed he ended his days in exile at Fulwell Park, Middlesex, just ten miles from Longford.

* * *

At the other end of the village street from the King's Head was (and still is) The Kings Arms. It is not a listed building but had been trading from at least the late 18th century. In 1818 two brothers, James and Richard Tillyer, who were gentlemen Baptist farmers employing many people in the parish, hosted a dinner at the Kings Arms after a day on which the non-conformists demonstrated the strength of the community co-operation. This event was unusual enough to be reported in the newspapers and was

63 Oxford Journal – Saturday 06 May 1826

The Kings Arms in the early 20th century

the result of the brothers taking the tenancy of nearby Stanwell Park Farm, owned by Sir John Gibbons. It was November, a time when the fields would normally have been prepared for the next year's harvest, but this ground was untouched. To avoid the brothers having to miss the harvest, the neighbouring farmers offered to give the brothers one day's work bringing with them their labourers and ploughing teams to help prepare the land. Between six and seven in the morning of an unusually fine November day 125 teams assembled on the land comprising 389 horses and a yoke of oxen. These teams, together with labourers and all necessary equipment started work and in the first hour twenty acres had been ploughed. The normal ploughing rate for a two-horse team would be no more than two acres a day. In that one day 100 acres were ploughed, harrowed and rolled and sixty acres were sown with wheat and 20 acres with tares.[64] The event attracted

> **Tares**
>
> Winter Tares is an annual fast growing vetch. It fixes nitrogen in the soil and is winter hardy. It can be used for weed suppression and animal fodder.
>
> www.kingsseeds.com

64 Tares: see panel

agriculturalists and yeoman from around the area to witness such a mass effort. At the end of the day the labourers' were presented with a small gratuity, and a substantial lunch with plenty of ale. The Gentlemen were treated to a good dinner at the Kings Arms in Longford.[65] This was one of the rare opportunities for farmers in the area to come together socially and to discuss farming matters. The event would lead eventually to the formation of a West Middlesex Agricultural and Market Garden Society in 1837.

One of the aims of the later Society was to foster good relationships, not only with fellow farmers, but with the labourers. The agrarian revolution and the enclosure of commons and wasteland caused hardship and poverty in some areas. Unemployment increased with the beginning of mechanisation in farming and this led to protests and unrest. The Middlesex farmers were anxious to prevent discontent among their workers.

In Longford there was no shortage of work. Those that did not work on the land had alternative employment choices, but people in other parts of the country had fewer opportunities. When work was hard to find, people went looking for it and the only way to do that was on foot.

One day, in spring 1827, Abraham White, at 37 a middle-aged man for that time, was walking through Longford overnight on his way to London. He came from a village near Newbury, Berkshire, and had been looking for work as a gardener, but after failing to find work in Maidenhead he continued walking. Walking at night was easier because the roads were quieter and he was ashamed of his shabby appearance. He was tired, hungry, and desperate to get some money so that he could eat. As he passed the Weekly House he saw a dung fork in the yard, which he thought he would take and sell to buy food. When he went into the yard to pick up the fork he saw the roughly built hen house and wondered if he would find an egg in there to eat. He was so desperate for food that he pulled at the boards of the hen house until he could reach inside. The temptation to take more than he needed was too great. He pulled out some fowls, and a number of eggs, stuffed them into a sack, and hurried on his way breaking an egg into his mouth as he went. He had got as far as the thirteenth milestone, two miles from Longford, when a patrol stopped him. The damaged henhouse had been spotted at 5am, and the patrol had been looking for anyone suspicious. The patrolman, Joseph Sawyer said,

65 Hereford Journal – Wednesday 11 November 1818

'What have you got here? What have you got, fowls?'

White replied, 'Yes, I bought them at Maidenhead – I have been walking all night, and am much fatigued'

'How many have you got?'

'Seven or Eight'

White then confessed that he got them from Mr Weekly's farmyard and he returned there with the patrolman. William Hester, Mr Weekly's husbandman identified the fowls. They were all returned, but a crime had been committed. White was sent for trial at the Old Bailey (Central Criminal Court) in London and accused of stealing ten live tame fowls, value ten shillings; twenty-seven eggs, value two shillings, one fork value one shilling. [66] Richard Weekly, William Hester, Joseph Sawyer all gave evidence. The prisoner pleaded distress. On 31 May 1827 he was found guilty and sentenced to seven years deportation. He was taken to Portsmouth and boarded the prison hulk, Leviathan, an old naval ship that had seen action in the Battle of Trafalgar. He entered the ship on 10 July 1827 and was issued with clothing, blankets, mess mugs and plate. He was set to work in gangs doing manual work ashore for 10 or 12 hours a day, all the while wearing heavy ankle chains.[67] He did this for four years until on 15 November 1831 he was put on a ship that took him to Australia where he disappeared from the records.

* * *

The busy Bath Road, provided a theatre, a thoroughfare, and an income for the village, but for the traveller it presented many dangers. Carriage and horse accidents, highwaymen and robbers competed with natural hazards. In Longford, being low-lying and near several rivers, mist and fog was a common peril. On Monday 19 November 1827 William Moody, the son of the proprietor of the London to Windsor coach company, was driving his father's stagecoach with passengers when in thick fog he suddenly saw a wagon in front of him and swerved to avoid it. The two front horses shied and hit the wagon, which broke the pole and traces. Mr Moody, was jerked off the box with his hands entangled in the reins and was dragged fifty

66 Old Bailey Proceedings Online (www.oldbaileyonline.org, version 8.0, 21 March 2019), May 1827, trial of ABRAHAM WHITE (t18270531-125).

67 https://www.ourfamilypast.com/article/topic/7397/haa007-breakout-2-prison-hulks-and-leviathan

yards along the road before he could release himself. He was taken to the local inn seriously injured, but eventually did recover from his accident.[68] None of the passengers were injured, but the following morning another Moody coach met with an accident in London when the driver struck the side of Temple Bar as he drove through it.[69] Both the driver and a passenger sitting beside him on the box of the carriage were seriously injured when they were thrown off onto the road. A month later the same coach company had an axle break on the road at Longford, but luckily the coach did not fall over and the passengers were uninjured.[70] The Moody coach company ran four coaches a day from Windsor to London and back and boasted that they completed the journey in only two and a half hours. [71] The coaches were a familiar sight in Longford where they would change horses. William Moody who survived the accident in the November mists of 1827 had other serious accidents from which he recovered, but his older brother, and his father both died in coaching accidents.

One of the natural hazards in the summer for the Bath Road travellers was the choking dust created by the wheels of the carriages breaking up the dried mud of the road. To lay the dust water was sprayed on the road. In 1827 the Colnbrook Turnpike Trust had spent £759 on trying to solve this problem. They had wells dug every two miles, installed pumps and bought new water carts. The pumps were made by Fowler & Co of Lambeth and were about two metres high in order to be tall enough to fill a barrel mounted on a cart. One has been preserved, today, at Longford near the 15th milestone. From March to October the road would be watered twice daily in dry weather, except for Sundays. This practice continued into the twentieth century until just before the first World War when the road surface was sprayed with tar.

Competitiveness between coach companies became apparent one Saturday night in February 1827, when rival coaches clashed, terrifying their fare-paying passengers. Mr Wyatt the proprietor of the Marlow coach was driving between the Magpies and Longford when he caught up with the Henley coach and they began to race each other. After driving furiously for a considerable distance one of the horses on the Henley coach

---

68 The Examiner – Sunday 25 November 1827
69 Berkshire Chronicle – Saturday 24 November 1827.
70 Berkshire Chronicle – Saturday 15 December 1827
71 Windsor and Eton Express – Saturday 12 May 1838

fell. The coach stayed upright and the passengers, although shocked and shaken, were uninjured. Seeing his rival stop, and seeing that no one was injured Mr Wyatt, normally a compassionate man towards his horses and passengers, did not stop to help his adversary but continued his journey.[72] The rivalry between coach companies was becoming bitter. In November that year a paid informer convinced the courts that Wyatt had been carrying more passengers than he was licensed to carry. On appeal this conviction was overturned, but not before damaging his reputation. Two years later, after failing to attract enough passengers Frederick Wyatt found himself in the bankruptcy court, but only two months later he had paid off his debts and was running a new service between Marlow and New Inn, Old Bailey, London.[73]

The continued rivalry between coach companies and attempts to put their competitors out of business by reporting them to the law led to an altercation in Longford in June 183. John Bowles, the driver of Gray's Windsor coach was driving through Longford when he suddenly pulled up outside the Kings Arms. He jumped off the box, red-faced with fury, and together with another man, who was holding a halter, they went inside the public house and into the parlour where two men were drinking tea. Bowles snatched the halter from the other man's hand and jerking one of the men at the table to his feet said, 'You b......, how would you like to have this halter thrown round your neck and dragged through a horse pond?' Saying that he threw the halter over the surprised man's head and dragged him down.

The man, Irving, was stunned by this aggression. His companion, Nightingale,

Longford pump on the
Bath Road today.

72 Berkshire Chronicle – Saturday 10 February 1827
73 Reading Mercury – Monday 17 August 1829

jumped up to protest and a scuffle broke out. Other people got involved and amidst the confusion the group spilled into the street. The hostility seemed to be caused by a rumour that Irving was an informer and it took an hour before the two were able to leave Longford.

Bowles was eventually taken into custody by three police officers who took him to Queen Street police office in London where he appeared before magistrates accused of assaulting W. Irving, a man who, unknown to him, was a police officer.

Irving gave his evidence first. 'I went to Longford, near Cranford Bridge in a horse and gig with Mr Nightingale, a local tradesman, to serve a summons on a person named Hester. After I had served the summons I went in the Kings Arms public house and had some tea in the parlour.' He then described how Bowles had attacked him.

In the Court Bowles said, 'It is certainly true what the officer has stated, and I am extremely sorry for what I did. I regret it very much, but I did not know at the time that he was a police officer.'

The Magistrate told him 'But whether he was an officer or not, what right had you to treat any man in such a manner?'

Irving told the Court, 'I have no vindictive feeling whatever towards the Coach driver, but both I and brother officers have been repeatedly attacked when we, in the execution of our duty, have to go a few miles into the country to serve summonses, and in many instances we run the risk of our lives.'

Magistrate: 'You acted perfectly right in bringing the case forward. If such conduct was to be tolerated it would be impossible for any officer to serve a legal process. I am glad that the accused is sensible of his error and on that account I will mitigate the penalty to forty shillings and costs.' Bowles immediately paid the fine.[74]

* * *

As the nineteenth century progressed, and steam power was revolutionising industrial processes, thoughts were turning to what this new energy source could do for farming. Other entrepreneurs were already producing innovative machines and Longford was about to witness the excitement of an experiment with one of them.

---

74 Windsor and Eton Express – Saturday 30 June 1832.

Chapter 10

The Threat of Steam (1829-1831)

Mornings started early at the Forge in Longford. The furnace had to be lit and brought up to heat before any work could be done and it was not unusual for the men to be active in the forge at 5am, but on this bright summer morning with the doors open to dispel the heat there was something unusual going on. There were rumbling and hissing noises in the distance and a slight trail of smoke moved along the top of the hedgerows.

The men went outside and stood on the Bath Road puzzling over what could be making the sound. The noise was getting louder and coming from the direction of London at a speed faster than a horse and carriage. More people were emerging from the cottages or looking out of their windows as the thunderous noise grew louder. When the noise-maker came into sight it appeared to be a large carriage with inside and outside seating and at the rear six large vertical tubes rising into the air from which a small amount of smoke was emitting. The whole vehicle was enveloped in a cloud of steam and dust from the road, but the amazing machine had no horses pulling it. This was 1829, and engineers were experimenting with steam propulsion. George and Robert Stephenson had already demonstrated a steam engine that could run on rails, but a public railway that could take passengers was still a year away. The incredible machine that was hissing its way through Longford did not need rails. This vehicle was on a trial journey from London to Bath and back. The intention was to demonstrate the feasibility of a steam carriage that could run on normal roads faster and cheaper than horse-drawn transport.

The sight, sound, and smell of the steamer as it rolled along the road on its six wheels was astounding to the people of Longford. It did not stop.

The water tanks needed filling every four miles and it had already halted outside Longford to fill the tank from the roadside pump. The seven people sitting on top of the open carriage waved to the villagers who were staring open-mouthed as they passed, but the man in the lower front seat kept his eyes straight ahead whilst holding the rod that was the steering mechanism.

Goldsworthy Gurney's steam carriage. Pyall engraving 1830.

The villagers followed the vehicle along the Bath Road. They were keen to see what would happen at the three narrow bridges it still had to cross. It easily cleared the bridge over the Kings river, but the next bridge was being repaired and a pile of bricks was stacked beside the road which partially obstructed the way ahead. In front of the steam vehicle was a slow-moving broad-wheeled wagon and as the steamer passed it, and neared the bridge, the Mail coach from Bath appeared at the top of the bridge advancing rapidly. The steamer driver shouted to him to pull up, but the coach driver, momentarily stunned by the sight of such a strange vehicle, kept going and there was a collision. The lead horses on the Mail were now so close to the steamer that they took fright, broke their traces, and bolted. To try to avoid the collision the steamer driver turned towards the pile of bricks and the impact damaged one of the wheels.

Both vehicles were on a schedule, and the accident was reported to have caused a delay of about a quarter of an hour whilst they were repaired. All of which gave work to William Passingham, the blacksmith at the Forge, and great entertainment to the people of Longford.

After a few mishaps along the way, including being stoned by people in Melksham, the steam vehicle reached Bath and on the following Monday, 3 August, made the return journey to Cranford Bridge without mishap and passed through Longford around 4.45pm. The whole journey from Bath had taken 11 hours including stoppages. It appears that, apart from the accident in Longford, no horse had taken fright at the steamer, the smoke nuisance was reduced by burning coke, and the journey was declared a success.

After hearing of this experimental and innovative journey, the Prime Minister, the Duke of Wellington, asked for a demonstration. This took place on 12 August, at Hounslow Barracks, in front of various Lords and Ladies, members of the government, the military and scientists. A carriage was attached to the steam engine in which sat the Duke and some of the guests. Mr Goldsworthy Gurney, the inventor, drove the vehicle around the parade ground in various patterns to demonstrate its manoeuvrability. After which a wagon containing twenty-seven soldiers was attached and the engine pulled this load with ease. The Duke of Wellington observed that it was impossible to calculate the benefits from such an invention.[75]

Mr Goldsworthy Gurney felt he had proved his vehicle roadworthy, and even with refuelling and taking on water, could travel at an average speed of 14 mph, which was faster and cheaper than conventional travel. He thought the future of steam omnibuses seemed bright, and entered into contracts to exploit the commercialisation of his invention, but there were detractors. The machine was a threat to the horse-drawn coach operators and they hit back. They persuaded the Turnpike Trusts to charge ten times more for a horse-less vehicle than for a four-horse carriage. To vary their toll charges the Trusts had to apply to Parliament for an amendment to their Act. Over fifty did so. A Select Parliamentary Committee was appointed to investigate the use of steam vehicles on the roads, which concluded that they should not be charged excessive tolls on the turnpike roads. The Committee felt that these vehicles would be of benefit to the public as they were safe, quick, cheap and less damaging to roads than horse-drawn carriages. The Commons passed the Bill containing these conclusions, but it was rejected by the Lords, some of whom had vested interests in

75 Star (London) – Thursday 13 August 1829

coach companies and the emerging railway industry. Mr Gurney's steam company fought the opposition for as long as they could but eventually became insolvent.[76] It took the demise of the turnpike trusts at the end of the nineteenth century and the acceptance of steam rail travel before once again innovative steam-driven road vehicles were seen on the roads. In the meantime the horse was still dominant.

* * *

The villagers of Longford saw fewer Royal carriages at the beginning of the nineteenth century. After nearly sixty years on the throne George III had died in January 1820 and the Prince Regent became King George IV. Although Windsor Castle was not to his taste, he did like living in Windsor Great Park and in 1814 commissioned a ranger's cottage in the grounds to be enlarged and transformed into a gothic cottage, which he called the Royal Lodge.

The King was now spending most of his time at the Royal Lodge, but the work of government continued. Therefore, Longford saw many of his Ministers and Privy Councillors stop at the Peggy Bedford on their way to Windsor. Some of the King's relatives also went to visit him.

To escape the record-breaking summer heatwave of 1826 the Duchess of Kent, and her seven-year-old daughter, Princess Victoria, travelled from London to stay with her sister-in-law, the Duchess of Gloucester, at Cumberland Lodge in Windsor Great Park.[77] On 2 August, young Victoria, was driven to the Royal Lodge to see her uncle, the King. The next day he gave her a carriage ride round the Royal Park and they ended up at his private menagerie at Sandpit Gate Lodge.[78] At that time Princess Victoria was second in line to the throne, but her uncles were still hoping to produce an heir that would precede her in the line of succession.

* * *

At the Weekly House, in Longford, the farming year of 1831 continued as normal. Richard Weekly was now farming 300 acres of land as both a tenant, at Perry Oaks, and his own land at The Farm in Longford. Approaching his sixtieth birthday, Richard was finding the farm management tiring.

---

76 https://en.wikipedia.org/wiki/Goldsworthy_Gurney
77 https://en.wikipedia.org/wiki/1826_in_the_United_Kingdom
78 Hibbert, Christopher, *George IV*, (London 1973) p.706

He was glad that his only son, Richard, now seventeen, had finished his education and he could teach him how to run the farm. Young Richard was not the brightest of 'apprentices'. His health was not good and he had not excelled at school. In order to learn the tasks that needed doing throughout the farming year he kept a diary, which started in January 1831.[79] His large spidery writing briefly recorded, in one sentence a day, where the men and horse teams were working and what they were doing, with occasional entries for family events.

Richard and his father were just finishing lunch when they heard riders enter the farmyard. They were expecting two family members, uncle Richard Weekly the tenant of Manor Farm, and Henry James Weekly, a cousin.

'Hello, Mr Weekly, fine day', said Richard, always very respectful of the principal farmer in Harmondsworth. 'Your dogs seem keen'.

'They are, young Dick. Raring to go'.

The horses were taken into the stable and the four men and their dogs walked into the fields. The autumn ploughing was well under way and there were five teams of men and horses working in one field, turning over the stubble from the harvest, their ploughs followed by a flock of birds swooping to pick up a tasty morsel on the ground as the teams proceeded in unison down the level field. The field next door was yet to be ploughed and the Weeklys headed for that, their dogs racing ahead, sniffing the ground for interesting smells.

The dogs soon found a prey as a large brown hare leapt up from its resting place (a depression in the ground, known as a form), where it had remained camouflaged until the dogs got too near. Immediately the dogs were in pursuit. They were faster than the hare, but could not make the sharp turns to match that of the leaping hare. The prey continued its advantage by leaping the hedge into a neighbour's field where it was eventually cornered and savaged by the dogs.

The labourers continued to plough, but looked on with interest at the hunting party. They did not begrudge their bosses having sporting leisure. It was the culture of the time for the gentry to be acknowledged in a class who behaved differently to the working class. There was no class envy, no social-climbing aspirations. Labourers knew their place and accepted it.

---

79 A transcription is in the author's possession, the original is held by the Wild family in Essex.

The farmers did not think of hare coursing as being cruel (it is banned today), but as a way of having an exciting afternoon whilst removing an animal that damaged their crops. Nor did they worry about trespass when the hare led them into a neighbour's field as it was considered acceptable to hunt across private property. However if the labouring classes were found catching hares it was a different story.

Trespassing on land to poach hares, rabbits and other game was a punishable offence and if caught poachers were prosecuted. On 6 November 1848 Benjamin Gilmore, a shepherd on the Weekly's Perry Oaks Farm, appeared before the magistrates at Uxbridge charged with having in his possession a hare, a quantity of wood, and some Swede turnips thought to have been stolen. He was also charged with assaulting police constable Robins whilst in the execution of this duty. He was fined forty shillings, or in default one month's imprisonment with hard labour.[80] Gilmore had been a shepherd at Perry Oaks for over five years, and two years earlier had received a prize at the local sheep-shearing competition. Now he was struggling. His wife had given birth to their second son, David, three months earlier and had been unwell ever since. He was trying to cope with the sleepless nights of a new-born, look after his wife, and a two-year-old son. Desperation made him steal wood for the fire and food for the family. Nevertheless he was prosecuted and his punishment was a heavy fine (more than one month's wages) that he was unable to pay. A normal employer would have dismissed him and his family would have been evicted from their tied cottage, but Baptists were forgiving. It is speculated that Richard Weekly paid his fine in order to help him in his misfortunes and to keep him as a shepherd, and he paid him back out of his wages. However this did not help his job security. Fewer sheep were now being kept on the farm and after paying off his debt Benjamin Gilmore moved his family four miles away to work as a shepherd for another Baptist farmer, Sir Robert Bateson Harvey at Langley Furze, Buckinghamshire, where he remained until his death in 1874.

The farm workforce on Perry Oaks farm was divided into teams, meaning teams of horses pulling one cart, or plough, with a driver and a boy. There were five teams and sometimes they helped other Baptist farmers by working the neighbour's fields. Most farmers had a cow to

---

80 Windsor and Eton Express – Saturday 11 November 1848

provide milk for the family. Richard Weekly also kept a bull and charged three shillings for the bull to service his neighbour's cow.

The farms interbred their horses so that there would be a continuing supply of young horses ready to take over from the old ones. Teams were employed to do various jobs outside of the farm such as taking crops or livestock to market, or grains to the mill at Colnbrook to grind for animal feed. Sometimes the teams worked together in a large field. To get the soil to a fine tilth the teams would plough the field one way and then plough again cross-ways.

The labourers were very versatile and far from unskilled. For example a team could be ploughing one day or spreading chalk (a soil neutralizer) on an arable field, the next. After harvest all the men worked together to build ricks. These would be hay, straw, or corn. The corn would be stored until it could be threshed in the winter months to obtain the grain. The ricks would be expertly thatched by the labourers.

As well as the men a number of women were employed to do the less manual work, although not less back-breaking. A core group of about eight women were employed all year round. This number was increased at haymaking and harvest time when all available help, including children, would be expected to help out on the farm. The women and boys were paid a lot less than the men although their work was just as vital. In February the women would be planting broad beans by hand. In March sorting newly harvested potatoes, pulling turnips, weeding, and removing couch grass. Haymaking took place in June and July. It was an important crop not only to feed their own horses in winter, but to sell to London stables. The corn harvest in August was labour intensive and a good man with a scythe could mow an acre of corn a day. The scythe had to be sharpened frequently on a whetstone.[81] In October the pigs would be fattened on barley meal, and a new flock of sheep bought at Laleham Market.

In December when a load of wheat was taken to Uxbridge market the carts returned with a load of 200 pantiles that had cost 16s. These were used to repair the roofs of the farm buildings, and sometimes to replace old thatch. Thatching roofs with local straw in Harmondsworth stopped around the year 1500 when locally made clay tiles became available, but some farm-buildings were sometimes thatched for cheapness. December

---

81 Seymour John, Rural Life, (Devizes, 1993)

was the time when some farmers laid off workers as there were fewer jobs on the farm, but the Weekly's farm labourers were employed all the year round, mainly on maintenance jobs.

When one day the rain was so heavy that all field work was stopped the men worked in the wheat barn moving the grain from one end to the other and in doing so caught 30-40 rats and a polecat. On another very wet day when the teams stayed in the stables, the men worked on cleaning out the seventeenth century pigeon house. [82]

Perry Oaks 17th Century Pigeon House. Photo A.S. Peacock 1939.

A dove or pigeon house was a status symbol and a privilege reserved for monasteries and the Lords of the Manor. [83] The fact that Perry Oaks had one confirms that it was once a sub-Manor of Harmondsworth Manor.[84] The pigeons were kept for meat and a pigeon pie was a dish for a wealthy man. The pigeon house also provided guano from the pigeon droppings which was a valuable fertilizer. Richard Weekly's lease dated 18 March

82 RCHME, Historical Monuments, p.63

83 Lake, Jeremy. *Historic Farm Buildings*, (London 1989) p.39.

84 https://www.exploringbuildinghistory.co.uk

1800 stipulated that at the end of his term as occupier, he should 'leave the Dove House stocked with thirty dozen of pigeons'.[85]

All farms had orchards, mainly to grow fruit for their own consumption, but later in the century the orchards of

> **Pigeons**
>
> Two men from General William Scot of Thorpe House, Surrey bought fifteen dozen pigeons from Perry Oaks farm. Two dozen for shooting and the rest to keep. Cost £9.

Perry Oaks were enlarged to cover a third of the farm. Richard and his son began the expansion of the orchard on 20 December 1831 when they went to Shrubbs Hill in Berkshire, an area renowned world-wide for its plant and tree nursery gardens. It was a ten mile ride from Perry Oaks along the old Roman South West road now called the A30.[86] They returned with 450 apple trees and the next day the planting began in the long orchard with all the trees planted by nightfall.

Richard's wife, Mary, inherited some of the Wild family land in Sipson, a hamlet of Harmondsworth, to the north-east of Perry Oaks. Part of the land, before enclosure, had been a road track across Hounslow Heath, and the stones that surfaced that track were still in the soil and a nuisance for the plough. On the day before Christmas that year, when there was a shortage of jobs on the farm one of the older long-serving men, Thomas Little, was given the task of 'pecking' up the stones. He managed to do forty-five yards of stone picking in the limited daylight hours of a mid-winter day. These stones were not wasted. They were carted off to another area of the farm to reinforce an existing track. Sundays and 25 December were the only days the men and horses had off, although there would still have been the stock to feed. The day after Christmas Day, the men were back at work either spreading dung or moving hurdles into the cart house.

* * *

While Richard Weekly and his son were busy on the farm, their landlord, Colonel Thomas Wood of Littleton, was fulfilling his duties as the Lieutenant-Colonel of the Middlesex Militia. George IV died in June 1830 without heirs and his younger brother became King William IV. The new King, when Duke of Clarence, was a familiar figure in the Longford

---

85 Wild, David, 'Reminiscences of Harmondsworth' in Sherwood, Philip (ed.), The Villages of Harmondsworth, (West Middlesex, 1993) p.51

86 Surrey Hisstory Centre. https://www.surreycc.gov.uk/culture-and-leisure/history-centre/marvels/nursery-records

neighbourhood. He had a close group of male friends in West Middlesex who used to meet once a fortnight at either the Bush at Staines, or the Black Dog at Bedfont and were renowned for their 'conviviality and good cheer'.[87] One of his friends was Colonel Thomas Wood who became his aide de campe when the new monarch inherited the throne. The Colonel's wife, Lady Caroline Wood, who was entitled due to her status as a daughter of the Marquis of Londonderry, became lady in waiting to his consort, Queen Adelaide, and the Woods frequently attended royal functions. The village of Longford was to see a great deal of the new monarch, and especially his Queen, and The King bestowed on it a generous contribution to the village's architecture.

87 Salisbury and Winchester Journal – Monday 26 June 1837

Chapter 11

Death at the Castle (1831-1835)

King William IV had been in the Navy for many years and felt more comfortable as an ordinary citizen rather than a monarch. As the third son of George III he had not expected to become King, and as he was not a lover of pomp and ceremony he was trying to avoid having a grand coronation. Eventually he agreed and the ceremony was planned for late 1831. Many of the foreign guests arrived early to enjoy the English summer.

On 20 May 1831 Queen Adelaide journeyed from St James's Palace to Windsor Castle in a carriage and four with outriders, stopping at the King's Head in Longford for the change of horses. Accompanying the Queen was her youngest sister, Ida, the Duchess of Saxe Weimer, with two of her children, who had arrived from Rotterdam the day before. Windsor Castle was undergoing extensive alterations by the architect Sir Jeffry Wyatville. He had been commissioned by George IV to redesign Windsor Castle in the gothic-style and to enhance and refurbish the state apartments. These were nearing completion when George IV died but were now ready for occupation.

On arrival at Windsor 'the Royal Party inspected the corridor and the whole suite of the splendid State apartments, and also those in the Devil's Tower, which are already fitted up for the reception of the Duchess and her family. Her Majesty then accompanied her sister over the new terrace and parterre, and from thence through the orangery and slopes to Adelaide Cottage. On their return they partook of an elegant collation, and left for London at half-past four o'clock.'[88] William IV had arranged for his

---

88 Berkshire Chronicle – Saturday 21 May 1831

brother's Royal Lodge, with its rustic thatched roof and verandahs, to be almost completely demolished. The building materials where then used to build Adelaide Cottage for his wife in the grounds of Windsor Great Park, not far from the Castle.[89]

Adelaide Cottage.

The Queen's sister and her children spent the summer with the Court attending Ascot, and every royal event until the coronation on Thursday, 8 September 1831. At the end of September the Duchess returned home, but her eldest daughter, Princess Louise, aged 14, was not very well and was left behind in Queen Adelaide's care in the hope that the English climate and the Royal physicians could improve her health. In February 1832 their Majesties with Princess Louise were in Brighton at the Royal Pavilion taking the sea air. The Royal party made the five hour return journey in a series of carriages on 28th February, but they did not stay long in London. The little princess was unwell and the Queen took her to Windsor hoping that the country air would aid her recovery, but by 14 March she was seriously ill. The Queen cancelled all her engagements to stay with her niece who was not expected to survive. After the intervention of various royal doctors the

---

89   This 'cottage' became the home of the Duke and Duchess of Cambridge and their family in 2022.

princess appeared to recover a little and the Queen, who had already sent for her sister, Ida, to come urgently from the Continent, continued with her engagements in London. In between engagements, the Queen made frequent trips, via Longford, to visit her niece. The little princess turned 15 on 1st April with still no sign of the arrival of her Mother who had been delayed. By the time Princess Ida eventually reached Windsor on 6 June, the Court had moved to Windsor to partake in the normal diary of summer events.

When the whole Court moved to Windsor it was a busy time in Longford, with the many carriages stopping to change horses and other travellers passing through on their way to Royal Ascot. Ever since Queen Anne had first ordered the preparation of a racecourse in Windsor Forest, where she watched horseracing events, there had been racing there.

The King and Queen arrived at Windsor on the night of Friday 1 June. They entertained their guests at a glittering dinner, and accepted the Provost of Eton, Dr Keate's, invitation to attend the Eton regatta on the Thames on 11 June. When the day dawned the weather was poor so the couple watched the races from the castle. The next day the whole Court attended the Eton Montem. This was a bizarre traditional event, held every three years by the boys of Eton College, who dressed up in elaborate costumes according to their role in the ceremony. Some were dressed as soldiers with wooden swords or poles, and feathers in their hats; others wore Scottish, Grecian or Indian dress. A motley parade of boys in their fancy dress marched to Salt Hill, Slough, to hold a mock ceremony. On their way the schoolboys would demand money or 'salt' from the carriages of spectators parked by the roadside who were witnessing the extravaganza. It was essentially a 'rag week' to raise funds, not for charity, but to send the head boy to university. Everyone took part in good humour, especially the Royal Family. It was an event too good to miss for eighteen-year-old Richard Weekly, from Longford, who went there to watch the colourful and unique event.

The Princess Louise's health was still declining.[90] In between royal engagements, the two sisters nursed the Princess. The King and Queen both attended the first day of Royal Ascot on 19 June, although Princess Ida remained with Princess Louise. Coincidentally the favourite horse in the first race and the eventual winner was called 'Ida'.[91] The King's welcome

90 Windsor and Eton Express – Saturday 02 June 1832
91 Oxford Journal – Saturday 23 June 1832

at Ascot had been muted. He had just passed the Reform Bill into law which reorganised the electoral system in Britain. It made representation in Parliament fairer for the electorate, but was unpopular with the upper classes and the House of Lords.

Just before the second race, as the King and Queen were conversing with their guests in the Royal Box, a shabby man in the crowd below threw a stone at the King, which hit him on the head just above the brim of his hat. The King staggered back, shocked but uninjured. The assailant was Dennis Collins, a disgruntled ex-sailor, with a peg leg, whose pension had been stopped after a dispute whilst he was staying at the Greenwich Hospital. He was now destitute and living on the streets. He threw the stone in protest about his circumstances, but later historians have wrongly attributed the incident as a protest against the Reform Bill.[92] Collins was accused of an attempted assassination – a treasonable offence – and sentenced to be hanged (later this was commuted by his victim to transportation). The assault on the King caused alarm amongst the nobility when they realised that, if the King had died, the succession would pass to thirteen year old Princess Victoria of Kent. As she would be under age her mother, the formidable Duchess of Kent, would become Regent, a situation nobody relished. The King's escape from death caused a resurgence in his popularity.

Less than a month later, on July 11 1832, Her Serene Highness Princess Louise Wilhelmina of Saxe-Weimar-Eisenach, Duchess of Saxony, eldest daughter of Prince Bernhard and Princess Ida of Saxe-Weimar-Eisenach, and niece of Their Majesties King William IV and Queen Adelaide, died at Windsor Castle, aged fifteen, of spinal meningitis.[93] Neither her mother nor her aunt could bear to be at the funeral which took place in St George's Chapel in Windsor Castle. Lady Howe stood in for them as chief mourner and William IV preceded the funeral procession in a carriage. The princess was buried in the Royal Vault, a chamber excavated under the chapel on the orders of George III, where, the following day, the very upset and emotional sisters visited her coffin. Princess Ida left Windsor Castle on 4 August accompanied by the Queen. After arriving at St James's Palace they then went directly to the Tower of London where at 12 noon the Princess Ida boarded the steam vessel *Attwood* to return home to the Continent.

* * *

92 Ziegler, Philip. *King William IV,* (London, 1971), p.236

93 http://theesotericcuriosa.blogspot.com/2015/06/vale-beloved-daughter-niece-princess. html

In Longford, in 1832, there were complaints about the dangerous state of the old wooden bridge at Longford Moor which was originally built for pack-horses, but now carried a flow of heavy coaches and carriages. One dark evening in March a mourning coach with four horses collided with a wagon on the bridge and the bridge was badly damaged. It was no fault of the drivers.[94] The bridge was just not strong enough or wide enough for two vehicles to pass.

The bridge crossed the artificial King's River (now called the Longford river), dug on the orders of King Charles I to divert water from the River Colne at Longford and send it twelve miles away to increase the flow of water to the fountains at Hampton Court. William IV decided to do something about the dilapidated bridge and in 1834 he ordered the construction of a cast iron bridge, bordered on each side by an elliptical arch, with a parapet of a trellis design. In the centre of the arch was a plaque with a raised crown and underneath "WR IV 1834". This is now a Grade II listed structure. The King's bridge and the waterway that runs beneath are still Crown property.

* * *

Kings bridge 2018.

---

94 Windsor and Eton Express – Saturday 5 May 1832.

Sipson House.

The new bridge was not only a boon for the carriage companies, but an asset to the local community. The Weekly's had to cross it to reach the Baptist Chapel at Colnbrook, but on 9 April 1832 Richard Weekly and his son set off in the other direction, towards Sipson, another hamlet of Harmondsworth on the eastern edge of the parish. Richard Weekly's wife, Mary ,was the daughter of the horse doctor in Sipson and when he died she inherited Sipson House. Father and son were now on their way to this imposing Georgian house, situated just off the Bath Road at the fourteenth mile post, to hand over the keys of the property to Mr and Mrs Cooper. John Cooper had bought land in Harmondsworth at the time of the Enclosures and was now moving his family from Westminster to the country to become a market gardener. When the Weekly's and Cooper's met outside the house for the formal handover, it was the first time young Richard Weekly had met their son, John Cartwright Cooper, a young lad of similar age. His contemporary immediately impressed young Richard by giving him some rabbit hutches. This started Richard on his own little enterprise, breeding and selling rabbits for fur and meat.

Sometime later another family moved near to the Coopers, called the Mittons and they were friends with Charles Dickens. Eventually John Cartwright Cooper married Mary Ann Mitton and Charles Dickens lent Mary Ann his carriage to take her to the church on her wedding day. Dickens had known Mary Ann since she was a small girl and always called her Dorrit. She was said to be the inspiration for his novel.[95] Dickens stayed

<hr />

95 Rust, Douglas. *Charles Dickens and His Local Connections,* West Middlesex Family History Society journal. June 1995.

with the family occasionally and must have drawn ideas from the area around Sipson House. Nearby was a cottage with its name on a board on the wall, which Dickens passed on his daily walks. Scroogeall cottage was a name he popped into his writer's notebook for future use.

June on the farm, was haymaking time. Just a day after the attempt on King William's life at Ascot in 1832, seven men began scything accompanied by four men and seven women turning the cut grass as it lay on the ground to help it dry into hay. Unfortunately that year there was only one day of cutting before the rain came and haymaking stopped for the rest of the month. By the beginning of July, when there was a desperate need to get the hay cut before it spoiled, there were thirteen men, one boy and eleven women all working long hours on haymaking. Without the hay there would be no feed for the horses in winter.

When winter came a village charity provided coal for the poor men of the parish and Richard Weekly sent one of his teams to Brentford docks to collect the coal which was distributed the next day. It was so cold in mid-January 1833 that a large pond, Shepherd's Pool, at the end of the lane from Perry Oaks ,where it met the Bath Road, froze over. The pool was formed by gravel extraction to keep the surface of the Bath Road in good condition for the coaches, and was very deep. On Sunday 13 January 1833 a passer-by noticed a man's head under the ice. There was speculation as to how he came to be *under* the ice and at the inquest two days later the coroner concluded it was 'self-murder' (suicide). The man was never identified and was given a Christian burial in St Mary's churchyard.

Horses were treated very well. They were the energy suppliers for the farm. The farm needed a continuous supply of young horses so the mares were often in foal. On May 4 one of them gave birth, but three days later the mare died with the foal by her side. The sadness of losing a mare was felt by everyone, and compounded when another horse, Old Jolley, was stolen from a field in August.

Time was set aside out of their farming schedule for the church and Richard's obligations as a Deacon. When the Colnbrook Pastor and his wife, Mr and Mrs Coleman, came to Perry Oaks farmhouse to dine on goose with the family, no one around that table that night could foresee that young Richard's sister, Mary, would, one day be the next Mrs Coleman.

In August young Richard together with his cousin Henry James Weekly went to Brentford fair to buy 370 lambs. Henry James was eleven years older than young Richard and had moved in with the family to help manage the farm for Richard, senior, who was now sixty-one and struggling to manage the two farms. Young Richard was too young and inexperienced to take on the tenancy of the 300-acre Perry Oaks and so it had been decided that Henry James would succeed Richard to the tenancy. Now that Henry James had a secure future he could think about marriage. A year later, on Monday 2 December 1833, the Weeklys and another leading Baptist family gathered at the St Mary's Church East Bedfont, two miles from the farm. They were there for the wedding of Henry James to his cousin Mary Rayner. Richard senior was a witness and so was her mother, Martha Rayner, Richard's sister. After the wedding Henry James brought his bride back to Perry Oaks farmhouse where they were to live with Richard and Mary and their children, and Richard's spinster sister, also called Mary. Four Mary's in one household must have caused some confusion.

As Perry Oak tenants, there were obligations to their landlord, Colonel Wood of Littleton. Hedges had to be maintained by trimming and banking and trees pollarded. Other obligations included allowing, and sometimes hosting, the Royal Staghounds and huntsmen on the land. In October the stag was released from a wagon (it would be recaptured alive later) and was pursued across the fields followed by the staghounds and the pack of sporting gentlemen on their horses. It might have been a spectacular sight, but it was the day after the field had been sown with wheat. The nicely ploughed and tilled soil was now trodden down and the seed dispersed. It was the curse of the farmer, but as a tenant of a large landowner and huntsman there was nothing they could do to prevent the hunt.

One day, when a team took ten sacks of wheat to Uxbridge market they returned with 1000 bricks. The bricks were for the laying of a new kitchen floor at Perry Oaks farmhouse. The carters also brought back the exciting news that Uxbridge streets were to be lit by gaslight.

Gossip was rife on market days and among some groups there was an undercurrent of discontent. The drive for more efficient farming was increasing the invention of farm equipment and labourers feared their jobs were at risk.

* * *

The increased mechanisation of farming was causing extreme concern for agricultural labourers who were already struggling to survive the Napoleonic post-war agricultural slump, high taxes, and low wages. They saw the machines as a threat to their jobs. People were starving.[96] Desperate people used desperate measures to fight back against the machines, and setting fire to prosperous farms was their way of protesting.

At 5pm on a dark winter night in late December a boy on a farm at Stanwell, just south of Perry Oaks, was crossing the farmyard when through a hole in the barn he saw a light. He knew instantly it was flames and rushed to tell the farmer's wife, Mrs Jordan. The farmer and his brother were at a Vestry Meeting two miles away at Stanwell Church and the labourers had gone home. Mrs Jordan called on her neighbours and they came running to help rescue the horses from the stables and the livestock in the yard. Messengers were sent for fire-engines and to inform Mr Jordan. The animals were saved but the barn, stables, cart houses, sheds, pigstyes, corn stacks and hay ricks were all a mass of flame. The Colnbrook fire engine was the first to arrive, then others. The water supply at the farm was too far from the buildings to be reached. Nearly all the premises were destroyed leaving just a shed and one stack of hay. Luckily the wind was not strong at the time. The labourer's cottages survived, but had to be covered with a tarpaulin and damped down to prevent them from igniting. The farmhouse also escaped the flames even though it was just a few yards from the barn. The barn and its contents, the produce of six acres of wheat, 30 acres of barley, and five acres of oats, was destroyed as were the stacks of wheat, oat, hay and clover from another 28 acres. The whole loss amounted to £4000. The property was insured. It was thought the fire was started deliberately.[97] There was a spate of 'incendiarism' at that time. The following evening a farm at Egham, Surrey, was on fire.

In December 1831 at a local farm, just off the Bath Road, two men were seen running away shortly before a fire was discovered.[98] Luckily, the fire was spotted in time and the farmer had already installed his own fire engine (pump) so the flames were soon extinguished.

96 Hammond,J.L, and Hammond, Barbara, *The Village Labourer 1760-1832*, (London, 1920) p.218

97 Windsor and Eton Express – Saturday 21 December 1833

98 London Courier and Evening Gazette – Thursday 15 December 1831

Poster calling a public meeting to discuss recent arson attacks.

After a series of arson attacks, the local farmers held a meeting at Bedfont to discuss what should be done about them. It was resolved that farmers should keep a night watch on their own premises, that Constables and Police Officers were instructed to keep a good look out for strangers and to apprehend suspicious characters. The government subdued the wave of protests by agricultural labourers with a clamp down on meetings and gatherings with severe punishments for those caught protesting. Protestors were liable to be imprisoned and then either transported to a penal colony or executed. A severe punishment for men who just wanted to earn enough to feed their families, but to some the punishment might have been preferable to dying of hunger. Agricultural labourers in some areas had been found starved to death in hedges whilst out looking for work.[99]

The arson attacks got worse. On the 13 February 1834 at 7pm Mr Isaac Cain's farm at Heathrow, not two miles from Perry Oaks, burnt down to the ground. It was such a huge conflagration that it could be seen from the market town of Uxbridge and by passengers travelling along the road from Uxbridge to London. One report said nine ricks of wheat and barley were consumed.[100] The extent of the fire left no doubt it was deliberately set alight, although none of Mr Cain's employees were under suspicion.[101] By the 21 February it was reported that a man named Green had been brought before the Magistrates on suspicion of causing the destructive fire.

99   Hammond, J.L & Hammond, Barbara, *The Village Labourer 1760-1832*, (Londojn, 1920) p.218
100   The Hereford Times, 22 February 1834
101   *Jackson's Oxford Journal* (Oxford, England), Saturday, February 22, 1834; Issue 4217.

After a short investigation of the case he was remanded until the following week.[102] William Green was eventually tried at London's Old Bailey on 10 April 1834 and accused of setting fire to stables at Isaac Cane's farm with the intent to endanger life. The prosecutor said he was unable to show that Green had been any nearer than two hundred yards from the building and therefore offered no evidence. The verdict was not guilty, William Green was a free man, and the perpetrator was never prosecuted. Even with all their precautions the farmers had no deterrent against the arsonists who always struck when the hard work of growing and harvesting the crop had been completed and the barns were full.

* * *

At Longford there was no sign of militancy among the workers. The Baptist farmers and their wives made the welfare of their labouring families a priority and for the labourers there was plenty of work and a cottage to go with it. Any sign of dissent would lose them a home for their families.

Richard Weekly senior, was now 62 years old. He had been farming Perry Oaks for over 30 years and he was exhausted. He was so unwell at the end of February that the doctor was called to him on four consecutive days. By the fifth day he felt better, but it had been a warning. He was not getting any younger and he must think about reducing his workload. Plans were now in place for him to hand over the tenancy of Perry Oaks to Henry James Weekly and move back to his own farm in Longford. The family would move back into the Weekly House but that was currently occupied by their manager, William Hester. So in April 1833 all the farm teams were used to transport 10,000 bricks to Longford with which to build a farmhouse in the Longford farmyard for Hester and his family.

* * *

The Weekly family moved back to the Weekly House at Longford at the beginning of 1835, leaving Henry and his wife, and Aunt Mary living in the Perry Oaks farmhouse and running the Perry Oaks farm. Richard Weekly now only needed three horses, two carts, two men and a boy to work the Longford farm.

* * *

---

102   The Morning Chronicle (London, England), Monday, February 24, 1834; Issue 20124.

The Farm
The farm house on the left and the Weekly House behind the barns on the right.

On the Bath Road, the travelling trade was getting busier. The journey to Bath now took around fifteen hours and there was a regular coach service from London, which left at 6am, or 4pm, and arrived in Bath at 10pm and 7am, respectively. There was also a service that left London at one in the morning which was particularly fast and could do the journey, on the empty streets, in twelve hours. A total of twenty-two daily services journeyed from London to Bath in 1834.[103]

All this activity required the Peggy Bedford to run a twenty-four hour service. The ostler would be organising the change of carriage horses, and the indoor servants serving the travelling public. Longford was used to strangers and everyone was given a warm welcome, even though some turned out to be opportunist thieves.

---

103   Rosevear, Alan. *A booklet on the Turnpike Roads around Reading,* (2004)

Chapter 12

Thieving and Grieving (1837-1840)

Thomas Henry Whipham was a barrister and local landowner. His Baptist family had owned land and property in the area for generations. On a warm June day in 1837 he took the Windsor coach from Belle Sauvage, Ludgate Hill, in London to the Peggy Bedford where he got off and stayed to have a meal. He had with him a large carpetbag with his clothes, books and shaving gear, and as the bar was crowded, he left the bag in a passageway where Elizabeth Jarvis, the barmaid, saw it. [104] Later two men knocked on the door in the passage that led behind the bar and asked for a pint of ale. She asked them to go into the taproom but they said they were only going to stop for a quick drink and would rather drink it in the passageway. One of the men then left and the other stayed just five more minutes to finish the beer and then left. It was only then that Elizabeth noticed the bag was missing.

Out in the yard John Clements, the horsekeeper, saw a man come out of the side door with a carpetbag. When William Willis, the ostler, heard that a bag had been taken he ran up the road and in about half a mile saw a man, and in front of him a man and a woman. None of them was hurrying along, but he saw the first man make a signal to the other that made him suspicious.

'Do you know the whereabouts of a bag that has gone missing from the Peggy Bedford?' he asked the strangers.

'We don't have nothing that doesn't belong to us'

104 *Old Bailey Proceedings Online* (www.oldbaileyonline.org, version 8.0, 16 April 2020), June 1837, trial of PATRICK PHILLIPS JOHN TYGH BRIDGET PHILLIPS (t18370612-1480).

The ostler glanced at the woman, who had not spoken, and said to her, 'You appear to have something under your cloak'.

He drew back the woman's cloak and saw the bag. He grabbed the second man and took him back to the inn. The others came with him where the Constable arrested them and took them into custody. Four days later all three were in court at the Old Bailey in London and after hearing the evidence the Judge sentenced the two men, John Tygh, 23, and Patrick Phillips 25, (in spite of one of them receiving a good character), to six months confinement which included three weeks in solitary. The wife, Bridget Phillips, was found not guilty.

* * *

Ten days after the Whipham robbery, on 20 June 1837, King William IV died at Windsor aged 71, six days short of a seven-year reign. The whole town of Windsor closed its doors and shutters as a mark of respect. King William had ten illegitimate children before he married Queen Adelaide but the nineteen-year marriage brought no legitimate heirs. The crown therefore passed to his eighteen-year-old niece, Princess Alexandrina Victoria of Kent – Queen Victoria.

King William IV had made Colonel Thomas Wood MP, the owner of Perry Oaks farm, executor of his will and soon after the King's death this role gave Thomas Wood a delicate problem. Queen Victoria herself tells the story of a visit she had from Colonel Wood on 22 July who was asking her to decide on points arising from King William's will. The young Queen, less than a month into her reign and weary of decision-making, said firmly, 'I would rather think about that matter first – perhaps I shall let you know tomorrow my determination on the subject.'

Colonel Wood persisted, 'I beg your pardon but I beg to ask another favour of your Majesty. The Queen Dowager has a great partiality for a few trifling articles of furniture which had been favourites of her lamented consort, but which she did not wish to disturb or to remove from Windsor Castle, without leave.'

Queen Victoria, who was very fond of the Queen Dowager, replied with great emotion, 'Oh, my dear Colonel, let the dear Queen have them by all means, and anything else in the Castle which she may desire.'[105]

105   West Kent Guardian – Saturday 22 July 1837

The Dowager Queen Adelaide was now living at Marlborough House in London, but she also had the use of Bushy House. The death of her husband affected her deeply and although she lived a further twelve years she was never in the best of health.

* * *

Richard Lay was walking back to his house in Longford from West Drayton railway station around 9pm in January 1839, when he saw the Mazeppa Worcester coach and its four horses stationary on the Bath Road. The passengers were out of the coach and standing next to a ditch on the side of the road. [106]

'What goes on?' he asked, and then he looked where they were pointing.

As he later reported. 'I saw a mare standing in the ditch. On going towards it I saw it had a bridle and saddle on. Then I noticed a man lying on his face in the mud. His head was immersed in the water, but there were no marks on him as if he had been attacked or robbed. I pulled him from the water. He was alive, but not sensible, although I do not think he was drunk. As I pulled him out I noticed two loaded pistols in his breast pocket. With the help of the coachmen we took him to the Kings Arms inn at Longford.'[107]

Several men helped carry the unconscious man into the pub and laid him on a bench. As concerned people surrounded the mud-covered man he began to regain consciousness, spluttering and coughing after his near drowning.

'What caused you to end up in the ditch?'

'I don't know. I can't remember'

Some people speculated that he had been knocked into the ditch by the Mazeppa coach. The ostler from the Peggy Bedford, William Willis, was despatched to examine the accident spot. He later reported that he thought the mare had been backed into the ditch as she was covered with mud and clay to above the haunches and the tail.

---

106   Marzeppa was the name of the coach. "named either after Byron's poem of 1819 or more probably, the show at Astley's from 1831 onwards." Vincent, David. *I hope I Don't Intrude: Privacy and its Dilemmas in Nineteenth-Century Britain*. (Oxford, 2015)

107   Evening Mail – Monday 04 February 1839, p.3 [The inn where William Brotherhood was taken was probably The King's Head, where William Willis was ostler, and not the Kings Arms as reported]

'Perhaps you would like to go to bed, sir, until you feel better', said the publican.

'No, no, I must get home. Can you order me a chaise?'

William Willis brought a chaise round and drove the man home. On the journey home to Hounslow, he was rambling 'They ought not to have served me in that way, as I stood a glass of grog at Slough' He gave no further explanation.

This man was William Brotherhood who, with his son, was a contract engineer for Isambard Kingdom Brunel and worked on large construction projects for the Great Western Railway. Only six months earlier he had seen the opening of the Wharncliffe Viaduct, at nearby Hanwell, that carried the railway line west to Bristol. He had been responsible for the ground works that enabled the building of one of Brunel's famous landmarks. It is now Grade I listed and of architectural significance. On the day of his accident William Brotherhood was returning from Sonning where his son was supervising the mile-long deep excavation through Sonning Hill for the Great Western Railway line. He was known to be a man of 'singular habits and manner'. As an example of his eccentricity he had just ordered two coats, on one the buttons were to be old guineas, and on the other old half-crowns.

When Brotherhood arrived home that night he went to bed and stayed there for several days still in a state of delirium. His friend, William Penton, on hearing that he was seriously ill visited him the following Friday.[108] At first Brotherhood did not know who his visitor was, but after a while recognition dawned.

'What happened, old chap? How did you come to be in the ditch?'

'Well, I left Reading at 4 o'clock on my favourite mare. I was riding quite fast as I got to Longford when the animal stopped all at once. I was thrown over her head and rolled into the ditch, just like a football. I was shook all to pieces. I have no idea why she stopped so suddenly.'

William Brotherhood died the following morning aged 51. The coroner at the inquest told the jury, 'In the absence of clearer testimony as to the cause of the deceased's death, it would be better for the jury to find a verdict that the deceased was found in a pond immersed in water, from

---

108   William Penton's daughter, Priscilla, was married to William Brotherhood's son, Rowland. At this time they had a mutual 9-month-old grandchild, Peter, who went on to become a renowned civil engineer and engine designer.

the effects of which he subsequently died, but how he came in the water, there was no evidence to show.'[109] It was a sad end to a well-respected man who had worked closely with Brunel to build the foundations for the Great Western Railway.

* * *

As an early example of a welfare state Queen Elizabeth the First, introduced the Poor Rate Act that compelled parishes to appoint an Overseer of the poor. This voluntary role was given to a member of the vestry meeting, an early parish council made up of leading citizens. In 1839 the role was given to a principal farmer, Mr Tillyer, who had the job of deciding how much each household should pay based on the rental value of each property. The money collected was paid into a fund that could be used to help the parish poor. In May 1839, at the Uxbridge Petty Sessions, the magistrates were hearing appeals against the poor-rate assessment in Harmondsworth. Joseph Reynolds, a Longford farmer, appealed on the grounds of the incorrectness, inequality, and unfairness of the rate he had been asked to pay. A surveyor supported his appeal. The complaint was not that Reynolds was overrated, but that other land in the parish, such as that of the current parish Overseer of the Poor, Mr Tillyer, was not rated sufficiently high. As some farms had poorer land than others Reynolds felt that those with better quality land should pay more. Other landowners had also complained about inequality, but were waiting to hear the result of Reynold's appeal before they applied to the magistrates.

Mr Tillyer, the newly-appointed parish Overseer, told the magistrates, 'The committee appointed to value the parish had taken a great deal of trouble in assessing the parish, and they had had many meetings. Not one of the committee had been allowed to have a voice in the valuation of his own property. The result of the committee's valuation was that the parish assessment had been raised from £5333 to £6417.'

Mr Dagnall, the Magistrate, said, 'I have no doubt the assessment might have been fairly made, but yet it might have been upon an erroneous principle. Did the committee go over all the land prior to assessing it?'

Mr Tillyer: 'We all know the property very well; but we did not go over it.'

---

109   Bell's New Weekly Messenger – Sunday 03 February 1839

Mr Dagnall; 'If that was imperative on the committee to do, it puts you completely out of court, for you admit that you did not go over the land.'

Mr Tillyer was asked three times if he thought his own land was properly assessed. At first he was diffident, then unsure, and on the third occasion he finally admitted that it was not.

Mr Dagnall: 'The rate cannot be legal unless the land is valued at its full value, and it is now proved that it is not so.'

Mr Tillyer: 'It is higher than other parishes.'

Mr Dagnall: 'That is no argument.'

The magistrates conferred and concluded that the rate was unfair and unequal and ordered it to be quashed and the parish would make another rate. [110] This judgement was a great relief to the appellant, Joseph Reynolds. He had been carrying around a red purse containing the rate money in case he had to pay it to the court. Now he could keep the two sovereigns, a £10 note and a £5 note safely in his waistcoat pocket. He was buoyant as he made his way home from the Uxbridge Sessions House that evening with William Godfrey, another appellant, who owned the Kings Arms at Longford.

The Kings Arms 1930.

110   Windsor and Eton Express – Saturday 11 May 1839

It had been a long day and Reynolds was hungry. Apart from two bottles of ginger beer at lunchtime and a brandy after the successful conclusion of the appeal, he had nothing all day. Both men returned to the pub and Reynolds asked for a plate of cold mutton and a pint of half and half (a mixture of mild ale and bitter) and glanced around the room. The room was full. There was a man sitting in the corner with dark sallow skin, brown hair and eyes. Two scars on his right eyebrow made him look villainous.[111] He had the look of a labourer but was not a local. It was not unusual for Longford inns to be full of strangers. The Bath Road saw travellers day and night passing its doors. Strangers were welcomed as they brought trade to the hostelries.

Reynolds and Godfrey were in a merry mood and later Godfrey ordered a half-pint of gin passing it around the room to everyone's delight. Then the landlord, James Spratley, paid for a further half-pint of gin, and finally Reynolds paid for a third. He did not drink any, but felt obliged to add to the general feeling of rejoicing at their success at the Session House. The gin had warmed up the whole room and there was jollity all round.

Joseph Reynolds noticed two women looking in his direction and as he caught their eye the two women came up to him just as he was taking a sip of his beer. He exchanged banter with the women and joked with one about the whip she was carrying, but he had to cut the conversation short as he felt the need to visit the privy. He excused himself and went out of the front door and round into the yard at the back. As he went towards the privy he saw the ostler crossing the yard and waved to him, then, as he left the privy, doing up his clothes, he saw the two women had followed him and were within a yard of him when they saw the ostler. They hesitated for a moment, and the ostler, who was about to lock-up, asked if he wanted to go into the stable,

'No; what the devil do you think I want to go into the stable for?' said Reynolds.

The ostler walked away and did not see the women put their arms around Reynolds. He pushed them away and they continued to run their hands over his body. One woman said 'I will kiss you', the other asked if he wanted a woman, and in the struggle they all fell down to the ground together, with Reynolds pinned underneath them and unable to call for

---

111   London, England, Newgate Calendar of Prisoners, 1785-1853

**The Transportation Sentence
for the Reynolds Robbery**

Joseph Stanley, aged 25, was transferred to the harsh conditions of a prison hulk for five months until his voyage was arranged. He was sent to New South Wales on the ship, Mangles, on 21 Nov 1839 and arrived on 27 Apr 1840.

The two women, Ann Edwards,25, and Matilda Ozier,21, where held in a prison until they set sail together on 10 December 1839 for a four-month voyage to Van Diemen's Land (Tasmania), where Ozier served her sentence in the service of G.P. Reid of New Town. and Ann Edwards was sent to work for Mrs Barrett in Tamar.

help. They were calling out for their accomplice and their victim caught a glimpse of a short swarthy man, the one who had been sitting on his own in the bar, moving toward them and then helping to hold him down. He felt his red purse being taken out of his fob pocket and he grabbed their skirts to pull himself up, but they pushed him down again. All three of them ran away – the man going one way and the women the other. Reynolds holding his breeches up as best he could ran into the inn and shouted 'I've been robbed'. The male robber was running towards London. Reynolds, sixty, was not fit enough to follow him, but went on horseback to call a constable.

William Thompson the horse patrolman on the Bath Road was told of the robbery and he went in search of the culprits. He caught up with them in Richmond, Surrey, and took them into custody. The man did not have the purse on him. At their trial at the Old Bailey all three of the thieves were found guilty of taking from Reynold's person, and against his will, a purse and beating, striking, and using personal violence to him. They were each sentenced to transportation for fifteen years.

* * *

Most of the labourers in Longford had a little patch of land on which they grew vegetables and sometimes kept poultry. Joseph Bryant, an agricultural labourer who was born in the village, lived at the end of the village and as well as growing vegetables kept six ducks in his garden. On the night of 31 July 1842 it was getting dark at 9pm when he put them in the shed and put a brick against the door before going to bed.

PC Thomas Duggin was on night patrol in the village when he heard an unusual sound for that time of night. He could distinctly hear ducks cackling, a noise only heard in daylight. A man with a basket was walking towards him.

'What have you got in that basket?'.

'Nothing'.

He looked inside the basket and saw two ducks.

'Where did you get these ducks?'

'From a man in Colnbrook', referring to a village two miles away.

'Who was the man?'

No answer.

'If you can't tell me his name I will lock you up'.

'I bought them off Bryant, who lives just over the bridge'– about a quarter of a mile away.

'Very well, we will go to Bryant and see'

At Bryant's house he called him up.

'Do you know this man?' pointing to Samuel Tomkins who was holding a basket.

'Yes, I do, but I haven't seen him for about a week'

'Then you didn't sell him some ducks at any time?'

'No. I have never sold him any ducks'.

The policeman told him to get dressed and to go to the public house where there was light. When Bryant left his house he noticed that his shed door was open and three ducks were missing. Nearby in a ditch was one of the ducks. When Bryant caught up with the policeman and the man, the policeman asked Bryant if he had lost any ducks.

He said, 'Yes. A white one, and a black speckled one, which was a very remarkable one, which I could swear to from a hundred'. He looked at the ducks in the basket.

'Yes. These are my ducks'.

Tomkins admitted that he had been drinking all day and was drunk. He said he saw the ducks in the road and did not know who they belonged to so he thought there was no harm in taking them.

Bryant replied, 'They could not get out—I shut them up at nine o'clock, and put a brick against the door.'

P.C. Duggin arrested Samuel Tomkins. As he was being taken to the police station, with Joseph Bryant accompanying them to make a statement, Tomkins said to Bryant,

'Tell them you sold me the ducks and I will see you alright'. Bryant ignored him.[112]

Three weeks later the case came before the judge at the Old Bailey. Having heard all the evidence and learning of his previous good character Tomkins, aged 28, was found guilty and as the jury recommended leniency he received a sentence of 14 days in prison.

Both Samuel Tomkins and Joseph Bryant came from a long line of Longford agricultural labourers. They were of a similar age and knew each other well, but the extensive Tomkins family had mixed fortunes and some were less respectful of the law than others. Samuel Tomkin's brother, Thomas, escaped from police custody after being questioned about an illicit still he was running. After his recapture in London he was tried and sentenced to imprisonment for three months. [113]

Joseph Bryant's parents had moved to the village to work and founded several generations of labourers. Joseph Bryant's son married a local girl and followed in his father's footsteps, but grandson George Frederick Bryant had more ambition. As soon as he was old enough he joined the Royal Horse Artillery, and served in India for a while. He had married a Middlesex girl and was the father of three children by the start of the First World War when he was immediately sent to France. He was serving as a Battery Quartermaster Sergeant when in 1917 he was injured and repatriated to Springfield War Hospital, Tooting, where he died of his injuries aged 36. He is buried at Wandsworth Cemetery and his name is inscribed on the Harmondsworth War Memorial plaque.

* * *

There is no better mirror of class culture in early nineteenth century Britain than that of the treatment of criminals. Magistrates, who were usually substantial land-owning gentry, were tougher on the lower classes than those they thought equal or above them in status. Even the newspapers were cautious about naming ennobled people involved in crime, scandal, or mischief. One August night in 1840 a 'certain' titled Officer from Windsor barracks took some of his friends, all noblemen and gentlemen, in his four-in-hand (a four-horse carriage) on a drunken spree. They smashed parish

112 *Old Bailey Proceedings Online* (www.oldbaileyonline.org, version 8.0, 17 April 2020), 22 August 1842, trial of SAMUEL TOMKINS (t18420822-2180).

113 Windsor and Eton Express – Saturday 28 June 1851.

street lamps in Windsor, broke windows and door knockers in Colnbrook, pressed rotten eggs into the hands of the tollhouse keeper in lieu of payment and finally ended up at the Peggy Bedford at midnight where they woke the household and continued to party. None of these participants were named or prosecuted as they had plenty of money to pay for all the damage claims caused by their spree. The worst condemnation the newspaper could think of was to call them 'freaks'.[114]

Eighteen years later and the magistrates were still being very inconsistent and unfair in their sentencing. The extensive grounds of the Peggy Bedford allowed for a degree of self-sufficiency. Pigs were kept and there was a kitchen garden and orchard. The sight of growing food was a temptation for the passing hungry itinerant, but if they were caught helping themselves the punishment seemed unduly harsh. A little boy called David Jesse was caught picking up walnuts from under some trees in the orchard. The walnuts were worth 2d and he was found guilty of theft. He couldn't pay the fine of seven shillings so he was given seven days imprisonment.[115] All child offenders would once have been held in an adult prison, but under the 1854 Reformatory Schools Act, courts could sentence offenders under the age of sixteen to be held in establishments to shelter, educate, and train poor children in the hope that they could be stopped from re-offending. A large Industrial training school for this purpose was being built in Feltham, six miles from Longford, but the complex was not finished until the year after Jesse's sentence.

* * *

Monday 10 February 1840 was a national public holiday for the marriage of the young Queen Victoria to her cousin, Prince Albert. After the wedding ceremony in St. James's Palace, and a wedding breakfast at Buckingham Palace, the couple left for Windsor.

Crowds lined the route to Windsor along the Great Bath Road. Some towns had erected celebratory arches under which the royal carriage passed. By the time the carriages reached Longford at 6pm it was dark, but a light in every window illuminated the village. Flags and decorations stretched across the street and the church bells from Harmondsworth and Stanwell were ringing out in celebration. The royal carriage, with its military escort,

---

114   Windsor and Eton Express – Saturday 8 August 1840.
115   Windsor and Eton Express – Saturday 16 October 1858

stopped at the Peggy Bedford to change horses as usual before continuing on to Colnbrook where there was a celebratory arch of evergreens. At Colnbrook the newlyweds were joined by a troop of Life Guards who were to escort the royal carriage into Windsor. The procession was approaching Slough when one of the horses of the mounted escort became skittish and a soldier called Lamb was thrown from his horse. He was taken to a nearby inn where he was found to have dislocated his shoulder. He later returned to his barracks at Windsor to recover. The next day, when the Queen heard of his accident she sent Mr Brown, a royal surgeon, to visit the soldier in the barrack hospital. He made a full recovery.[116]

The honeymoon was short, and only two mornings later three carriages left Buckingham Palace containing the bride's mother, the groom's Father and brother, and several other relatives to visit the newlyweds at Windsor.[117] This caused a flurry of activity in the Peggy Bedford's stables, where the carriage horses were changed. Two days later, on 14 February 1840, they were once again changing the horses for the newlyweds' return to London with the route thronged with cheering people.[118]

After the excitement of seeing their young Queen on her wedding day, and many subsequent sightings, Longford and the licensee at The Peggy Bedford had built a special rapport with the Queen. A relationship of trust that would be demonstrated in a very special moment with a future King.

---

116   Windsor and Eton Express – Saturday 15 February 1840
117   Dover Telegraph and Cinque Ports General Advertiser – Saturday 15 February 1840
118   Windsor and Eton Express – Saturday 15 February 1840

Chapter 13

Royal Visit (1842-1848)

Peggy Bedford heard the sound of the distant bugle. So did the ostler. So did the cook. All at once everyone started bustling about. Peggy ripped off her apron, smoothed her skirt and put on her hat. In the stables, the men stopped what they were doing and ran to get four well-groomed horses from their stalls. Cups and plates were assembled on a tray in the kitchen. Soon the jingling of multiple harnesses could be heard as the cavalry entered the village and came towards the inn.

First to be seen was a troop of Lancers, then a gleaming black landau with a crest on the side of the door and bright red wheels, followed by another military troop. As the carriage came to a halt outside the inn two smartly liveried footman leapt from the back of the carriage and opened the door pulling down the steps and standing back to attention. Slowly a young diminutive figure stepped down from the landau. Peggy, who was waiting to greet her, dropped a deep curtsey and then as she stood up gestured in the direction of the door of the inn said, 'Welcome, your Majesty'. Queen Victoria had come to visit.

In the rural village of Longford, usually busy with carts of farm produce and men and women on errands everyone had stopped to watch this magnificent spectacle of royal pageantry. Little Willy Archer a young child from the next village, Colnbrook, had walked there with his friends especially to see the Queen.[119] They stood respectfully holding their caps in their hands as the young Queen turned and waved in their direction before walking through into the building, a building she had visited many times

---

119   Uxbridge & W. Drayton Gazette – Friday 09 February, 1917.

before. Ignoring the bar on her left, hastily emptied of clients, she turned right into the large majestic Queen Anne panelled parlour with china in recessed cupboards on each side of the fire-place, and furniture fit for any aristocrat.[120] The Queen sat down and Peggy moved to the tea-tray freshly placed on the side table. She poured the tea into the cup which she then placed on the table next to Her Majesty. The table already held plates of sandwiches and cakes. This was a regular stop for all Royals travelling to and from Windsor and her Majesty's food and drink preferences were already known. This time the Queen was accompanied by her infant son, the Prince of Wales, on his way to Windsor to be christened in King George's chapel on 25 January 1842, and with him was his wet-nurse, Mrs Brough.[121] Peggy, the licensee of the inn that now bore her name, hovered in attentive obedience at the side of the room, cooing and ahhing when she saw the Prince in the arms of his nurse.

'Go and get some refreshments Mrs Brough. Mrs Bedford will hold the baby', said her Majesty to the nurse. The sleeping bundle was handed over, and the nurse went through to the kitchen. Peggy could hardly believe she was holding the future King Edward VII.

In the fifteen minutes the Queen remained in the parlour the four Windsor Grays had been changed on the carriage by the stable-men, and when the Queen was ready, and the baby safely returned to the nurse, the Royal party and its escort continued on its journey to Windsor. As the carriage left the village en route for Colnbrook the turrets of her Majesty's destination could clearly be seen in the west across the flat farmland. It was one of the last Royal visits to Longford. Soon decades of royal journeys by carriage to Windsor would end.

The Peggy Bedford had stables for sixty horses and not only kept the royal Windsor Grays, but teams for the Royal Mail coaches and other companies using the Great Bath Road to travel between London and the west of England. All this was changing. The age of the railway had begun.

Prince Albert was a supporter of all forms of new technology and was keen to encourage the young Queen to try the new mode of transport. The Queen was a bit more cautious. She had always travelled sedately by carriage and she worried about the effect on the body of travelling at speed on a train. By the middle of 1842 Prince Albert had persuaded the Queen

120   Uxbridge & W. Drayton Gazette – Friday 26 January 1934.

121   Ridley, Jane, *Bertie: A life of Edward VII,* (London, 2012), p.15.

to take a train journey from Slough Station to Paddington in a specially commissioned royal saloon. She would not allow it to go faster than 40mph, but she delighted in the fact that it was quicker and more comfortable than a carriage ride. From then on she made all journeys to Windsor by train. The royal horses were no longer stabled at the Peggy Bedford and the tradition of the regular royal stop had ended – with one exception.

In January 1844 there was a surprise visit to Longford from Queen Victoria and Prince Albert. They were scheduled to arrive at Windsor Castle from Buckingham Palace between four and five on Saturday afternoon. The special train had been waiting at Paddington since 3pm to take the Queen to Slough where the royal carriages and a military escort were waiting to proceed to the Castle. When the detachment of the First Life Guards arrived at Slough ready to escort the royal party to Windsor they received orders to ride to Longford. Spare carriage horses, from the Windsor stables, were also sent to Longford to await the arrival of Her Majesty. The change of plan had been caused by the news of the death of the reigning Duke of Saxe Coburg Gotha, Prince Albert's father, which meant the royal couple decided to travel without pomp in a closed carriage and four with the postilions wearing mourning attire and without a large military escort.[122] If it was a surprise to the military it was an even bigger surprise for Peggy Bedford who had to make ready the grand parlour and prepare some refreshments. The villagers might have seen the royal carriage, but few would have guessed the Queen was inside.

This was not the end of the stirring sound of chinking harness, and the electrifying sight of colourful uniforms, for well into the twentieth century the Household Cavalry moved their headquarters from Buckingham Palace to Windsor during the summer. They rode their horses with their plumed helmets and shiny breastplates through Longford and the excited school-children were given the day off to enjoy the spectacle.[123]

* * *

There is no mention of a variety of apple called the Cox's orange pippin in the nineteenth century reference book, *The Apple*, because at the time it was published this apple was a tiny sapling in the garden of Richard Cox of The

122   Newcastle Courant – Friday 09 February 1844

123   Wild, David, *Reminiscences of Harmondsworth,* in The Villages of Harmondsworth, (London, 1993), p.41

Lawns.[124] Richard Cox had been a brewer in Bermondsey and retired to an imposing Georgian house with a large garden situated between Longford and Colnbrook. His relaxation was gardening and he grew the apple tree from seed around 1830. It was thought to have been a cross-pollination between a Ribston Pippin and a Blenheim Orange.[125] When he realized it was a unique and tasty apple he gave cuttings to Messrs R Small and Sons, nurserymen of Colnbrook, and from 1840 they began marketing the trees to local growers. It was not until the apple gained first prize in the Royal Horticultural Society's Grand Fruit Show of 1857 that its reputation took off. The original tree remained in the garden of the Lawns until it blew down in a storm in 1911.[126] After Mr Cox's death in 1845 the Lawns cottage and seven acres of additional land were sold. Later a railway company bought some of the land to build a branch line through the town of Colnbrook. In 1908 H.J. Wild of The Farm, Longford, bought the remaining three acres. Richard Cox and his wife are buried in Harmondsworth burial ground.

Part of Mr Cox's large garden was a paddock on the Bath Road which was used as a cricket ground. The farmers of the Longford area, now selling most of their produce at Covent Garden, challenged their fellow London tradesmen to a cricket match. In July 1864, the Longford Cricket team played a Covent Garden eleven at The Lawns. This was an all-day match and after two innings Longford won by 35 runs in front of an 'unusually' large attendance and a band. At the end of the match, the outstanding Longford batsman, Mr M. Lott, who took five wickets, was played off the field by the band with 'See the conquering hero comes', which reduced him to tears.[127] The Longford cricket team had never been defeated.

* * *

The stables of the White Horse public house, were not large enough to accommodate the horses for the regular coach companies, but they provided a good service for the general public. The people of Longford saw horses every day on the farm and on the highway, but they never lost their respect for the animal that was the main supplier of energy and transportation in their lives. However, not everyone had the same regard for the animal.

---

124   Hogg, Robert, *The Apple*, (London 1859)
125   Rust, Douglas. The Middlesex Apple. Gazette, Wednesday November 25 1992.
126   Bate, G.E. *And so make a City Here: The story of a lost Heathland,* (Hounslow, 1948)
127   Uxbridge and W. Drayton Gazette – Tuesday 5 July 1864

In May 1844 the Secretary of the RSPCA brought to court a case of cruelty to a horse. William Moseley of London was driving a chaise towards Windsor and stopped at the White Horse at 5.45am.

The ostler, James Stevens, thought the horse was exhausted, and told the landlord that he did not think the horse would get to Windsor. However Moseley insisted that it was fine and continued on his way but when he reached the New Inn at Windsor the horse dropped dead. Mr Moseley told the court that he was not used to driving and would not do so again. He was full of remorse. He paid the 40-shilling fine 'without hesitation' as well as court and RSPCA costs of £3.13s. 6d.[128]

> **The White Horse**
>
> An inn since 1601. Grade II listed building with 18C brick elevations to 16C timber-framed building. Now whitewashed, with tiled roof. Two storeys, four bays. Brick dentil cornice. Horizontal sliding sash windows in centre bays on each floor. On first floor blank outer panels. On ground floor blocked door at left and entrance in modern porch at right. Inside has very low ceilings and much exposed timber especially upstairs, where the bay posts suggest a small open hall with smoke bay and chimney inserted later.
>
> https://britishlistedbuildings.co.uk/england/heathrow-villages-ward-hillingdon

The White Horse – early 20th century.

---

128   Windsor and Eton Express – Saturday 4 May 1844.

The White Horse was the location for an inquest in February 1848 on Mary Groves. She was the servant of Mr Filbey, a draper of Hammersmith and a few days earlier he had been alarmed at her behaviour as she appeared to be showing symptoms of insanity. Mr Filbey sent for her family in Longford. On Tuesday night her mother and another woman hired a cart and horse to fetch her home. When they arrived to pick her up she appeared to be better but near Brentford, on the return journey, she collapsed on her mother and died. Mr Adams, a surgeon of Colnbrook, said the death was caused by an overflow of blood on the brain.[129] Mary Groves, just 25, was laid to rest in St Mary's churchyard, Harmondsworth on 13 February.[130]

There was another inquest at the White Horse later that year when the body of James Butler, a haydealer from Hayes, was found on the road between Colnbrook and Longford on the evening of 11 September 1848. He was riding on top of a load of hay when the chain of the harness broke and he fell over the horse and the cartwheel ran over him. The horse and cart following him also ran over his body. The verdict was accidental death.[131] Even with the slow pace of horse travel driving was still a precarious occupation.

* * *

Now that farm produce was being sold daily at Covent Garden market in London the carters employed by farmer Weekly had to work hours that suited the trading hours at the market. Therefore they would leave the farm sometime after midnight, then they would stop for a break to rest the horses at a Hounslow tavern and arrive at the market in central London in time to unload and set up the farm's stall ready for when the market opened. It was the practice for several carters to leave from the farm and on their return journey they would load all the empty market baskets onto one wagon whilst another wagon visited a military stable or similar establishment to load up with manure for the return journey. This valuable resource was spread on the fields after ploughing. There was little variation to the carter's routine until one morning at the end of 1847.

---

129   Windsor and Eton Express – Saturday 12 February 1848

130   St Mary's Parish records London Metropolitan Archives; London, England; London Church of England Parish Registers; Reference Number: DRO/123/019

131   Windsor and Eton Express – Saturday 16 September 1848.

Chapter 14

Mischief and Mayhem (1847-1857)

One morning in November 1847 two carters from the Weekly's farm at Longford were returning from Covent Garden at 6.30am when, as they crossed Longford Bridge, they saw a large object in the water. It looked like a sack containing something heavy and with the help of fellow farm-workers they were able to pull it from the water. Inside they found pieces of an ironclad wooden strong box. The police were called who recognised the object as matching the description of a box stolen from the ticket office of the Paddington Terminus of the Great Western Railway a few days earlier.

Mr Collard, the superintendent of the railway police rode out from London to examine the find. He concluded that there was no doubt that it was the box that had been stolen between 2am and 3am on 15 November 1847. During his round that night Mr Nash, a Great Western Railway police sergeant, found the door of the second-class passenger office open. The door was not damaged so it was thought a skeleton key was used. The thieves then went through several other offices forcing open doors and drawers and taking notes, gold and silver and removing a strong box. The box contained gold and silver coins valued at around £1200-£1500 [£127,000-£160,000 today], and to get at it the thieves had removed some screws at the back of the chest and then unscrewed the lock. They then dismantled the box and tied the parts together to place in the sack. [132] The discovery of the box was the evidence the authorities hoped would lead to the arrest of the villains but no one was ever charged with the crime.

---

132 Morning Post – Tuesday 30 November 1847

This robbery, however, was one of three similar high-value thefts from the Great Western Railway and suspicion fell on one of their employees although nothing could be proven. This employee, Henry Poole, left his job and set himself up with his wife in a substantial house in Exeter. He continued his villainous ways and in a variety of disguises managed to elude capture, but on 1 January 1849 there was a raid on a post office mail van on a London to Truro train. Poole and his companion, Edward Nightingale, were discovered in a first class carriage with registered packages that had gone missing from the mail van. The pair were arrested on suspicion and, after a preliminary hearing in the magistrates court, they were sent to trial at the Crown Court in Exeter in front of Lord Chief Justice Denham. After a long trial they were found guilty of this particular robbery and sentenced to fifteen years which was commuted to seven years transportation, but the other crimes remained unsolved.[133] Poole was transported to the British colony of Bermuda, a place where only men sentenced to theft and serving seven years transportation were sent. His time there coincided with Sir Charles Elliot's term as Governor. Sir Charles was a keen supporter of prison reform and instead of concentrating on punishment, he believed prisoners should be rehabilitated. He introduced a system where prisoners could earn 'marks' for good behaviour and for showing signs of rehabilitation from their former life. He must have been impressed with Henry Poole for only two years later he wrote to London petitioning for a reconsideration of Poole's conviction. It was probably unsuccessful at that time, but later when a ship called *Sir George Seymour* returned to Portsmouth in 1855 with 140 English convicts and 200 Irish convicts Poole was on board. He was taken to Millbank prison in London, but released on licence the following month. Thereafter he disappeared from the records.

The high number of Irishmen on the ship carrying the returning criminals was due to the Great Irish famine of 1845-1852, when through desperation many were driven to steal. England was also experiencing poor grain harvests at that time and supplies from Ireland could not supplement the crop. The Corn laws imposed by the UK government after the end of the Napoleonic wars in 1815 were designed to restrict imports of corn which caused the price of grain to be held artificially high. This was good for landowners who made a bigger profit on their crops, but it kept the bread prices high and out of reach for the poor. It was only in 1845 that the

133   Manchester Times – Tuesday 27 March 1849

government relented, partly due to the famine, and repealed the Corn laws to allow grain to be imported which lowered bread prices and reduced the unrest which was building among those that were close to starvation.

For the Middlesex farmers the formation of the West Middlesex Agricultural Society in 1837 helped to cement relationships between farmers and workers. The first week of October every year was reserved for the Society's annual ploughing match and agricultural show. Each year it was held on a different farm. It was a day of fun and excitement for both gentry and labouring families, with everyone dressing up in their best clothes for the occasion. The farmers entered their produce, and their ploughman and other skilled workers competed, not just with local farmers, but also with open classes from neighbouring Counties. Labourers' entered produce from their own gardens in the relevant classes and they and their families had fun guessing the weight of the bullock and admiring decorated carts. The highlight for some labourers and farm servants was receiving monetary rewards for long-service, loyalty and good craftsmanship. These payments were sometimes equal to a week's wage and this recognition of their service was greatly appreciated and subliminally prevented any local unrest due to poor wages or conditions. After the event the ploughmen and their driving lads received refreshment on the field, but the local farmers, landowners, local Members of Parliament and nobility all enjoyed a lavish meal near to the location of the match. [134] In October 1838 two hundred and fifty men sat down to dinner at the Peggy Bedford following the second annual ploughing match. The dinner started at 3pm and cost twelve shillings a head (a week's wages for a labourer) which included a bottle of wine. After the dinner there were speeches, and ribaldry which went on late into the evening.[135] It was a platform for the local MPs to make political statements about the state of the farming industry and other participants to make speeches about their problems and concerns, their triumphs and successes. There were toasts, comic songs (usually about farming) and the whole gathering was a bonding of farmer and landowner, gentry and politician. This annual event became a landmark in the Middlesex farming year and flourished for nearly 100 years.

The show was also an opportunity for traders and manufacturers to exhibit new innovations to the farmers. In 1848 the society, now including

---

134   Windsor and Eton Express – Saturday 29 September 1838

135   Hampshire Chronicle – Monday 15 October 1838.

Market Gardens in their title, held the Annual Show at nearby Bedfont and a new steam threshing machine was demonstrated.[136] In 1856 the Longford wheelwright and blacksmith, William Passingham was exhibiting his patented plough sheers.

* * *

The Baptist farmers favoured employees who were also in their faith, or at least expected the labouring families to go to the chapel on a Sunday. Joseph Keen was brought up a Baptist in Gloucestershire, but came to Middlesex to look for work. He managed to find work as an agricultural labourer with Mr Philp from a farming Baptist family in both Longford and the next door parish of Harlington. Keen worked for farmer Philp for eight years alongside the farmer's nephew, Joseph, with whom there was antagonism. After his employer's death the nephew inherited the land and Keen continued to work for him, but the resentment was building and after a few angry words Joseph Philp dismissed him in November 1849. This meant he not only lost his job but his tied cottage. By January 1850 Keen and his wife and baby were lodging with John Exell in a cottage on the Bath Road at Longford, next to Mad Bridge. John Exell, a basket-maker, lived not far from a four-acre orchard owned by Joseph Philp.

On Saturday 30th March Joseph Keen and a friend, Thomas Peters, spent a few hours in West Drayton drinking seven quarts of beer between five men and then they walked back together to Longford, and parted at about six or seven at night. Keen was still resentful over his dismissal and told Peters he intended to get even with Philp. Later that night about 9.50pm the man he lodged with heard him go downstairs and out of the door. Keen walked along the main road towards the orchard where he used to work for Philp. As he walked he passed the shoemaker, Josiah Heath, who wished him a 'good night' and he made the same reply.

The next morning, being Sunday, no one was working in the orchard, but a neighbour had noticed that a great many of the trees had been chopped down and alerted Mr Philp. Mr Philp and police-sergeant Thomas Duggin went to the four-acre orchard to survey the damage. They found 131 standard apple and pear trees, worth £19, had been chopped down and when looking around for evidence saw a number of footprints in the soft light soil which led to each tree and then across a hedge into a meadow.

---

136   Windsor and Eton Express – Saturday 30 September 1848

They followed the footprints across the meadow and they stopped at a wall alongside the cottage in which Keen lodged. Mr Philp and Sergeant Duggin knocked at the cottage and spoke to Joseph Keen.

As Joseph Keen came to the door Duggin said to him, 'Mr Philp suspects you of having cut down trees in his orchard. Get your coat and your shoes and come with me.'

'These are the shoes I had on on Saturday'

The policeman took the shoes, and Keen watched Duggin fit his shoes into the track against the wall.

The policeman said, 'I am confident this is the shoe which made that mark'. Keen denied it. They then went to the orchard and tried the shoe in the footprints next to the trees and found they corresponded. They returned to Keen's lodgings so that Duggin could search his belongings. 'Have you got a bill-hook?'

'No, only this hatchet'

They could find no pruning knife or any other tool and the hatchet was not very sharp. The policeman thought that although many trees where chopped off in one blow others were hacked at and this tool could possibly have done the job. Mr Philp was not so sure, nor was he sure that Keen's boots had made the impressions. He was reluctant to think badly of a fellow chapel-goer. 'But, the nail marks from the sole of boot fit exactly.'

'Nevertheless I would like to see more evidence before I prosecute',

A second policeman examined the shoes and the footprints and came to the same conclusion that the nail marks were identical. On this corroborative evidence Philp agreed to prosecute and the case went before the judge at the Old Bailey in London on 6th May 1850.[137] After hearing all the witnesses and in spite of receiving a good character, Keen, aged 28, was found guilty and sentenced to seven years transportation. He was taken to Millbank prison and transferred to a prison hulk where he was kept in shackles for almost three years before being put on board *The Pyrenees* bound for Western Australia. He left behind a pregnant wife and a child. Their fate is unknown but they did not appear in the Harmondsworth census a year later.

* * *

---

137   *Old Bailey Proceedings Online* (www.oldbaileyonline.org, version 8.0, 17 April 2020), 6 May 1850, trial of JOSEPH KEEN (t18500506-927).

The Weekly family's life revolved around the Colnbrook Baptist Church where Richard senior, was a Deacon. For twenty years the church had been presided over by a charismatic pastor, William Coleman, who was deeply respected by all who knew him. His wife, Sofia, had died in the early summer of 1845 after which his warm friendship with the Weekly's daughter, Mary, blossomed. When William Coleman proposed marriage to Mary the couple worried that his hasty remarriage might damage his spiritual reputation amongst the congregation so he resigned as Pastor and took up another post in Bexley Heath, Kent. They were married quietly in West Ham London just over six months after his wife's death. Mary was 40 and William 71, but they would only have three years together. After he died, Mary brought his body back to Colnbrook to be buried in the Colnbrook Baptist burial ground, and Mary moved back in with her parents and brother, Richard, in the Weekly House.

On 8 January 1849 Richard Weekly senior rose from his bed feeling better than he had for a long time. He came downstairs and, although it was cold outside, he went for a walk in the garden. When he did not return for breakfast the family went out looking for him. He had collapsed and died in the garden of the house in which he was born. He was 77 and had been frail for some time. He was buried on 23 January in the grounds of the Colnbrook Baptist Chapel where his grandfather had been a founder member in 1708.[138]

For the farm and its workers the seasonal routine continued under the supervision of his son, Richard, and the farm manager, William Hester, with the ongoing support and experience of Henry James Weekly who was farming the adjacent Perry Oaks land. That support was not to last long. Four months after Richard's death, Henry became ill and died. Richard, the fragile son, was going to be reliant on his faithful farm manager to help him run the Longford farm, although he still intended to be in charge of recruiting.

Farm labouring was hard work, but for most men it was their only option. The farmers needed the labourers and the labourers needed the farmers. Getting enough, and the right sort, of workers was for Richard Weekly, as with many other Longford farmers, a constant concern. Young boys in the village could be trained up, but it took time before they were really useful. Placing an advertisement in a newspaper would not attract

138   The Gospel herald; or, Poor Christian's magazine, Volumes 17-18, 1849

an illiterate labourer. It was more common to hire workers at thrice-yearly hiring fairs. As the name suggests these were usually large gatherings of farm workers, servants and labourers who dressed in their Sunday best and wore something in their hat that indicated their skill such as a whipcord for carters or woven straw for thatchers.[139] Employers would move among them enquiring about their experience and situation. Once suited the emblems of their employment would be replaced by bright ribbons.[140] Labourers would be hired for a one-year term but some stayed with their masters for many years. When employee and employer were suited they sealed the contract with a shilling which soon got spent in the pleasures of the fair that accompanied this event.[141] The labourers when they began work would be found lodgings and supplied with food and light beer. The food would be mainly vegetables. Single farm workers would live-in with the family. The labourers would be paid between nine shillings to seventeen shillings a week depending on their skills and how often the farmer had rehired them. In order to retain the labourer for a whole year and prevent them leaving prematurely when they were needed most at harvest time the farmer would only pay them a proportion of their wages each week, and save the rest until the completion of a year, paying them interest on the saved amount. In winter, when the days were shorter, their money was reduced but often they would be given a supply of coal to help them out. At the end of their term they could move on with their accumulated savings or hope to be rehired on the same or better terms. Over the years some managed to accumulate enough saved wages to buy themselves a little piece of land. Those looking for work seldom had a written reference or a character reference from their previous employer and there was little time to make enquiries about a person so the employer had to use their own judgement on the individual's character.[142] Employing new people on the farm was often a leap of faith and a test of mutual trust but it did not always work out well.

Richard Weekly attended the High Wycombe Michaelmas Hiring Fair in September 1856 and engaged a young lad called Robert Izzey as a live-in farm servant at three shillings and sixpence a week plus sixpence a

139   Mingay, G.E., *Rural Life in Victorian England,* (Stroud,1990)

140   Oxford Journal – Saturday 03 October 1903

141   Wikipedia. https://en.wikipedia.org/wiki/Hiring_and_mop_fairs

142   Stirling Observer – Thursday 31 October 1867

week extra at harvest time. At the end of his year he would receive thirty shillings. Izzey started work the following Monday and on 20 October he became ill with a fever. Unbeknown to Richard, before he hired him, Izzey had been kicked by a horse and although he sustained no major injury the fever could have been the result. After a period at home with his parents Izzey recovered and returned to work just before Christmas for five days, and then had a relapse. After that Richard Weekly refused to take him back and paid him two shilling and sixpence for the five days he had worked. Robert Izzey and his parents applied to the magistrates and in March 1857 Richard Weekly was summoned to show why he refused to receive his servant back into his service after illness. Izzey's father corroborated his son's story and said that he was not aware he had been taken on trial. Mrs Coleman, Richard Weekly's sister and housekeeper, told the court she remembered Richard Weekly telling the boy he would take him on trial for three shillings and sixpence a week and if he suited he would give him four shillings a week plus five pence extra at harvest time and thirty shillings next Michaelmas.[143] Richard Weekly was later able to prove his sister's statement that the lad was taken on trial, and the case was dismissed.

Workers were only paid for the hours they worked. There was no sick pay or holiday pay. Richard Weekly wanted reliable workers and so it was usual for new hirings to be taken on for a trial period. This was to judge their character, work ethic and reliability. It was unfortunate for Izzey that he was taken ill so soon after starting work and it might have affected his future work prospects. Later that year Robert Izzey was charged by William Randall with stealing apples from his orchard. He had already been before the Bench for similar offences. This time he was ordered to pay twenty shillings in fines and costs or on default twenty-one days in prison.[144]

Managing a farm, the workers, and the weather required a lot of planning and foresight, but as Richard Weekly was to find out, life-changing events can strike at any time.

---

143   Windsor and Eton Express, Saturday 21 March 1857.
144   Windsor and Eton Express – Saturday 25 July 1857

Chapter 15

Changing Times (1859-1868)

Richard Weekly lingered over his breakfast in the Weekly House. He was in no hurry to return to the hot humid farmyard where he had been since six o'clock that morning supervising the three men and a boy and assigning them fieldwork for the day. 'Would this heat ever end?' he thought to himself. The summer of 1859 was one of the hottest of the nineteenth century. The long hot days often ended in damaging thunderstorms with many newspaper accounts of deaths, fires, damage, and floods. It was a difficult time for farmers.

Richard was worried about his crops. He needed enough produce to sell daily on his stall at Covent Garden. In these summer months soft fruit was the main crop and although it ripened quickly in the heat the frequent thunderstorms brought torrential rain that beat the plants into the ground. This left the soil saturated for a while until it seeped into the fast-draining brick earth of the region. The four rivers that crossed the Bath Road at Longford failed to cope with sudden heavy rain, and flooding was inevitable. Even when the floods subsided the mud left behind on the Bath Road formed deep tracks which the sun then baked into solid furrows and impeded the travellers using the main highway.

After his early start Richard had returned to the Weekly House to have breakfast with his sister Mary, and then sat in the cool of the morning room. At 45 he was by no means an old man, but his health had never been robust and the heat was too much for him. He closed the internal window shutters to keep out the sun. He felt safe sitting here beside his huge empty fireplace in this ancient house whose eighteen-inch walls shielded him from the heat of the day. As he sat in his chair, he watched as a chink of sunlight shining between the shutters grew weaker and he knew another storm was brewing. He dreaded the effect it would have on his already flattened and saturated crops, but he had learned to live with natural events. It was God's Will.

As he dwelt on that thought an image of his dead father came into his head. His father, a successful farmer of not only his own land, but 300 acres of tenanted land in adjoining Perry Oaks, was a shadowy figure in his early childhood. The farms took up much of his time and energy, and what he had left was given to the Baptist Chapel where he had been a Deacon for fifty years until his death aged 77, ten years ago. Richard had started working alongside his father at seventeen. His father had made the farms prosperous in a time of uncertainty for the farming industry and he attributed his success to his faith.

Richard's faith was not so strong. He wondered if he had been a disappointment to his parents. The whole family had moved back into the Weekly house in 1835 after giving up the Perry Oaks tenancy. After his father's death Richard had inherited the Longford farm, but when his mother died three years ago he wondered why she had made his cousin John Weekly her executor and not him. Was she disappointed in him?

The Weekly House 1910

Both Richard's parents had been very devout members of the Colnbrook Baptist Church and attended services regularly but Richard did not join them very often. Richard's allegiance to the farm outweighed his spiritual conscience and his adherence to some of their beliefs. The Strict Baptists did not forbid the consumption of alcohol but preferred to encourage temperance. Richard liked a drink now and again, and would slip out of his house, and round behind his ancient barn where a small path led into the back yard of the neighbouring Kings Arms public house. Keeping the Sabbath as a day of worship was another church rule that he had flouted when work on the farm seemed more important to him. Two months earlier his cousin John Weekly of Longford had been elected a Deacon at Colnbrook Baptist Chapel which was a tribute to John's devotion to their church, but a reminder that it should have been Richard following in his father's footsteps. [145]

These thoughts were going round in his head as Richard sat in his chair looking at the ancient beamed fireplace, and reflecting on his failure as a son. The room felt hot, even with the shutters closed, and as the fading light between the shutters infused the gloom he had a sense of foreboding as if the gates of hell were beckoning.

Suddenly there was a flash and an ear-splitting explosion of thunder which shook the building, and a bright bolt of lightning shot down the chimney and out of the fireplace towards him knocking him backwards out of his chair. He felt a searing pain pass through his body as he crashed to the floor and everything went dark.

Mary rushed into the room and saw her brother lying still on the floor, unconscious, his clothing burnt and smouldering and the exposed skin burnt black. She screamed, fearing that he was dead, which brought their servant, Ann Wilson, running into the room. The ladies stood around weeping and shocked. It needed Thomas Rush, the carter, sprinting in from the yard to calm them down and to realise that Richard was still alive although unable to move.

Tom was despatched to Colnbrook to fetch the doctor.

Although he regained consciousness Richard never fully recovered from this incident. He was left partially paralysed and with very little eyesight. However, he was exultant at his survival which he was convinced was a

---

145   Windsor and Eton Express – Saturday 16 April 1859

message from God, a sign that however remiss he had been in the past God was with him and wanted to bring him back to the right way. He resolved to be a better Christian, but his injuries made walking difficult. His strange gait caused a great-nephew to refer to him as 'Shaky Weekly' and he was no longer able to ride his horse and even getting into a horse and trap was difficult for him. His great resolve to be a better worshipper by attending the Colnbrook Baptist Chapel regularly seemed a forlorn hope until he had an idea.

Richard realised that what was needed was a Baptist chapel in Longford so that residents like him who were old or infirm could still have a place to worship. He commissioned Thomas Drake a fellow Baptist to build a chapel and two cottages, at a cost of £260, on a piece of land at the end of the village near Kings Bridge. There would be two semi-detached two-storey cottages for his labourers, and alongside it a single storey chapel capable of holding about 60 people. A chapel chimney would be needed so that a fire or stove could heat the building for the comfort of worshipers and Richard particularly requested that the chimney should have a bend in the stack. In medieval times a kink was sometimes built into a chimney stack in the superstitious belief that it would prevent witches entering the house and doing mischief, but Richard's request had a more pragmatic purpose. It was designed to deflect a direct hit from a bolt of lightning from coming down the chimney and into the building. He had learned a harsh lesson and did not want a repeat of his accident.

The chapel was full for its official opening on 8 December 1859. It was named the Zoar Chapel meaning 'little' but later this name was changed to Zion chapel. The stone name plate on the building (now a privately-owned house) still shows where the name was altered, and underneath are Richard Weekly's initials and the date.

Name plate.

Although the Longford Baptist Chapel was officially opened in December it was convenient to hold the anniversary service in June. The following June, with the Chapel too small for the expected congregation, Richard Weekly allowed a large barn on his farm to be used.[146] Having a big celebration in the summer when haymaking and harvesting kept everyone busy on the land, risked a poor attendance, but year after year the anniversary services were held on the farm and attended by up to seventy people.[147]

The Longford Baptist chapel with its strange chimney and the two cottages next to it which were all built in 1859.

* * *

Whilst the Baptists in Longford were thriving, the Quaker Meeting House was experiencing the opposite effect. It had been the first dedicated Quaker meeting house in Middlesex in 1676 but as other meeting houses were built in the county attendance was declining and the decision was made to combine it with Westminster and to call it the Westminster and Longford meeting, with all the meetings held in London. On 28 June 1865 the last meeting of the Society of Friends was held at Longford. The building was bought by a local farmer who turned it into two dwellings for his labourers, and renamed it Hunts Cottages.

---

146   Windsor and Eton Express, Saturday 9 June 1860.
147   Windsor and Eton Express – Saturday 18 July 1863.

The old Quaker Meeting House, became labourers cottages.

Mr Samuel Hunt was an influential farmer in Harmondsworth and in October 1865 he chaired a 'spirited' public meeting in the schoolroom to discuss the prospect of both Harmondsworth and Longford receiving a supply of manufactured gas from the Colnbrook Gas Company. It was agreed that Mr Hunt would lead a deputation of Harmondsworth citizens, including farmers Jarvis, Philp, and Grey from Longford, at a meeting with the directors of the Gas Company. The directors agreed to supply the villages, but were worried about the cost of laying a gas main of the length that would be needed to service the two villages. This did not put off the village delegation; five individuals in the parish had offered to pay half the cost of laying on the gas supply.[148] It was a turning point for the villages. Residents, who could afford it, could now replace candle-light with gas light; they could cook with it and heat their homes, and the farmers could run their steam threshing machines on gas instead of coal. Longford was modernising.

* * *

148   Windsor and Eton Express – Saturday 14 October 1865

Since his accident Richard had been too incapacitated to continue running the farm. He had his sister and three house servants to look after him in the Weekly house but he needed someone to manage the farm. He had no wife and no children and after a family conference, it was decided to look for an experienced, but spare, member of the extended family to assist him. His cousin, Mary Weekly, had married William Wild of the Langley branch of the Wilds and they had six sons. The discussion over the most likely candidate among the sons to take over the Longford farm was based on practicality. By 1859 their father was 65 years old and had handed the management of his 150 acre farm to his two eldest sons who were unmarried and fully engaged in running the family farm. The next two sons were already 'apprenticed' to other Weekly cousins whose large farms required the help of the next generation. That left the next available candidate which was Henry James Wild who although only 22 was eager and knowledgeable. He was happy to have the opportunity to help his disabled second cousin.

With the Weeklys all failing to produce heirs and the Wild family, with whom they had intermarried through three generations, producing an abundance of sons it meant that within a generation the old guard changed. The Weekly land in all the hamlets of Harmondsworth was inherited by the Wild family and the two-hundred year reign of the Weeklys, descendants of Wycliffe the Reformer, was about to end.

* * *

Since the introduction of the railways, Longford had seen fewer fine coaches and people of importance travelling through the village, but in April 1864 the villagers caught a glimpse of a person who was fast becoming a cult figure in England at that time. General Guiseppe Garibaldi who had united Italy was regarded as a hero. On his visit to Britain, aristocrats vied to entertain him and thousands of people swamped the streets wherever he went. The Dowager Duchess of Sutherland invited him to a luncheon at Stafford House in London on the first day of his visit and the next evening held a glittering reception for him.[149] The Duchess, a close friend of the Prime Minister and the Queen, later invited him to stay at her country house at Cliveden in Berkshire. Although there was a railway station nearby at Taplow the Duchess wanted to show her pride in having this great man

---

149   Livingstone, Natalie. *The Mistresses of Clivedon*, (London, 2015), p. 306.

visit her country house. They travelled in an open carriage drawn by four greys along the Bath Road. In the carriage was Garibaldi's son, Menotti, and the Dowager Duchess's son, the Duke. Just before they reached the London side of the Harmondsworth parish boundary, at Cranford, they stopped to change horses at the Berkeley Arms (now demolished).

The Duke and the General's son alighted from the carriage and went into the inn leaving the other two occupants in the open-topped carriage. As they waited, a middle-aged man with a clerical collar came puffing and wheezing up to the door of the vehicle. This heavy-built man with a large head and one eye-lid drooping over his grey-blue eyes had run along the Bath Road on hearing that the great General was in the carriage. Removing his hat he placed his hand on the carriage to steady himself, and in a slight Somerset accent asked, 'I have the honour of speaking to General Garibaldi?' to which the General nodded.

'I should not have intruded on your notice, if I were not aware that one of your most intimate friends is related to our family.'

'May I ask who that is?'

'Captain Roberts!'

The General seized Dr John Allen Giles' hand saying, 'Captain Roberts is indeed one of my closest friends, and I am delighted to meet any of his family in England.'

Dr Giles, scholar and Cranford curate (former vicar of Harmondsworth), turned to the Duchess and said, 'I beg your pardon but I am so out of breath that I can hardly speak,' which made her laugh. He explained to the Duchess that the General's achievements tempted persons to cut short all ceremony, and he then asked if he may send something for the General to Clivedon and she agreed.[150] He later sent them both a copy of his book *Memorials of Alfred the Great*.[151]

Dr Giles shook hands with the General, received a polite bow from the Duchess, and as the Duke and Menotti returned to the carriage they raised their hats to him. The carriage then proceeded along the Bath Road towards Longford. Garibaldi regarded himself as 'brother of the working man' and

---

150   Bromwich, David, (ed.), *The Diary and Memoirs of John Allen Giles*, (Somerset, 2000), p.363

151   Garibaldi's copy now owned by the author.

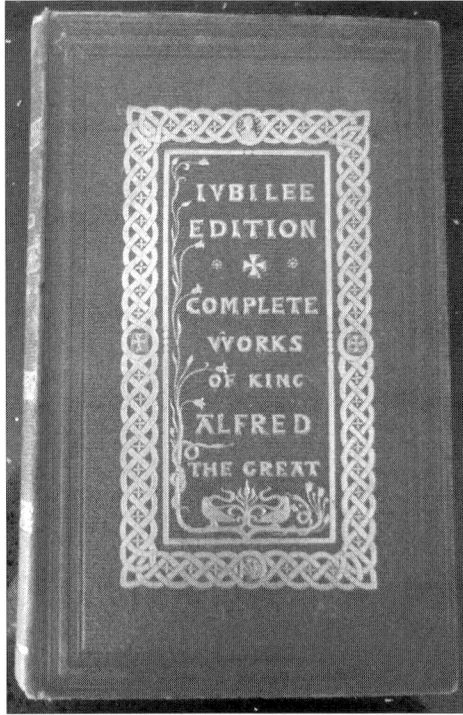

The actual book given to Garibaldi.

Dr Giles inscription inside the book.

the public identified with him. As he made his way through Longford many people left the fields to wave and cheer their hero.[152]

Garibaldi's stayed at Clivedon for a few days dining with the Dowager Duchess and her aristocratic friends who were all besotted with him. During his three weeks in Britain Garibaldi had intended to travel to Scotland and Northern England to meet worker's groups, but his enthusiastic welcome was worrying the ruling and political classes who felt Garibaldi might encourage a popular uprising amongst the workers. For Garibaldi the social whirl was becoming overwhelming and exhausting. When it was suggested that he should shorten his trip he agreed. He left England at the end of April promising to return, but never did.

* * *

Henry James Wild's move to Longford marked a new generation of farmers in the village. Richard Weekly, now free from the responsibility for the farm, was able to absorb himself in the meetings and affairs of the Baptist chapel. At the church meetings Richard made the acquaintance of a lady from the congregation, Elizabeth Philby, who came from Datchet, and they were married in 1861. She was 40 and he was 47. The household in the Weekly House was expanding and Henry James Wild found it more convenient to organise the farm from the farmhouse in the farmyard once occupied by farm manager William Hester, who had now moved to a smaller cottage. It was also a good house to bring a bride home to, and in 1867 Henry James Wild married Mary Ann Gregory a fellow Baptist.

The farm now separate from the Weekly House was always known in the village as 'The Farm'. Henry Wild now had complete control of the farm and its workers. He took on a young lad, John Woodward, who had been born 9 July 1852 in Harmondsworth into a labouring family. John enjoyed work at the Longford Farm. It was a mile's walk each way from his parent's cottage in Harmondsworth, but at least he could contribute to the household income and help feed his three brothers and sisters. In July 1866 John was alone in the yard at Longford putting the harness on the cart horse. He backed the horse into the cart house to where a fully-laden hay cart was waiting. As he was trying to attach the shafts to the harness the heavy horse suddenly pulled away, knocking him to the ground and bringing the cart on top of him. He had no time to call out and no one

---

152   Bucks Herald – Saturday 16 April 1864

noticed the incident until another employee, George Whitley arrived back to the yard in the late morning after a trip to West Drayton. As he entered the yard, Mrs Elizabeth Weekly, pointed out the carthorse which was heading for the harness house and she asked him to stop it. He grabbed the reins and led the horse back to the cart house where he saw the fully laden hay cart with its shafts up. Then he spotted something under the cart. With assistance he was able to get John out from under the cart but he was already dead. At an inquest held on the following Monday the verdict was Accidental Death.[153] Young John Woodward was laid to rest in St Mary's burial ground exactly a week after his fourteenth birthday.

The year 1866 was a sad time for the entire Weekly family, and the Colnbrook Baptist Chapel, as more of the family succumbed to old age. Mary Coleman, sister of handicapped Richard, died aged 60, and two married cousins also died childless. All were laid to rest in the chapel's burial ground

Richard and his wife Elizabeth were now alone in the Weekly House with three servants. Their time was fully engaged on church matters and

Dorcas Society

A charitable community-based organisation usually attached to a church to make and provide clothes to the less fortunate. Named after a disciple of Jesus who sewed clothes for the poor, (Acts of the Apostles 9:36-43). The organisation was founded in the 1800s when branches were formed in Britain and America. There are still Dorcas societies in some parts of the world today.

good works in the Community. Richard was too handicapped to stray far from home, but his wife was more active within the Colnbrook Baptist community. She helped the Chapel form a branch of the Dorcas Society which had been set up to sew and provide clothing for poor families. Elizabeth was the 'visitor' or representative for Longford. Initially the Society was formed to provide ladies, who were about to give birth, the loan of a box of linen for their confinement. The boxes would contain sheets and pillowcases and other items for the women and basic clothing for the baby. Often there would be soap and a bag of oatmeal. Sometimes it contained a small bible although until later in the nineteenth century few wives of labourers could read. After a month, when the box was returned in good order, a set of baby clothes would be given as a 'reward'. The volunteer 'visitor' in each group decided who was most in need of the box. Funds for the society had to be raised by events or subscriptions. Longford had a

---

153   West London Observer – Saturday 21 July 1866

box in November 1868 and a newspaper article encouraged other ladies to contact Mrs Weekly to offer their help. [154]

In spite of him having poor health from birth and incapacitated by the lightning strike nearly twenty years earlier, Richard 'Shaky' Weekly became the last surviving male member of the Weekly land-owning farming family. There were other Weekly's living at Longford, but these were only spoken about in surreptitious whispers.

---

154   Windsor and Eton Express, Saturday 7 November 1868.

Chapter 16

The Last Farmer Weekly (1871-1881)

While Elizabeth and Richard Weekly occupied the Weekly House and did good works around the village, Henry James Wild was running The Farm with his wife Mary Ann. By 1871 they had a two year old son, William, and a ten-month old daughter, Marion, who would go on to marry a Baptist preacher. Henry had rented additional land and was farming a total of 90 acres with the help of 10 men and 9 boys.

The previous year another Weekly in Longford had died. He was John Weekly, Richard's cousin, who died after a long and painful illness, aged 79, leaving a widow, Joanna (nee Wild), of the same age to whom he had been married for 54 years. They had spent their lives farming 408 acres at Fugman Farm, Bag Lane, Hayes, but on retirement had handed it over to a nephew, John Wild, and moved to their smaller 58-acre farm The Firs (now called Springbank) in Longford which had been left to them by his father. The couple, who were first cousins, did not have any children of their own.

After John's death, Joanna, now 81, continued to run her Longford farm and called herself a farmer in the 1871 census although most of her farm was being farmed by Thomas Weekly, a second cousin of both the late John Weekly and Richard Weekly. This cousin came from a branch of the family that had been shunned by the richer Weekly relatives for three generations. Joanna had taken him on in the spirit of Christian forgiveness and because she needed someone she could trust. His grandfather, would have inherited the tenancy of Manor Farm in Harmondsworth, if he had not scandalised the family in 1808, at the age of 19, by running off to marry an illiterate 15 year old girl, called Rebecca Plowman. She was not a Baptist and marrying outside the faith meant he was ostracised by the tight-knit Baptist family.

Springbank. 2018.

His father did give Thomas and Rebecca a run-down cottage on the Moor in Harmondsworth where they raised four boys and three girls on what he could earn as an agricultural labourer. When the children grew up they produced another generation of four sons and three daughters between them. It was ironic that the pious landowning Weeklys of Harmondsworth did not produce enough sons to keep the land in the family name, but the 'black sheep' branch had no trouble producing sons, grandsons and great-grandsons, although many were short-lived.

When John and Joanna Weekly inherited Springbank farm it was on condition that they paid an annuity of £36 per annum to the 'black sheep' Thomas, now living in retirement in his cottage in Harmondsworth. In a circular twist of fate this annuity came from the rent his grandson Thomas was now paying Joanna Weekly to farm her land.

This grandson was living in a cottage in Longford with his wife Sarah, and although they did not have children of their own, in 1871 they had living with them a cousin called Ellen Kemp. A year later two new-born baby boys are found dead in a sack in the Queen's river.[155] Suspicion about who could be the mother fell on Ellen Kemp. A piece of cloth similar to that in which the boys were wrapped was found in the barn on Thomas Weekly's market garden. Mrs Weekly challenged Ellen Kemp who said, 'What next, I wonder; I never put them there, nor ever had one.' At an inquest on the boys in which PC James Whitehead, stationed at Longford, gave evidence of finding a bundle in the river, the coroner decided that the boys were probably still-born and unknown, and that there was no criminal case to answer.

The annuity obligation on Joanna Weekly's farm lasted two more years until grandfather Thomas died aged 84, a great age for an agricultural worker at that time. In his lifetime he did not return to the Baptist faith and therefore his family missed out on the support structure the church offered, but he did redeem himself in the eyes of his own descendants. He took on the burden of raising two grandsons when one of his sons died young, and later contributed to the upkeep of two orphaned grandsons who were in the workhouse and raised another one himself.[156] This grandson, Richard, a cousin of the Longford Thomas, was aged 25 when his grandfather died in 1873. Young Richard inherited the cottage and now had a home to offer his sweetheart, Mary Williams, and they married in the spring of 1874.

Richard and Mary only had eight years together before Richard died aged 33, and his wife died two years later. They left four young children all under eight years of age. With no Baptist family support the children were consigned to the workhouse in Stanwell where they spent their childhood until they reached the working age of 14. The girl, Ada, went into service and died unmarried aged 30. The oldest of the three boys, aged thirteen, asked the Workhouse master if he could emigrate to Canada. Thomas Walter Weekly knew Dr Barnado's Society had a scheme for sending young orphan boys to Canada to work on farms and, after arrangements were made, he was on the *SS Circassian* on his way to Montreal a few months later. The second son was apprenticed to a baker and later went to the United States and ended up as a restauranteur in Los Angeles. The last brother became a sailor and travelled the world until finally settling in Australia. The three boys never lost touch with each other and met up

155   Windsor and Eton Express – 15 June 1872.
156   Windsor and Eton Express – Saturday 07 August 1858

whenever their travels allowed. They had all overcome the disadvantages of their early life in the workhouse and thrived, the last brother dying in 1957. They were too young when their parents died to remember their early life in Harmondsworth and would not have known that they were the last remnants of the once powerful and influential Harmondsworth Weekly family that had dominated the parish for three centuries.

* * *

Henry James Wild was now the main employer and leading Baptist in Longford. Farming was going through difficult times in the 1870s and 1880s. Cheaper food was being imported, especially grain from the United States, and there was also a period of poor harvests caused by adverse weather.[157] Longford was only 71 feet above sea level and in 1879 heavy rainstorms flooded many parts of South East England including the Great Bath Road at Longford.[158] The Farm was able to ride out the agricultural depression by concentrating on growing horticultural crops for the London Market.

The farm had a fifteen-acre orchard growing apples, pears, plums, cherries, damsons and walnuts. Underneath the trees were soft fruit bushes of gooseberries and currants.[159] Fruit was a profitable crop in the summer season, but as agriculture went into a decline new horticultural crops were grown to keep the farms viable. Labour was still a vital element. Towards the end of the nineteenth century the agricultural labourer was at the bottom of the list of occupations, considered the last resort for the unemployed, but the Weeklys would help anyone in need. They would employ people with no questions asked and with no character reference and in return they expected them to work hard, be punctual, and go to chapel on Sundays. Drinking in the pub was frowned on, but not forbidden. Spare produce could be purchased at a nominal cost and also milk, but any form of stealing of produce would result in the sack. Sometimes fines were imposed for arriving late for work (15 minutes of pay deducted), or breaking the head off a Brussels sprout plant when picking (half an old penny), or for eating a plum (six old pennies). The farming week had a strict routine. The men would get paid on a Saturday afternoon when 'Shaky' Richard Weekly, still nominally the boss, would raise the sash-window in the ground-floor

157   Harrison, J.F.C. *Late Victorian Britain 1875-1901*, (London, 1990), p.16

158   Berrow's Worcester Journal, Saturday, 30 August 1879.

159   Windsor and Eton Express – Saturday 9 June 1860

Morning Room at the Weekly House. Inside, at the base of the window frame, was a hinged piece of wood which, when raised, served as a table. Each employee would be handed an envelope with their pay for the week. Only Sundays and Christmas Day were non-working days and there were no paid holidays.

Keeping the land continuously cropping was the aim. Spring spinach ended in early May. Brussels sprouts, savoy cabbages, cauliflower, kale and broccoli were sown in February and March and then planted out in May. From July cauliflowers were picked and then Brussels sprouts at the end of August, which would crop continuously until February. In February the tops of the Brussels sprout plant would be cut and sold as greens. In late autumn savoy cabbages would start to be picked and would continue into the winter. Kale and broccoli were not marketed until after Christmas and they would continue to be available until April. Cabbage was the main crop. In the last week of July spring cabbage was planted which needed careful seedbed preparation and had to be grown on land that was not too rich to avoid the production of leafy plants. The plants had to be hoed and then left during the winter. After the winter equinox nature would start to wake up and the growing processes continued with hand hoeing at three week intervals then nitrate of soda added to the soil. Early plants had raffia tied round the outer leaves so the plant would produce hearts, and then cutting and marketing by the end of February.[160] The annual cycle continued and the enrichment of the soil with manure was needed to produce the best results.

Initially market gardeners would be paid to clear the horse manure from London stables, but later this arrangement was reversed and the farmer paid the stable for the manure. Sheep droppings were good fertiliser, but as the Longford farms moved away from livestock to grow more horticulture crops the flocks were phased out. Chicken breeding was a growth area when manpower was short. These produced several streams of income. The young chicks could be sold to poultry farmers, and the hens kept for egg sales or sold for meat. The droppings were also a good fertiliser.

Richard Weekly in the Weekly House was now effectively the last farmer Weekly, although he had handed over all his farming responsibilities to Henry James Wild. Richard died in 1878 aged 65. He had survived his

---

160   Lucas, Alfred E. and Calder, R.J. (ed.), *"The Great A.W. Smith"* (Ashford, Middlesex, 2000) p.54.

terrible injuries from the lightning strike nearly twenty years earlier and overcome his blindness and physical handicaps to lead a pious life which he hoped had redeemed him in God's eyes.

He was buried in the Colnbrook Baptist Chapel's small burial ground, which was reserved for the burial of the most ardent local Baptists. He had married late and had no children. He left the Weekly House to his wife Elizabeth who lived there until her death. His legacy was the Longford Baptist chapel that was in constant use until 1971 and is now a private house.

In 1881 Henry James Wild and his wife invited all the children, teachers and friends from the Colnbrook Baptist Chapel Sunday School to a picnic tea on Tuesday 5 July at The Farm. The decorated horse-drawn vans took them from the Chapel to Longford where they were welcomed into the shady orchard. There they ate strawberries, cherries and other fruit that were growing in abundance. Even though the journey was just over a mile from where they lived it was a rare treat for the Sunday School children, and a generous gesture by the Wilds. For their six young children, two sons and four daughters, it was a great day for them all to enjoy having fun with their fellow Sunday school members.[161]

By 1886 the spate of farm arson attacks from earlier in the century had ceased, but there was still the fear of accidental conflagrations. In November that year a large shed belonging to Farmer Gray, nearly opposite the Weekly's farm was seen alight at four in the morning. Henry Wild sent for the two local fire brigades. Captain Rayner of the Colnbrook Fire Brigade got the horses out of their stable and police sergeant Hinton helped with the appliance. On arrival they found the shed well alight. By this time, the Harmondsworth brigade had also arrived and the two brigades managed to extinguish the fire after an hour's hard work. Mr Henry Wild was praised for his prompt action and Mrs Wild provided a hot breakfast for the men. It was thought a stable boy had left a candle alight when he left for London about 3.30am that morning.[162] Ten years later Henry Wild's son William was a member of the Colnbrook Fire Brigade and when one of three thatched cottages in Longford caught fire, the owner immediately ran to William for help. When William returned there he could see the flames were coming out of the cottage door and nearly catching the thatch. The

161   Windsor and Eton Express – Saturday 09 July 1881
162   Windsor and Eton Express – Saturday 27 November 1886

fire appliance had been sent for, but with many helpers and a good supply of water, the local people managed to extinguish the flames before the appliance arrived, leaving the cottage badly damaged.[163]

Henry James Weekly had a profitable business and in 1881 was employing thirteen men, one boy and five women. The steady rhythm of the farming year continued its seasonal annual progress with most of the land now cultivated as market gardens and all of the produce sold on his stall in Covent Garden. The very last person with the Weekly name to occupy the Weekly House was Elizabeth Weekly, the widow of Richard 'Shaky' Weekly. She died there on 2nd January 1899 aged 77.[164] An obituary in the local paper described her as a great loss to the village of Longford. 'She had been in delicate health and a few days before her death was seized with an attack of bronchitis which proved fatal. She gave pecuniary support to the chapel that her late husband had built in Longford, and was kind and generous to her poorer neighbours and a great support to her relatives and friends. She had been a member of the

The Weekly House

Weekly house and barns in 1937.

The house is of brick and has a coved eaves-cornice on the east and west sides. Inside the original staircase has turned balusters and square newels with ball terminals and pendants. There are some original floors and a fireplace with a moulded surround, shelf and panelled overmantel with flanking pilasters. The barns, east of the house are timber-framed.

An inventory of the Historical Monuments in Middlesex 1937. Royal Commission on historical Monuments.

Baptist chapel at Colnbrook for many years and took a keen interest in the welfare and progress of the chapel, and especially of the Dorcas Society. She was interred in the burial ground behind the Colnbrook Baptist Chapel following a long procession of carriages and vehicles which drove through the town where the inhabitants displayed signs of mourning. Among the many mourners were members of the congregation, family, friends, two former pastors and other local clergy, with the employees of her husband's former farm acting as pall-bearers.'[165]

---

163   Windsor and Eton Express – Saturday 5 March 1898.

164   West Middlesex Gazette – Saturday 14 January 1899

165   Ealing Gazette and West Middlesex Observer – Saturday 14 January 1899

As the farms of Longford prospered with their fertile market gardens, for the hospitality trade in the village the prospects were not so good. The railways had ended the long-distance carriage trade and only local traffic passed through the village. There was a railway station three miles away at West Drayton and in 1882 the Peggy Bedford received some unexpected guests.

Chapter 17

Scandal (1882)

Bessie was excited as she woke that Saturday morning. She was going on a secret journey that would change her life, although she could not imagine the direction it would take. She helped her mother with her three younger siblings at their respectable house in 81 Warner Road, Camberwell, London, and then, at half-past five, she put a tight fitting brown ulster coat (an overcoat with sleeves and a short cape) over her dark blue serge dress. On her head she put a round black felt hat trimmed with black velvet and around her neck were two necklaces and on her wrist a silver watch.[166] She had a small bag containing a change of linen and half a sovereign in her pocket. She said nothing to her parents about where she was going. The secrecy was all part of the adventure.

She got to the Oval, at Kennington, and there waiting for her was the man of her romantic dreams. He was a slim, good-looking, well-dressed man, who looked at her tenderly.

'I was afraid you would not come,' he said.

'You should not have worried. I would not have disappointed you.'

Frank Norris and Bessie walked to Vauxhall Station and took a cab to Bishop's Road Station (now called Paddington Station). In the cab Frank said, 'You will have to return home on Monday'.

Bessie looked at him in horror, 'But I thought we were going to be together forever'

The look of distress on her face made him say, 'Don't flurry yourself about it; you know I don't mean you to return on the Monday.'

166   London Daily News – Thursday 18 May 1882.

Frank bought two tickets to West Drayton, Middlesex. They got out off the train at West Drayton station and set off on the footpath to Harmondsworth. Bessie was glad she was wearing flat shoes for after passing through Harmondsworth village they walked on to Longford and eventually arrived at the Peggy Bedford. They were dusty from their three-mile walk. It was unusual for travellers to arrive on foot, but the respectable looking couple with London accents attracted no more attention than admiring glances for the strikingly pretty young lady of medium height with dark brown hair and dark eyes. George Bacon the son of the landlord greeted them.

'Can you give us accommodation for the night?'

'Of course. Please sign the register'

The man wrote, 'Mr and Mrs Churchill, Dulwich'

They were shown to a room with no sitting room where they remained all weekend.

This was Saturday the 13 May 1882. A month earlier, the girl, full name Elizabeth Stewart, was walking fast down Camberwell New Road when a smartly dressed young man started walking beside her and spoke to her.

'I bet I will race you to the bottom of the road'[167]

He walked with her for a while and then left her, but a couple of evenings later they met accidentally and stopped to speak to each other. They made an appointment to meet again, but although she kept it, he did not. She was disappointed. She was flattered by the attention of such a good-looking man who was so obviously refined and worldly. She did not tell her parents about the meeting as she knew they would not approve of her talking to a stranger. However she continued to meet the man and they had eight or nine casual walks together, On each occasion he would walk her back near her house and leave her. From these conversations she assumed he was a gentleman of means and she fell for his charms. He started hinting at marriage and persuaded her that if they went away to Dieppe or Jersey then, after the scandal had been hushed up, they would return to England and be quietly married. She was convinced he was sincere and agreed to the elopement.

On the Monday morning, after their weekend at the Peggy Bedford, Frank said he had to return to London on business and when they arrived

---

167   *Old Bailey Proceedings Online* (www.oldbaileyonline.org, version 8.0, 22 October 2021),
       June 1882, trial of FRANK NORRIS, Unlawfully (t18820626-714)

there, around 1pm, he took her to a coffee-shop and hotel at Vauxhall where they stayed the night. After breakfast the next morning he left her there and did not return that night or any night after that. There the story came to a shattering disillusionment for the naïve young Bessie Stewart when her seducer, twenty-three year old fantasist Frank Norris, finally told her, that he was married and that he was a clerk in a gas company's office and not a man of independent means. He urged her to return home but she was too frightened of her parent's reaction.

During the week at the Vauxhall lodgings there was an exchange of letters in which he told her he would take her home on Saturday. His letter read, 'I received your dear letter directly I got indoors last evening, and I must say you are a loving little soul to write to me and tell me how you love me. I ought to be the happiest man on the earth to know I have won the warm love and confidence of such a darling as you, my Bessie. I am worrying myself this morning about your going home dear. Just think if your papa will not let me call to see you, but I should think he is bound to. So good-bye dear, with my best love and lots of kisses. Ever believe me, your loving husband, Frank.'

Frank was right to worry about her father's reaction when she returned home. Mr Stewart was a builder's foreman and used to dealing with people. Bessie had been missing for a week, and her frantic parents had put a plea for her return in the newspapers. To try to soften up her father Bessie had sent him a letter.

'My Dear Father and Mother. I dare scarcely hope ever to claim those relations again. I have sinned, but am bitterly punished. I have my punishment (which is almost more than I can bear) in a guilty conscience. I was tempted, and fell into temptation, but was soon able to see my error. When I think over the past I cannot imagine how I could have left so happy a home as mine was, and such kind parents, for someone who could offer me an empty title, riches, and the rest of this world's foibles. I am heartily sorry for my misdoings; and though I know I do not deserve to be looked upon by you again, I trust you will forgive me. After I left home on Saturday, I was driven away to the West-end of London. I was so confused and miserable. I had repented then of going away. I know I was taken to a grand house and dressed up, and then was almost carried down to a magnificent room, where there was a clergyman who mumbled a few words. I then felt a ring pressed on my hand and I knew I was no longer free, but bound up to a man for ever. I do not know what happened to me next, for I was lost, fainted I believe. When I came to myself I was in a grand bedroom, and a woman was there, who said she was my maid, and that the room was my own 'boudoir'. This woman then gave me a hideous satin dress, and helped me to put it on, and then I had to go down to dinner. I was then taken in a carriage to the theatre. I went home with the man who took me away but I did not see him again till ten o'clock on Sunday morning at breakfast. He took away my little silver watch which my dear father had given me and replaced it with a gold one. In fact, he loaded me with presents,'[168] The letter went on to say that she had managed to escape her abductor, Sir Philip Nugent, by bribing a manservant and was now staying in a little room and asked their forgiveness and signed herself 'your repentant daughter, Bessie Stewart'.

Bessie wrote the letter as Frank dictated it, then said, 'Do you think my father will believe such an incredible tale as that?'

'Yes; if it is any ordinary commonplace affair he won't believe it.'

'Please take me home, Frank, if you don't I will throw myself off Westminster Bridge.'

Eventually Frank agreed to take her home. She waited in the next street whilst he knocked on the door of 81 Warner Road at 11 o'clock at night. A little boy opened the door and then went to fetch his father saying 'There is a gentleman to tell us something about Bessie.' Her distraught father rushed to the door. Frank said, 'I found Bessie in distress on Westminster Bridge, and as a friend I have brought her home. She wants to ask forgiveness for going away'.

'There is no occasion for forgiveness; where is she?'

'She is in Wellington Road. You will find her there', but as the cowardly Frank made to depart the father grabbed him and said, 'I will go with you'. They walked together with Frank still grumbling and trying to make his exit. Mr Stewart said, 'If I could find Sir Philip Nugent, whoever he was, who took my child away, I would send a bullet through him.' Frank said, 'You shouldn't talk so; people will think you silly.'

Mr Stewart, still holding on to him, turned and said, 'I will let people know whether I am silly or not.'

---

168   Exmouth Journal – Saturday 03 June 1882

Bessie was not where Frank had left her and they walked back to the Stewart house with Frank's arm still being held tight by Mr Stewart. 'I am going to hold you on suspicion until I find my daughter.'

'But I am a respectable man and you will ruin me.'

'You can proclaim your innocence when I have found my child,' and he marched him off to Camberwell Police station where he left him and returned home. Three minutes later Bessie was knocking at the door and when she confessed that he was the man who had taken her Mr Stewart went back to the police station and charged him with absconding with an under-age girl. This news startled Frank Norris and he said, 'You will have to prove it', whereupon a birth certificate was produced which proved she still had two months to go to her 16th birthday. Frank said Bessie had told him she was eighteen years of age. It seems that both parties had duped each other. Frank was refused bail before he appeared in court at the Old Bailey. Bessie, her father, the police and George Bacon, the son of the landlord of the Peggy Bedford, were all witnesses at the trial. The Jury without hesitation pronounced Frank Norris guilty and he was sent to prison for twelve months with hard labour. This salacious case was reported in detail in newspapers all over Britain.

Bessie, her reputation in ruins, was sent away by her family to stay with friends in Worthing. Her escapade had brought shame on her family and with it her chances of marrying a respectable man. She was a fallen woman. Before her elopement she had been a pupil-teacher, but nine years later she was a live-in house-maid in London. After that she disappeared from the records. Frank's wife and son continued to live in London and on all subsequent census forms she referred to herself as a wife, but Frank did not live with them. By 1888 he was living with another woman and had another son. There are no marriage records for either of these 'wives'. In 1890 Frank and his new family emigrated to Vancouver, Canada, where he became a hotel keeper, and he and his wife had five more children. He died in 1942.

The newspaper reporting of the scandalous abduction brought infamy on both participants, but the publicity was good for the Peggy Bedford whose name appeared in all reports. The hotel's trade had been in a slow decline since the end of the coaching era, but it was to be an innovative mode of transport that brought renewed trade to The Peggy Bedford Inn.

Chapter 18

Landlords (1859-1893)

The Peggy Bedford lost its charismatic landlady in 1859 aged 78. Her fame was such that nearly every newspaper in Britain reported her death. She had been the licensee of the King's Head for fifty years and her death was the end of an era for the hotel's history. Her demise coincided with the decline of the long-distance carriage trade and the growth in popularity of the railways. Royalty and long-distance travellers no longer stopped to change horses and refresh themselves at the well-known inn. The hotel now had to rely on local trade, putting it in competition with the other three pubs in the village.

After her death the Peggy Bedford inn was put up for sale on 27 May 1859 to be sold in one lot. The large house had substantial stables, outbuildings, and pleasure gardens. There was also a productive four-acre orchard, and two meadows totalling 10 acres.[169]

The inn was bought by retired coach painter, Charles James Twite who, to make the hotel more attractive to visitors, improved the pleasure grounds and advertised them to Londoners as a destination for days out in the countryside. In 1877, he announced that every Sunday the gardens would be open to the public, with gravel walks and shrubberies, a bowling-green, summer-houses and a fish pond and he would 'provide on the shortest notice', wines and spirits, teas and dinners.[170]

169   "At the Mart. To-morrow." *Times*, 17 May 1859, p. 12. *The Times Digital Archive*, link. gale.com/apps/doc/CS201495729/TTDA?u=bou_ttda&sid=TTDA&xid=06171cc6. Accessed 19 Dec. 2020.

170   Middlesex Chronicle – Saturday 13 October 1877.

Mr Richard Weekly

KING'S HEAD INN,
LONGFORD, MIDDLESEX.

Particulars and Conditions of Sale

OF THE

KING'S HEAD INN,

LONGFORD,

WITH THE

Stabling, Out-Buildings, Garden, a Highly Productive Orchard,

AND

TWO ENCLOSURES OF MEADOW LAND,

CONTAINING IN THE WHOLE

ABOUT 14 ACRES,

ALL OF WHICH IS

COPYHOLD of the Manor of Harmondsworth,

Subject to a Quit Rent of 6s. 4d. per Annum.

For Sale by Auction,

AT THE AUCTION MART, LONDON,

On FRIDAY, 27th May, 1859, at 12 o'Clock,

IN ONE LOT.

MR. RICHARD MOSS,

AUCTIONEER,

12, *King William Street*, City, E.C.

Solicitors,—

Messrs. FARNELL & BRIGGS,

Isleworth.

Messrs. HOWARD & DOLLMAN,

141, *Fenchurch Street, City.*

E. COLYER, Printer, 17, Fenchurch Street.

Richard Weekly's own copy of the Sale Particulars.

Social clubs would organise an outing, colloquially known as a beanfeast, for their members. These trips were eagerly anticipated by the participants. They were often the only holiday they received all year. One such outing, in 1880 saw four brakes (horse-drawn open-top charabancs with bench seats and brightly striped sun awnings) carrying fifty people arrive at the inn with the employees of the Chiswick Improvement Commission. They had left Chiswick at 9.30am and had a 'pleasant' run through the towns of Kew, Brentford, Isleworth and Hounslow where they saw militia tents pitched in a field beside the road, and in the distance could see the land-based Feltham Schools (reformatory) Training Ship, 'fully rigged and manned'.[171] The party stopped for lunch at the Bell at Bedfont after which some of the party visited the six-hundred year old church, where a wedding was taking place. Back in the brakes they completed the three-mile ride to the Peggy Bedford. At their destination the men (no women were present), in between heavy showers, played games of cricket and quoits or walked in the garden noting that the grounds 'are not in the best state of preservation', until 2.30pm when they sat down to a substantial dinner in the spacious dining room. After the meal the Chairman and others made speeches which were followed by drinking several toasts. The Chairman hoped that they were all suitably grateful to the Commissioners for giving them the one-day holiday. He also cautioned that they should stay sober so that they would be ready for work the following day. The workers then returned to the grounds to play games and started back to Chiswick about 9pm.

Some members of other social groups, however, were tempted into mischief when they saw growing food for the first time. James Baker, 17, Henry Dearing, 15, and Thomas Adam, 17, all youths from London who were part of a beanfeast outing, were spotted by two policemen carrying a bag of apples and pears. They were unable to give a satisfactory explanation for where they got the fruit and so they were taken into custody. The local police had been watchful for day-trippers stealing local produce. At the Magistrates Court PC Whitbread said that on Bank Holiday Mondays a lot of damage was committed at Harmondsworth by excursionists. They stripped fruit trees and grubbed up potatoes and threw them at one another. Baker, Dearing and Adam were each fined ten shillings and another youth of the same party was fined five shillings for unlawfully having some wheat in his possession.[172]

---

171   Acton Gazette – Saturday 05 August 1882
172   The Bucks Herald Saturday 7 August 1880.

Bank Holiday visitors to Longford were only welcome as long as they behaved themselves. One Whit-Monday afternoon six lads from London arrived at the Peggy Bedford in a horse-drawn van and were served beer.

Tankard

Around the ancient bar counter hung pewter mugs which since the seventeenth century had been used to serve ale. Now no longer used they were displayed as symbols of a bygone age. These mugs were collectable and when the lads left they were seen by Cornelius Murphy, aged 13. He noticed that the last man was carrying a pewter pot that he put in the back of the horse-drawn van. Another pot was already in the van. They drove off, but young Murphy told the landlord what he had seen. The police were called, and when PC Davis saw the uncovered van driving towards London at 9pm. he asked the driver to stop who refused and increased his speed. Another policeman, PC Joyce, who was mounted, stopped them. The van was searched and two pots, valued at thirty shillings, were found in a sack under the seat of the driver. The driver said he had brought them from the College Arms, but the monogram was identified by Mr Thompson, the landlord of the Peggy Bedford. All six men denied any knowledge of how the pots got into the van. They were each fined twenty shillings or a fortnight's imprisonment.[173]

* * *

Miss Peggy Bedford had been well-regarded as an inn-keeper, and had built up the inn's formidable reputation, but some of her successors were not so diligent. A tenant licensee in the 1880s, Francis Boynton, seemed to lose

173   Uxbridge and W. Drayton Gazette – Saturday 20 June 1908.

interest in the whole business, closed the inn, and moved his family into a cottage in Harmondsworth. He failed to honour his lease's requirements to keep the public house in good repair. When the owners tried to replace him he refused to surrender the licence and the owners had to apply to the Courts to get the licence transferred, by which time Mr Boynton was already in prison for not paying his rates.

Another Landlord, far from making sure his customers did not becoming drunk and disorderly, had to be kept under control by his own staff when he was in the same condition. In 1890 the landlord, Henry W. Neville Clapp, was summoned for being drunk on his own premises. An off-duty policeman, PC Steel, was at home in Longford when Mrs Clapp knocked on his door at 7.15pm and asked him for help getting her husband to bed as he was the worse for drink. He followed Mrs Clapp into the tap-room where Mr Clapp was sitting at a table. The policeman asked him to go outside as he wanted to speak to him, but the landlord stumbled down the steps into the arms of the policeman who had to hold him up the whole time he was speaking to him. The policeman told him not to go back into the tap-room, but to go upstairs to bed. Clapp swore and told him to mind his own business, and the policeman responded by saying it was his business when he gets a request from the Landlord's wife. It took the wife and the policeman and the landlord's younger brother half an hour to take him upstairs and into bed.

Mrs Clapp regarded the policeman as a close friend of her husbands and was not expecting him to report the incident to his superiors, which he did the next day. Three days later Mrs Clapp confronted him, 'I hear you have reported this case' and the constable confirmed that he had.

When the case came to court PC Steel, in the witness stand, said that Mrs Clapp had a black eye given her by her husband. He admitted accepting a cigar from Mr Clapp before they got him to bed but he was adamant that he had not accepted a glass of whisky and water. In mitigation the defence lawyer said Mr Clapp was under notice to quit the premises by the 20th of March when he would retire from the business altogether so a conviction in the case would not make a difference as he would not be applying for a licence in another house. Mrs Helen Clapp gave evidence that her husband, some time ago, had been attacked on the highway and beaten about the head, since which time he had not been able to tolerate any spirits. Within the last two months he had suffered the bereavement of both his father and mother. On the night in question she saw her husband drinking whisky and knowing the effect it would have on him fetched PC Steel and asked him, as a friend, to help her get her husband to bed as he had more influence over him than anyone in Longford. She said she gave him threepence so that he might go into the tap-room and get a glass of ale which she saw him drinking at the bar. Later she drew him a glass of whisky. PC Steel said he would stay a little longer as he was not on duty until 10pm.

Mrs Clapp said it was not true that Mr Clapp needed assistance getting upstairs. She then offered PC Steel another whisky and after drinking it he left. She denied her husband had given her a black eye. She had a small bruise from knocking her face on a saucepan. The barmaid, Sophia Day, gave evidence that she served PC Steel with a glass of ale that evening and he only drunk half of it. Later she saw him with Mr and Mrs Clapp drinking whisky and she saw Mr Clapp go up to bed unaided. The constable left at 8.40pm.

Another witness Joseph Harrison, a carpenter of Longford, was at the hotel that evening. He saw PC Steel order a glass of ale which he paid for and drunk half of it. He then saw Mrs Clapp fetch a glass of whisky and a glass of water, twice. He saw Mr Clapp go up to bed smoking a cigar and wished him goodnight. There was no one with Mr Clapp. He appeared excited, but not drunk.

The bench considered the verdict, but decided that the evidence was so conflicting that they could not justify a conviction and dismissed the case. He could keep his licence.[174] Mr Clapp was a tenant of the Harmon Brewery Company of Uxbridge who replaced him with Lewis Chappell soon after this incident.

Although the inn was not making money it was still popular with day-trippers, and its function room busy with local meetings for trade unions, benefit societies, auctions and inquests. However the pub needed to find another way of boosting income. This arrived in the form of an innovative vehicle that gifted the inn with another form of clientele. The wide flat Bath Road and the convenient distance from London made the inn a perfect destination for those with new-found mobility in the form of a bicycle.

The Cycling Touring Club had been formed in 1878. At that time the popular bicycle was the penny farthing, but by the 1885 the 'safety bicycle'

---

174   Uxbridge and West Drayton Gazette – Saturday 8 March 1890

had been invented and the popularity of the sport exploded. Although a bicycle cost £3, which was a month's wages for a young man, this aspirational item caused cycle mania in Britain. Mr Chappell, conscious of the rising interest in cycling, managed to recover the inn's reputation for good hospitality by advertising it as a destination for cycling club outings.

The newly formed Isleworth Cycling Club, had its first run in April 1890 with a ride to the Peggy Bedford, where they rested and had refreshments before cycling back to Isleworth. So pleased were they with their outing that they paraded through Isleworth on their return.[175]

Cyclists, colloquially known as wheelers, had their own newspaper cycling correspondents writing specifically for the sport, and describing suggested destinations. In 1891 the Peggy Bedford was described as a 'picturesque hostelry' serving good ale 'as clear as crystal and of the right amber colour' that 'puts fresh strength into tired muscles'.[176] In March 1895, there was a change of landlord at the Peggy Bedford, and the same newspaper correspondent described the licensee of the 'ancient and most pleasant hostelry' the Peggy Bedford as a gallant sea dog because of his time in the Navy. This was Captain George Springett, a retired merchant marine seaman from Kent, 'who looks as if he could give and take hard knocks', and who was responsible for the pub being a great place for the 'better class of wheelfolk' with attractive gardens in which a cuckoo could be heard by day and where nightingales sung of an evening.[177] He was the publican for over ten years and became a parish councillor.

As well hosting cycling groups, the Peggy Bedford still catered for summer beanfeasts. The inn and its pleasure gardens welcomed this expansion of trade, but sometimes the groups became a little unruly. In July 1895 twenty-two members of a whist club journeyed from London in a brake pulled by four horses. A dinner had been pre-ordered at three shillings and sixpence per head to which they sat down at about 2pm. The horses were stabled and the brake put in the yard and the gates locked. Around 6pm, after dinner and an amble around the pleasure grounds, the party were about to settle their bill and leave when the bill was disputed. George Springett, refused to open the gates to release their wagon until it was paid. One of the party, Walter Empson, said, 'If you won't open

175   Middlesex Independent – Wednesday 23 April 1890
176   The People – Sunday 7 June 1891
177   The People – Sunday 19 June 1898

these gates I will break them down.' Shortly afterwards Mr Springett went outside to find one of his gates had been pulled off its hinges. Empson was walking away from it. When Springett tried to restore the gate Empson pushed him. The brake driver drove the vehicle out and the party got into it and drove off. Springett harnessed his horse and galloped along the Bath Road, overtook the brake and stopped at the Harlington Police Station and asked Police Sergeant Boutler to stop the brake that was coming along the road. When he did so Springett identified the man responsible, and Empson admitted to the policeman that he did it and claimed to have offered to pay for any damage. Springett disputed that this was said and prosecuted Empson for payment for repairs to his damaged gate of £2.2s.6d.

This action landed both parties in court. The organiser of the outing, Mr Savage had not been present on the day, but he went down to Longford the next day to inspect the damage. He saw that there was a two-foot piece of wood missing from one of the gates that he thought was probably rotten, he thought the damage repair would cost about four shillings.

The driver of the brake, who often took parties to the Peggy Bedford, said he asked for the gates to be opened at 5.30pm, but was told they could not do so until the bill for the dinner was settled. He offered to pay for the stabling, but the dinner was not his responsibility. He had his horses hitched and ready to go at 5.45pm and then noticed some people lifting the gate off its hinge but diplomatically said he could not identify them and he did not see any damage to the gate. The magistrates considered the evidence and decided that the forced removal of the gate was malice in law and convicted the defendant who had to pay a fine of 20s, and £4 4s in costs.[178] Springett had brought the case because he was determined to 'carry on his business in a proper and respectable manner'.[179] In other words he wanted people to know that he would be tough on wrongdoers.

Now that cycling clubs were well established and oil lamps for bicycles were being manufactured, the visitors to the Peggy Bedford were travelling from further afield. The Shepherd's Bush (in West London) cycling club made evening runs to the Peggy Bedford in the summer.[180] Another newly formed cycle club in Hammersmith made Peggy Bedford the destination for their opening run and whilst they took tea in the inn they held an

178   Uxbridge and W. Drayton Gazette – Saturday 17 August 1895.
179   West Middlesex Gazette – Saturday 17 August 1895.
180   West London Observer – Friday 20 May 1898

The Peggy Bedford at the beginning of the twentieth century with its two sentinel elm trees outside the main entrance.

election for officers and committee members.[181] A year later the club had introduced a 'special ladies day' at the Peggy Bedford. This was not long-distance cycling, but a series of novelty cycling competitions. There was an egg and spoon race on bicycles, a cycling obstacle race, a Gretna Green race (men cycling with ladies on their crossbar), a slow cycle race, a tug of war, skipping, ring tilting on bicycles, and gentlemen's hat trimming. The evening concluded with a lantern parade and concert. [182]

* * *

The Kings Arms, at the other end of the village, was popular with local imbibers. In November 1887 at 10.15pm three young agricultural labourers left the Kings Arms in a high state of inebriation and spoiling for a fight. Fred Darbon was so drunk he did not see PC Innes standing nearby. Fred held up his fists in a fighting stance and aimed a blow at Fred Scott, who fell down. The policeman said to Darbon, 'You're drunk. Go home'. Both opponents then walked to the White Horse pub, a few yards away, and Darbon went in where he was refused a drink at the request of the policeman, and as he left the pub he was again instructed to go home.

181   West London Observer – Friday 17 June 1898
182   Acton Gazette – Friday 19 May 1899

'I will go home', he said as he struck the policeman in the eye and pushed him into a hedge hurting his spine. As he fell to the ground Scott and a man called Henry Tillyer began kicking him before Scott hit him on the head with a stick.

The crowd who were witnessing the scene pulled the men off the policeman and while the policeman was getting to his feet the two drunks again rushed him and hit him in the face with their fists knocking him down, and then fell on top of him again. Two brothers named Gray pulled them off.

When PC Innes got to his feet he grabbed Scott, but was set on by Darbon and Tillyer and had to release him. Then he grabbed Darbon and drew his staff (truncheon), and once again an attempt was made to attack him by the other two, but he managed to stop Scott by striking him with his truncheon. Tillyer was held back by Francis Gray.

Someone in the crowd then hit the policeman on the right side of his head and he fell down releasing Darbon. Darbon made an attempt to hit the policeman, but was prevented by Isaac Gray who took hold of him, threw him down, and held him there. PC Innes then took charge of the prisoner and Isaac Gray procured a horse and cart and, with the assistance of both Gray brothers, Darbon and Tillyer were taken to the police-station, where they continued to be violent. PC Whitbread afterwards apprehended Scott. PC Innes was confined to bed for several days and was still receiving medical attention some weeks after the assault.

In Court Darbon made a rambling statement in which he denied assaulting the policeman who he said had hurt himself when he fell into a hedge. He said he was angry at being pushed about by a policeman. Both men had previous convictions. They were sentenced to two months imprisonment with hard labour, after which Darbon thanked the magistrates for their kindness in not giving them the full punishment of six months. The Chairman of the magistrates praised the conduct of the PC Innes and Francis and Isaac Gray. As the prisoners were led away Darbon asked 'Is the case settled now?' and was told that it was. He continued, 'Because I want to know if, when I come out, [if] the policeman is to come up to me and pull me about when I have had a drop of beer, but not interfering with anyone. I want to know if he is to interfere with me and pull me about, because, if he does, it might cause another bother, as I don't like to be pushed about when I am drunk.' There was laughter in court.[183]

---

183   Middlesex & Surrey Express – Saturday 10 December 1887

* * *

Some writers have written specifically about the history of the ancient road from London to Bath. Charles H. Harper, in 1899, contrasted a contemporary cyclist who could complete the whole return journey in record breaking time of less than twelve hours while a stage coach of two hundred years earlier would take three days to do the journey, one-way, and was called 'The Flying Machine'.[184] He also relates the relief of the stage coach passengers when they got beyond Hounslow Heath and were safe from the notorious highwaymen.

Cigarette card showing the Quicksilver Royal Mail coach.

Even before the end of the nineteenth century the nostalgia for the old coaching days had begun, and the public were excited by the sight and sounds of stage-coaches. It is similar to people today who have a romantic concept of travelling on steam railway engines, but who forget the reality of the noise, dirt and dust that accompanied the journeys. In 1893 a group of enthusiasts organised a day out of vintage mail coaches from Piccadilly to Slough, Berkshire, stopping at the Peggy Bedford to change horses. Sixteen stage coaches took part in the parade, including the Quicksilver which in 2019 was restored and is now the last surviving Royal Mail coach[185]. Negotiating the traffic, which as well as horse-drawn

---

184   Review of Charles G. Harper, *The Bath Road: History, Fashion and Frivolity on an old Highway*, (London, 1899) in Morning Post , Tuesday 12 September 1899.

185   https://www.bonhams.com/auctions/22705/lot/153/; https://www.devonlive. com/news/local-news/last-surviving-royal-mail-carriage-3217120. YouTube: https:// youtu.be/h7VWXY2PAOI

vehicles also included many 'wheelers', the journey took three hours. After lunch at Slough and a tour through the beautiful Burnham Beeches the coaches returned to London, but when they reached Hyde Park Corner the traffic was stationary. There was a suffrage demonstration taking place in Hyde Park which caused the parade to divert to a different route only for it meet another demonstration near Parliament Square for the Women's Temperance Society. The participants in the parade grumbled about the delays, but agreed that the complete nostalgic trip had been enjoyable.[186]

* * *

Away from the inns another important trade in Longford was the forge, which was owned by blacksmith and wheelwright John Passingham. The forge was an essential part of village life and the travelling trade. The Passingham family had been long-term blacksmiths and wheelwrights in Harmondsworth and Longford for many years. Now, in the Forge at Longford, John and his son William were continuing the family tradition, but as the nineteenth century came to an end it would bring gossip and disgrace to William Passingham.

186   The Field – Saturday 17 June 1893

Chapter 19

The Wheelwright's Shame (1896-1899)

The forge at Longford changed hands in 1827 when the executors of William Godfrey put all his Longford property up for public auction at the Peggy Bedford. This property included the blacksmith's workshop and three adjacent cottages, several brick-built stables, two orchards and a meadow.[187] The whole lot was bought by William Passingham, a blacksmith and wheelwright in Harmondsworth village centre. William, who had two young sons, saw this as an opportunity to provide a business for each of them.

As was the custom at that time, the sons were expected to follow their father's trade. Son John eventually took charge of the Longford forge and married Ann Piecey. They had five daughters and two sons, John and William. These sons worked alongside their father in Longford learning his trade. They were blacksmiths

The Forge

The Forge building we can see today was once part of a much larger complex of cottages, barn, and workshops. In the eighteenth century it was a bell foundry. Owned by Thomas Swain. He had been born in West Bedfont (on Harmondsworth southern border) and learned to make bells from Robert Catlin in St Andrew's Holborn. In 1739 he inherited the business of his master and moved the foundry to Longford.

Although Swain was making church bells for churches in London, Surrey and Sussex, these would have been made in situ in a large pit dug as near the church as possible in order to make transportation easier. The type of bells Swain was making in Longford were crotal bells. A spherical bell with an attachment at the top for hanging and a free-moving ball or 'pea' enclosed. These were usually grouped together and attached to horse harness.

Thomas Swain owned the forge from 1749 to 1782 when he died and was buried in St Mary's churchyard at Harmondsworth.

187   Morning Advertiser – Wednesday 16 May 1827.

The Forge on the side of the Bath Road, July 2018.

and wheelwrights, and as well as steel-rimmed wooden wheels, made agricultural wagons, plough shears and various other agricultural items. They employed several men in addition to the family members.

John Passingham, grandson to the first purchaser of the Longford forge, married and moved away from the village to work for another blacksmith. His brother William stayed in Longford and in 1890 was working, and living with his father John. William was a gentle, caring man. A committed member of the Baptist Chapel, and a highly-skilled craftsman working in iron and wood. Running the business and looking after his elderly widowed father left little time to find a wife.

A new tenant moved into one of their cottages. He was retired draper, Frederick William Sharp who lived there with his wife and their handicapped adult son. Being in close proximity to the forge William had a neighbourly relationship with them and their married daughter, Florence Tudor, who frequently visited her parents. When William's father died in 1892 the Sharp family consoled William who not only had to deal with his father's death, but also had sole responsibility for the forge and its business.

Four years later the condolences and support were returned when Florence's young husband died suddenly. Florence, a slightly flighty person who relied heavily on her parents for emotional support, was devastated by Walter Tudor's death. She, like many woman of her generation, had been shielded from dealing with financial matters and had never worked outside the home. She saw her role as supporting her husband and keeping his household running smoothly. She only knew how to manage the house and be an obedient wife. The couple had no children, and without an income Florence was at a loss as to how to deal with the situation.

'What shall I do now, Mr Passingham?'. Her tear-stained face looked up imploringly. He found himself saying, 'Don't worry we will sort things out.' He felt sorry for her. He looked across the room at her father, Frederick, who also looked at a loss. They had just returned from the funeral. William felt the family was looking to him for advice and he felt it was his Christian duty to help this lady who was so obviously in need of support. He sat her down and talked through her circumstances. He advised her to give up her rented home and move back in with her father. He would arrange for her furniture and belongings to be moved to Longford and stored in his barn.

Having moved back in with her parents in Longford the cottage was crowded. Florence had her belongings close by in the barn at the Forge, and she had to plan for her future. This was her dilemma. She had no independent means. She was not bright or educated enough to become a governess and thought of herself too much of a lady to go into service. She could not stay with her parents who had enough problems looking after her handicapped brother. Her solution, she decided, was to remarry. Widows with children often remarried soon after bereavement, usually to widowers with children who then had a mutually beneficial relationship. She had no children to encourage a hasty remarriage but she was in need of support both financially and emotionally. She soon realised that the object of her salvation was just across the yard.

William Passingham was 40, unmarried, running a successful business, and a respected member of the community. He was ready to take a wife and maybe raise a family to inherit the business. He had not been free to consider marriage whilst he lived with his father. He found himself attracted to the young widow now living with his tenants and flattered by the way she was so attentive and charming whenever they met. He felt sorry for her situation, but also began to see her as an ideal companion, a chapel-goer, and woman used to being a wife who could provide him with a comfortable home while he took care of business. He started to court her and brought her jewellery. She welcomed his attentions. Whatever her true feelings for him she realised she was in a desperate situation and this man was the solution.

Her parents' move to Southall, Middlesex, a few months after her bereavement was the step that prompted William to make a hasty proposal of marriage, and they married at Holy Trinity Church, Southall, on 9 July 1896 just seven months into her widowhood. On the marriage certificate she stated her age as 34 when in fact she was 45. If William was looking forward to starting a family he was probably going to be disappointed.

The marriage was a disaster for both of them. Florence was very unhappy. She missed her parents, her former husband and their town life. She could not adapt to her new rural surroundings. As a country wife there were extra duties to perform such as feeding chickens, helping to grow fruit and vegetables, and being part of a close community. Living in rural Middlesex was a culture shock.

The new Mrs Passingham declined in health. Prior to her marriage her father was aware that she was 'addicted to drink', a fact hidden from William until after the marriage when he was shocked to see his wife drinking whisky and beer all day long and neglecting her household duties.[188] Far from having a wife to help him so that he could concentrate on the business he found himself having to take time away from the business to look after her. Outwardly they appeared a contented couple but behind closed doors both were deeply unhappy.

The situation continued for two and a half years. William attended the funeral in January 1899 of a lady he greatly admired, Elizabeth Weekly from the Weekly House, with whom he lodged for a while in 1881. Mrs Weekly's kind and generous spirit had welcomed him and his sister Sarah into her home, and since then she had been a source of wisdom to him over the years. Whilst she had been unwell he did not feel able to confide in her about his troubled marriage. Now it was too late.

Three months later, his wife Florence, on 16 March 1899, had her 48th birthday. This combined with her probably being menopausal, put her in a deep depression. Her marriage was a fraud. The marriage had successfully

---

188   Quote from Frederick William Sharp, Uxbridge Court session, reported in West
Middlesex Gazette – Saturday 17 June 1899

freed her from money worries as William had settled £20 a year on her and allowed her five shillings a week spending money. All other household bills were paid by William. She had her pet dog and a bird to lavish with affection, but her life was empty.

Two weeks later she had a fit and lapsed into a coma. William wrote a letter to her father, who, with his wife travelled from Southall to see her and found her very ill. On 14 April they visited again and on 19 April William wrote to Mr Sharp to say his daughter required supervision and he was thinking of sending her to Bedlam (Bethlam Lunatic Asylum). Horrified, her parents came and took her back to their house. A month later when she felt ready to return home William refused to have her back. By then he had realised there was no future for their marriage.

In June the whole affair ended up in the Magistrate's court at Uxbridge The local poor law Guardians at the time would respond to people in need only if they failed to find someone else who was obliged to support the needy person. Usually a husband was responsible for maintaining his wife and children, or if the woman was single the onus fell on the Father. The court summoned William Passingham and accused him of failing to maintain his wife. The two parties: Florence and her Father; and William Passingham; faced each other in court with their solicitors by their side. The case hinged on who had deserted whom. A case for desertion by the wife could only be met if she had voluntarily left her husband. A husband could only be accused of desertion when he refused to have her back without good reason. Only in a proven case of the wife's adultery could the husband avoid having to maintain her for the rest of her life.

It was a glorious warm summer day on Monday 5 June 1899 when the magistrates convened to hear a protracted list of witnesses detailing the marriage troubles of Mr and Mrs Passingham in excruciating detail.

The father's story:

'My daughter is about 40 years of age' (actually 48).

'Mr Passingham did not know she was addicted to drink when they married, but she was not a confirmed dipsomaniac. Up until the time she became ill on 1 April she was treated very kindly by Mr Passingham. As soon as we heard about her illness my wife and I went to see her. She appeared to be very ill. We visited again on 17 and 19 April. Mr Passingham was abusive to Mrs Sharp and myself. He said he had seen his family and a lawyer and taken their advice. He intended to send her to Bedlam, but I said I would rather take her home and put her under her mother's care till she got well if he would provide a fly [hired carriage] which he did. My daughter was placed in the carriage and called for her husband most piteously. He did not come but sent a workman to close the carriage door. I deny abusing Mr Passingham or threatening to take my daughter away and saying he would never see her again.'

'On 1 May I wrote to Mr Passingham to say his wife wished to return to him, and in reply received a letter from his solicitor saying he declined to have his wife back or maintain her.'

The nurse's story:

'I am Laura Alice White of the Temperance Co-operative Nursing Association, Portland Place, a trained nurse, called by Mr Passingham on 13 April and Mrs Passingham was placed in my charge. Mrs Passingham was violent. The doctor told me she was suffering from delirium tremens. She seemed frightened of everyone who came near her and this confirmed to me that she was indeed suffering from this complaint. From 13th to the 16 April she was delirious. On 15th I went to see the doctor for advice and on 16th further help had to be got in. When Mrs Passingham became conscious she wanted nothing to eat but showed a disposition to drink and drained all the glasses and bottles in the bedroom. On 19 April her parents came to the house. Mr Sharp asked her if his daughter was fit to be removed and I referred him to the doctor. Mr Sharp went to the doctor and came upstairs and told her the doctor said it was alright, she could go away. He asked me to assist his daughter into the carriage which was at the door. Before going to the doctor the father had instructed me to tell Mr Passingham to order a fly which he did.' [this was an important point as to who ordered the carriage and therefore who was forcing the issue of Florence leaving.] The nurse said, 'I helped Mrs Passingham into the carriage. Mrs Passingham was not sensible and did not know where she was going. We had difficulty getting her into the carriage.'

The chief Magistrate interceded at this point to say that a husband could not escape liability unless it was proved that the wife went away willingly. 'By the husband's consent the wife goes with her parents to be taken care of by her mother. Those are the facts we have found.' 'Then when the wife is ready to go back the husband refuses to receive her.'

The defence counsel and the Court clerk argued over the technicality of whether the husband's refusal to cohabit amounts to desertion within the meaning of the Act.

The wife's story:

'I remember my father and mother visiting me on 17 April, and I remember leaving my own house and calling for my husband. I did not mean to go away permanently. Mr Passingham's income is about £300 a year.' On cross examination she said, 'I have not been addicted to drink. I have never had anything but what my husband gave me.' The defence council asked her if she had neglected her house duties, but the Magistrate interceded and said, 'This has nothing to do with the case. If the husband made a bad bargain [bad choice] he must stick to it. It does not alter the fact she was his wife.'

Florence Passingham continued with her evidence: 'They knocked me about forcing the medicine down. My husband said he wanted to put me in a madhouse. I was sensible the whole time. I was alright when I got to my father's home and did not stay a single day in bed. I did not go home, as I thought it was my husband's duty to fetch me. I never dreamt he was going to turn round. I always intended to go back.'

The doctor's story:

'I am Dr Southey of Colnbrook. On 13 April I visited Mrs Passingham. She was suffering from coma which might have been produced from a fit or from having too much drink. I recommended a nurse to look after her. The coma passed off and she became first of all in a hazy condition and then very violent indeed. She would not take her medicine and had to be forced. As she got better and there was no paralysis I held the opinion the illness was from drink and that she had delirium tremens. I do not think she was in a fit condition to sign a will, yet she could have told where she was going. She was capable of recognising her father and mother. When I last saw her she could answer any reasonable question. She is recovered now.'

The prosecution council asked the doctor about her fitness to sign documents.

'On 19 April she would not have been in a fit state to have signed a deed of separation.'

The husband's story:

'Soon after the marriage my wife would drink whisky and beer every day. I had to habitually neglect my business to look after my wife. She never did anything but sit down and drink. She would not do anything in the house. On 19 April I had a conversation with her father and told him I could not bear the strain and expense any longer. Mr Sharp said he would take her away on his own responsibility, providing I sent her belongings. On 19 April, Mr Sharp came to my house and went upstairs and I saw him no more that day. Mrs Sharp said she would take her daughter away and I should never see her any more. The nurse came to me in the shop at 4.30pm and told me to order a fly at the De Burgh [public house], West Drayton. I ordered the fly on the way to Uxbridge. It was booked to Mr Sharp. I refused to pay for it. I did not get back home till 8pm and my wife was then gone. Mr Sharp never mentioned anything about my wife going to be nursed by her mother nor was it agreed to by me. I sent her clothes to her in accordance with her father's wish. They have not been returned.'

Asked by the Clerk about his wife's condition.

'On 19 April my wife was not fit to be left by herself. I have refused to maintain my wife or take her back. My wife had £20 a year. She has had it every year since she has been my wife. I did not disagree with Mr Sharp taking his daughter. I ordered a fly and knew my wife was going away in it.'

He was asked about his income by the Chair of the Magistrates: 'I only make £120 a year and sometimes not so much as that.'

The Bench concluded that the defendant [Mr Passingham] had deserted his wife and she was no longer bound to cohabit with him. He was ordered to pay fifteen shillings a week to her from 10 June; and fourteen shillings costs of the court and three guineas towards the counsel's expenses.[189]

Thus the couple had a legal separation order and Florence received a regular maintenance sum, but this was not the end of the legal wrangling and more salacious and acrimonious scenes were to take place in court. In the meantime, with his reputation in ruins and the embarrassment of having his private life exposed to all the gossips, William put his business and property up for sale just three weeks after the court case. The property included a newly-built cottage and outbuildings, a very large barn,

189   West Middlesex Gazette – Saturday 17 June 1899

blacksmith's shop, garden and other premises together with the goodwill of the very old-established wheelwright's business which had been in the Passingham family for 60 years. Also included were three brick-built and thatched cottages which brought in a rental income of £60 12s per annum.[190] It must have been heart breaking for a highly skilled craftsman to give up his family's business at the age of 42, but more public exposure was to come.

When Florence heard that the Passingham forge and business were to be sold on 13 July and vacated in seven days, her father moved quickly to obtain an injunction to prevent her husband from disposing of her furniture and jewellery that were still in store at the premises.[191] The Judge at the Uxbridge County Court granted the injunction and the property was moved into storage for which Mr Passingham counter-sued for the storage costs of £17.4.0d. On 15 August, the warring couple were once again in front of the magistrates. This time to hear an action taken by Florence Passingham to recover her property. [192] The court listened to the evidence for two hours whilst the salacious history of the marriage was retold. William was scolded by the Chairman of the magistrates for having committed contempt of court by going against the Court's injunction and disposing of two bracelets that he had given to his wife during their marriage. Florence was not well enough to attend the court so her father gave evidence on her behalf, then William took the stand and explained the circumstances of his acquiring her furniture. He told the Court that when her former husband, Mr Tudor, had died they lived in three rented rooms and she did not have the money to continue the rent. He helped her by paying £2 for the rest of the rent due and taking all her possessions back to his premises. He thought Mr Sharp, her father, would arrange for them to be removed and stored, but he did not, so he arranged storage and would return the furniture as soon as he had his counter-claim for storage expenses paid. He always intended to return her possessions. In view of the antagonistic court proceedings that had been brought against him by his estranged wife he felt he was owed for the care and maintenance of the furniture. Likewise he felt that as he had given the jewellery to his wife for her own use they were part of her property which he as her husband

190   Uxbridge & W. Drayton Gazette – Saturday 08 July 1899

191   Uxbridge and W. Drayton Gazette – Saturday 15 July 1899.

192   Middlesex County Times – Saturday 19 August 1899

still had ownership of. William's solicitor told the court that he was happy to submit to an order to return the furniture at any time once his counter-claim for storage expenses was paid, or the sum recovered from the sale of the stored items. The Judge did not agree with the solicitor's plea.

The judge reproved Mr Passingham for an act of 'gross impropriety' and 'direct contempt of Court'. Mr Passingham, now angry, made repeated and serious accusations against his wife, to which the Judge, equally irate, expressed strong objections to the disclosure of unnecessary information 'of an aggravating nature' that had not been solicited by either counsel. Passingham said he had given his wife the jewellery after they were married on one condition that she would 'always act as a wife to him', a condition she had failed to carry out. After considerable discussion the Judge held that the husband, neither by act or word, had made his wife understand such a condition. He ordered that all her goods should be handed over to her father in trust for his daughter and that Mr Passingham should pay the whole costs of their conveyance to her father's house in Southall, which must be done within seven days. The two remaining items of jewellery should be handed over together with the £9 he received for the sale of the other two items, a diamond bracelet and a pearl bracelet. Mr Passingham's counter claim for £17 4s for housing and repairing the goods in question, would be dismissed and her husband would have to pay the full costs of the action.[193] William was portrayed as the villain. His humiliation was complete.

Almost as soon as the Court's verdict was announced William left the area. He said goodbye to the rest of his family and made for Southampton where he boarded a ship for Cape Town. It was a radical step to take, but his chagrin and humiliation left him little choice. He had to get away to avoid any other obligations he had to his wife. Whether he knew that her non-appearance at the Court on 15 August was because she was already under the care of the Bethnal House Asylum (a private lunatic asylum), or whether it was expediency, he knew he had to go. Barely two weeks later his wife was the subject of discussion at a meeting of the Staines Poor Law Union. The Bethnal House Asylum wished to find an authority to fund Mrs Passingham's treatment who they considered a pauper patient. They had applied to the Uxbridge Poor Union who had passed the request to the Staines Union, who promptly passed it back saying in their opinion

193   Middlesex County Times – Saturday 19 August 1899.

the husband should be responsible for her expenses. The bill finally landed back at the feet of the Staines Poor Law Guardians. In January 1900 Bethnal House Asylum were asking for 19s 3d a week for her keep, The magistrates had made an order for the husband to pay, but as he was abroad they could not enforce the order. The Father said he had no money and his daughter had no money in her own right, nevertheless the court ordered the father to pay 11s 6d a week. Mrs Florence Passingham died in 1902 in the asylum aged 51.

William Passingham did return to England, at least once, and gave an address in Ealing. His early life and well-earned reputation in the non-conformist community of Longford was shattered by an injudicious alliance and the subsequent disgrace. He died in Cape Town in 1927. His death marked the end of another multi-generational Baptist family in Longford, but as the new century was approaching more changes were on their way, and Longford embraced them.

Chapter 20

The New Century (1900-1909)

It was a dull grey day in Longford. The men were in the fields; the horses were drawing the carts; and the women, sleeves rolled up, were sweating over their boilers doing the traditional Monday wash – but this day was going to be different. By 8am, on 23 April 1900 the first of eighty-four motorised vehicles of all shapes and sizes passed noisily in front of their homes along the Great Bath Road churning up clouds of dust from the earthy surface. The motors were mainly cars, large and small, but there were also motor bicycles, motor tricycles, motor quadricycles (for two people sitting side-by-side), and steam vehicles. Wealthy Britains were excited by the potential of the internal combustion engine, but there were few British motor manufacturers at that time so most of the cars passing through Longford were European-made. Among the drivers was the Hon. Charles S. Rolls driving his own 12 h.p. Panhard. Six years later Rolls would join with Henry Royce to found a British motor manufacturing company.[194]

The sound of the vehicles brought people from their houses and fields. Everyone stopped to stare at this unusual sight. The car drivers travelling in their open-topped vehicles were dressed for the weather. They wore thick coats, peaked caps and glass goggles to keep out the dust. Some were dressed from top to bottom in furs others in oilskins and sou-westers.

Their passengers, many dressed in appropriate colours for St. George's Day, waved to the crowds that had gathered along the route to watch. Although the vehicles were restricted to a speed of twelve miles an hour, for the villagers that was fast enough. Horses, carts, chickens and people

194   Cycling – Saturday 28 April 1900

had to hurry from their path. Hundreds of cyclists followed the vehicles in their dusty wake and endeavoured to keep pace with them.

These vehicles were taking part in a 1000-mile road trial to Edinburgh and back which would take three weeks to complete. It was organised by the newly formed Automobile Club (it did not receive its Royal title until 1907), who wanted to increase its 600 membership by demonstrating the durability of powered vehicles. A sum of £10 was the prize for every vehicle that completed the run. The tour began at Hyde Park Corner at 7am that day and the initial stage followed the Bath Road.[195] For Longfordians who witnessed this parade it would have brought mixed feelings. For centuries village life had revolved around the horse, now they were witnessing change. The inns were pleased to welcome drivers of any vehicle. Farmers, if they could afford it, would consider using a more efficient vehicle for pulling the plough, but for the workers there was uncertainty about their future as technology spread into the fields.

The farm workers need not have worried. The horse would still be a vital part of Longford farming life for another three decades. The bicycle, though, was now an established mode of personal transport and was also bringing business to the four Longford inns. One of the non-farming newcomers to the village had made his fortune from manufacturing bicycles. In 1897 Thomas Fuller Toovey bought the freehold of the island at Longford, which included Island House, for £1080. He spent another £800 on the property before moving in on 28 June 1898.[196] The house had a large dining room with a bay window, overlooking the river, and a porch with conservatory. Upstairs were two large bedrooms and one small bedroom with no fireplace, and three maids' rooms on the second floor.[197] Mr Toovey made the house his home, and rented the rest of the island, including Colne Cottage that had been built on the site of the old mill, to Mr Perrin, a button merchant.

Thomas Fuller Toovey was only forty years of age but he had made enough money from the manufacturing and selling of bicycles to retire early. He was born in London and as early as 1875, before the more popular 'safety' bicycle had been invented, Toovey was selling 'combination' bicycles from his premises in Croydon. Not content with turning his

195   Newbury Weekly News and General Advertiser – Thursday 26 April 1900
196   In the 1910 land survey.
197   1910 valuation report.

creative mind to bicycles he also invented, and was making, early washing machines which he claimed could do a whole days wash in two hours.[198]

His company, The British Cycle Manufacturing Company, was manufacturing in Liverpool and selling in Croydon. In 1884 he sold his London retail business for £2,200, which at that time was 'making a net profit of £1300 per annum'[199] He and his wife Lilian bought the Island House at Longford as a retreat from their hectic life in London.

Although he professed that he wanted a peaceful retirement he soon involved himself in local politics. In December 1898 Mr Toovey was chair of the Harmondsworth ratepayers association.[200] He attended a public meeting to choose Parish Councillers on 4 March 1899 and although he nominated several parishioners, he refused to stand himself saying that he had not been resident long enough and that he had moved to the parish for a quiet life.[201]

Toovey was one of the first motor car owners in Longford. He had a 8 h.p. Peugeot which he drove over a wide flat bridge spanning the River Colne tributary to park it in the former stables on the island. He thought he was a careful driver, but in September 1901 he was summoned by Slough Magistrates for not displaying a red light behind his car.[202] He said, 'I have both front and side lights. I have driven a motor car for two and half years and was not aware that I had to carry a red light.'[203] He was fined £1.7s.6d. The couple continued to enjoy their retirement in Longford for another ten years until Lilian died in 1911. Toovey remarried, in Liverpool, in 1914 and brought his new wife back to Longford, but a country life was not to her liking and they left Longford shortly afterwards.

Another cycle manufacturer made Longford his home. He lived a short walk from the Island in a house on the Bath Road next to the forge, now called Springbank. His name was Arthur Markham. He was 53 when he settled in Longford. He had come into cycle manufacturing after making his fortune in competitive racing.

---

198   Croydon Chronicle and East Surrey Advertiser – Saturday 13 January 1877

199   London Evening Standard – Monday 28 July 1884

200   West Middlesex Gazette – Saturday 24 December 1898

201   West Middlesex Gazette – Saturday 04 March 1899

202   West Middlesex Gazette – Saturday 02 December 1905

203   Reading Mercury – Saturday 07 September 1901

There was little social mobility in class-structured Victorian England. You had to accept your place in society. You had to survive in the class into which you were born. A boy would follow his father into his trade or a girl would go into service until she was married and then her future depended on her husband's achievements. For young men, exploiting their natural talent was the only way of improving their status. Arthur Markham, at five foot eight inches, was tall for that time and weighed just over nine stone. When he found he could run faster than other boys he saw this as his opportunity to improve himself. Sport was of widespread interest to all classes of society and a lot of money changed hands at events. Spectators would gamble on the outcome of a race whilst the competitors would be focused on the prize money. If a gentleman felt his champion was better than another's then they would put up money for a match to determine the result. Publicans would put up prize money to sponsor events that would draw crowds to their establishments. Arthur Markham found that he excelled in endurance running. At the age of 18 he won a ten-mile race at Woolwich and then continued to win races. Two years later he faced an experienced runner, W. Coe, in a ten-mile race for a wager of £10 'a-side'.[204] Coe, two years older, was the favourite and took an early lead, which he held for most of the race until Markham sailed passed him near the finish to win the event.[205] By the time he was 21 a new sport began to attract Markham's competitive spirit. Early versions of the bicycle were being developed and Markham saw the potential for its use in competitive sport. The early machines were cumbersome and on rough roads prone to accidents. The development of the bicycle was still in progress but competitive sporting events accelerated the design and manufacture of more efficient machines. Markham spent his prize money from his running events on a bicycle with wooden wheels propelled by foot pedals on the front wheel and began competing in races. He became so proficient that on Whit Monday 1868, aged 23, he won the first official British cycle race at the Brent Reservoir in North London and received a silver cup from the local publican who had promoted the event. All this time Arthur had been doing his day job as a painter and glass stainer but by 1872 he had enough prize money to open a cycle shop in Edgware Road, London, and later another in Shepherds

---

204   A-side means each party stakes the agreed sum of money, which is held by a stake-holder and the winner of the contest gets the whole amount, i.e. for a £10 stake the winner gets £20 giving him a £10 profit.

205   Bell's Life in London and Sporting Chronicle – Saturday 06 October 1866

Bush. He was designing innovative machine such as tandems, tricycles and, towards the end of the century, was producing lighter bicycles with tubular enamelled frames. He even made one that could be dismantled and carried in a carpetbag on a train journey. He continued to compete in both cycling and running races, and later sponsored and promoted younger champions. By 1898 Arthur had moved his family to Longford where his daughter Florence Evelyn was born, and christened in the parish church on 26 January 1899. Around 1904 his wife, Louise, became ill and the family returned to London to live over the shop at 345 Edgware Road. He sold Springbank to Henry James Wild for £420 who bought it for his newly-married second son, John Wild, to live in. The bicycles Markham designed and built are on exhibition in cycling museums around the country. He died of heart failure in June 1917.

* * *

Next to Springbank is the forge. After Mr Passingham left the village, his reputation in tatters, he sold his wheelwright and blacksmith's premises and business, along with a newly-built cottage, to Ambrose Cure. Ambrose Cure married his sweetheart, Maude, in London and brought her back to Longford where they settled into the Longford community. He also joined the Uxbridge branch of the Freemason's in November 1899. However 31-year-old Ambrose Augustus Cure did not stay long and by 1902 was selling up the household furniture, plant and effects of a wheelwright and blacksmith to move abroad.[206] Ambrose Cure, principally a coach-builder, was finding there was little call for his skills. The transport business was in transition. With fewer horse-drawn vehicles, and people making the move to cycling and motoring, there was less need for wooden wheels and wooden carts. The couple emigrated to South Africa where he continued his trade as a blacksmith. His wife had first a daughter, Audrey, and then a son, Thomas William. They returned from Cape Town to England, with their two small children, in September 1904, but by the end of 1905 they had set off on the 56-day voyage to Australia.

Ambrose Cure did not sell the freehold of the Longford premises until June 1906, when the auction details still referred to it as Passinghams, and suggested it might be suitable for manufacturing or as a Motor Garage. With the proceeds of the sale Ambrose Cure bought a dairy farm in Byron

---

206   Uxbridge and W Drayton Gazette – Saturday 8 Marchg 1902.

Bay, New South Wales. His wife Maude died in 1924 but he remarried in 1930, and continued to live there until his death in November 1955.

Longford village 1915 and the White Horse pub.

* * *

It was during 1908 that the Bath Road was first sprayed with tar to improve the surface, just in time for a heavy fall of snow at the end of December which froze the Longford river and made the road so treacherous that horses were slipping and falling.[207]

Under the Motor Car Act of 1903 cars now had to be registered and drivers had to hold a licence.[208] The Act raised the previous maximum speed limit from 14mph to 20mph. This alarmed the Longford residents. The road through Longford was especially busy at weekends with cyclists and motorists making excursions into the Middlesex countryside, causing congestion. A local enquiry was held to discuss the matter. This resulted in

207   The Times, 29 Dec 1908, p.6.
208   A mandatory test of driving ability was not introduced until 1935

the speed limit through the village being fixed at 10mph.[209] The village was determined to keep its residents safe.

One such resident was Henry James Wild at The Farm. He was now in his sixties and leaving his four sons to run the business. The farm grew market garden crops that were sold at Covent Garden. In the summer this was mainly fruit. An author in 1907, passing along the Bath Road, admired the 'thousands and thousands' of plum, cherry, apple, pear, and damson trees, and innumerable currant and gooseberry bushes. [210] The growing and cropping of market garden produce was labour intensive. Even in the early twentieth century working conditions in the market gardens were still harsh. Planting, hoeing, picking, and sorting was done by hand and few farms had amenities for their staff like brick built restrooms or toilets. Women did many of the menial jobs. All root vegetables were washed in the packing shed, which had concrete floors sloping towards a drain. Rubber boots ('Wellingtons') were not in common use until after the First World War so women packers wore thick leather boots that absorbed the wet. They wore long black woollen skirts hitched up at the back with a kilt pin, three petticoats, woollen stockings, and flannel knickers that went below the knee and kept their stockings up. A heavy crocheted shawl was worn around their shoulders over coloured flannel blouses and a hessian apron was tied on with twine around the neck and waist. When washing vegetables they might wear a waterproof apron. On their heads they wore a scarf or a man's flat cap held on with a hatpin. Generally there would be one 'mother' figure who acted as a spokesperson for all the field women.

There were rules that the farmworkers had to follow. Smoking a clay pipe was forbidden, but flouted, and no drinking or swearing was allowed. Their ages ranged generally from seventeen to seventy and at peak harvesting times gypsies added to their number. In the summer some women worked eighteen hours a day. Typically they would work from 8am to 5pm in the field then go into the packing shed to sort and wash the produce until 8pm, sometimes joining in a general sing-song as they worked. If the weather had been wet they remained in their wet clothes until then, and if it was winter and frosty their aprons had been known to freeze to the bench.

---

209   https://www.sabre-roads.org.uk/wiki/index.php?title=Speed_Limit#Roads_ Act_1920

210   Stephen Springall, Country Rambles round Uxbridge, 1907

The market men worked in the packing sheds to pack the washed vegetables into baskets or crates and load the wagons that took them to market. A tarpaulin was thrown over the load and roped down. The wagons would be at Covent Garden by 2am to begin unloading before the market opened. At Covent Garden the produce would be sold in circular wicker baskets.

Covent Garden bushel baskets stacked up on the Ashby stall.
The Ashbys farmed Manor Farm in Harmondsworth.

The customer would take the goods away in the basket but would have to pay a refundable deposit. A token was given as a symbol that the deposit was paid and when the customer returned the basket he would get his refund. Each wholesaler at the market would have his own named tokens.

As technology advanced steam traction engines were experimentally used to pull trailers of produce to Covent Garden. The early vehicles had insufficient power to pull a fully laden trailer, so more powerful steam vehicles were developed. These clanking, hissing, machines passing through the empty night time streets brought many complaints and were eventually banned. The horse and cart continued to take produce to market until early petrol engine cars were converted into farm vehicles.

Covent Garden tokens issued by H.J. Wild of Longford.

* * *

The Weekly House had a new occupant in 1900 and for the first time since it was built the occupant was not named Weekly. William Henry Wild, 32, eldest son of Henry James Wild married Alice Pinar and moved into Richard Weekly's former home. It was William's job to be at Stalls 1 and 47 at Covent Garden each night to sell the farm produce. The rent for these stalls, in June 1902, was five pounds two shillings every half-year. H.J. Wild and Sons had these two stalls for many years and the rent never changed in that time.[211]

* * *

It was dark when, in the early hours of the morning, William Henry Wild quietly closed the front door of the Weekly House and went into the farmyard where the fully laden wagons of produce were beginning to make their way onto the Bath Road for their fifteen-mile journey to Covent Garden. William climbed aboard the last wagon to leave, which was standing waiting with the carter at the reins and the horses impatient to get going. William carried a large wooden box under his arm that he tucked under the seat. It was a quiet, uneventful, journey. In the dark only other wagons, with their flickering oil lamps, were on the road and they were able to make good progress to Hounslow where they stopped to rest the horses and get a bite to eat before they continued their journey.

---

211   The National Archives, E/BER/CG/E/07/06/016

Weekly House 1996. Where the buttress now stands was a chimney which was the flue for the cooking range in the single storey kitchen. Alongside the kitchen there were store rooms and a sunken dairy.

Once at Covent Garden Market, as the carters were unloading the baskets of produce, William lit an oil lamp and set up the box he had carried from home. He opened it and unfolded four legs that supported a folding desk containing his ledgers and receipt books. It was now 4am and with the baskets stacked around him he waited for his first customers.

'How much?' said one fingering the cauliflowers.

William named his price, but the customer edged away.

Another customer came along and looked around, but moved on. These early customers were from the larger hotels and restaurants. They were looking for the best quality and were willing to pay for it, but they were shrewd buyers. Each market day there would be variations in the seasonal supply and quality of the goods available so there were no fixed prices. William did not worry if his first offer was rejected. The buyer might return after looking around the market, or he might find a better price elsewhere. If his offer was rejected a couple of times William assumed that there was similar quality at a better price elsewhere, so the next customer was offered a lower price. When Walter Fewell came alongside his stall he greeted him warmly. Walter was the leading greengrocer in Chelsea and a wholesaler. He was an important and regular customer and he would always offer him a good price.

'How's the cough, Walter?'

'Getting worse. My doctor tells me I should move out of London.'

'Just what you need – country air'

'It would mean selling the shops, but then what would I do? I only know about fruit and veg, and, anyway, where would I move to?'

'Well, we have good clean air in Longford. As a matter of fact there is a small fruit farm for sale opposite my house. Why not come down and look at it?'

'I'll think about it'.

The two men completed their business transaction and the porters loaded Fewell's wagon with his purchases. This casual conversation was to make an impact on the future lives of both families.

By now other buyers were looking around. As the pale light of dawn broke the shopkeepers and buyers of smaller quantities would look around the market. William lowered his prices now. What was left was either of lesser quality or he still had a large quantity to sell. These later buyers risked finding some items sold out, but they might get what remained at a cheaper price. By 7am it was the costermongers or barrow-boys who are looking for a bargain. They were practised in haggling and would offer to clear the rest of the produce on the stall for a silly price. They knew the seller wouldn't want to take produce back to the farm.[212] With the produce sold and the empty baskets stacked on the last wagon, William Wild packed up his desk and, climbing onto the seat beside the carter, they drove back to Longford. He arrived back at the Weekly House in time for a late breakfast, the rest of the morning would be spent on his accounts, and finding out from his brothers what produce would be ready for sale the next day. After lunch he went to bed ready for his early start for the next day's trading.

Meanwhile his wife would be organising the house servants and the dairy maids. Most farms had a cow or two, mainly for domestic use. The

---

212   Calder, R.J. (ed.), *"The Great A W Smith"*, (Middlesex, 2000)

milk processing was done in the dairy which was a stone-walled white-washed building on the side of the Weekly House facing the farmyard and partially sunk into the ground to keep it cool. It had slate slab shelves with wide enamel pans into which buckets of milk were poured and left for the cream to rise before being skimmed off to make butter. There was also a scullery next to the kitchen where linen and clothes were washed. The scullery had a zinc bath, a copper to heat water and a round zinc bowl on a long handle to scoop out hot water from the copper. It also had a heavy mangle with wooden rollers.

Working on the farm was physically hard for both men and women. For those workers who had not managed to save money for their retirement they often had to continue doing heavy work long into their old age. If they became too frail to work they had to rely on Parish Poor Relief but by the end of the first decade of the twentieth century help was at hand. In 1909, people over 70 could claim a government pension of five shillings a week. It was the beginning of the welfare state, and in the following decade the Liberal government was to make more changes that would affect not just Longford, but the whole nation.

Chapter 21

The Calm before the Storm (1911-1913)

On the night of Sunday 2 April 1911 there were 354 people living in Longford. One of those diligently filling in his census form that night was Walter Fewell at his fruit farm called Heath Gardens. On the form, Walter wrote that he was head of the house, 54, and a market gardener and employer. On the next line he added his wife, Eliza Margaret, 49, who had no employment (being a housewife was not considered an occupation). Walter wrote that they had a house of eight rooms, not including the kitchen and scullery; that they had been married twenty-seven years and had had five children two of whom had died. He then listed the rest of the household: daughter, Winifred, 25, son Victor, 10, his widower father-in-law, John Emmins, 73, and finally their live-in general domestic servant, Emily Victoria Neal aged 13.

Emily Victoria Neal, known as Vicky, was the daughter of Caroline Neal, who owned the sweetshop in the village. Plump-faced, brown-eyed, Vicky had romantic dreams for her future. She was not unhappy working for the kindly Fewell family, but her imagination was fed by the stories she read in penny novels. One of her favourites was called, 'I Want to Enjoy Myself', which described a girl who runs away from home to travel to London to go on the stage, and in her young head she dreamed of going on the same adventure.

A year later, at 5am on the morning of 25 July 1912 she piled her brown hair on top of her head and put on black stockings and boots, black serge coat and skirt, a blouse, a black straw hat with a black bow in front, and she crept out of the house. She was carrying a bundle of clothes containing another pair of black boots, a blue cotton dress, and a change of underclothing. She walked along the Bath Road to the White Horse, but because she wanted to avoid going past her Mother's sweetshop she turned left at the pub, walked past the Barracks onto the island, and at the end of the island, crossed the footbridge and set off across the fields to Harmondsworth. Two carters saw her walking towards West Drayton station where she caught the cheap early-morning workers' train to London.

At Heath Gardens, the family rose that morning to find the stove not lit, the breakfast table unlaid, and no sign of Vicky

'Winifred, go up to the attic and see what has happened to the girl', said Mrs Fewell.

Winifred came downstairs a few moments later with a piece of paper in her hand.

'She's not there,' said Winifred, 'her bed has been made and this was on it.'

Mrs Fewell read the note. It said, 'I am going away'. It gave no indication of where she was going.

'Winifred, put on your hat and go and ask Mrs Neal if she knows where Vicky is'.

At the other end of the village Mrs Neal was sorting the newspapers on the sweetshop counter. When Winifred handed her the note she became frantic. She had no inkling that Vicky would think of running away, although she knew her daughter filled her head with the novels she read. The following morning her parents received a letter, posted at Upper Baker Street Post Office, which said, 'My Own Darling Mum. I am going away to try my luck in London. I want to enjoy myself. Don't worry or trouble about me. I will let you know when I get something to do.' With the letter was a five shilling postal order which was the one month's wages she normally paid her Mum, but there was no indication of her whereabouts.[213] Her desperate mother got Reynolds newspaper to publish a picture of the 14-year-old girl with a letter that said, 'Vicky. Should you see this notice please come home at once? If you are unable to do so, send a telegram that father may fetch you. We forgive you for running away, and want you back, Mother.'[214]

---

213   Uxbridge & W. Drayton Gazette – Saturday 27 July 1912

214   Reynolds's Newspaper – Sunday 28 July 1912

On a Sunday, two weeks later Vicky Neal returned home. She told them she had taken a situation near Marble Arch.[215] Homesickness had evaporated Vicky's dream of emulating her fictional heroine. She returned to Longford and her position with Mrs Fewell.[216]

Mrs Neal's sweet shop opposite the Peggy Bedford.

Vicky found happiness fourteen years later when, in 1926, she was married in Harmondsworth parish church to James Nelson Lee a bricklayer. Two days later, they sailed from Southampton on a Canadian immigration service ship. James Lee had already been to Canada in 1922 and stayed for a year at Egleton, Toronto, where his sister lived. The newly-weds paid their own passage and had £100 in savings. At last Vicky was having the adventure she craved as a teenager. They arrived on 5 July 1926. It is not known how long they stayed in Canada, but by 1939 they were back living in Harmondsworth.

Mrs Neal's sweetshop sold penny sweets from a barge-boarded thatched building situated near the Quaker house. The building, had previously been used as a farriers and additional stabling for the Peggy Bedford inn. When it became residential, an external chimney was added at each end of

---

215 Uxbridge & W. Drayton Gazette – Saturday 10 August 1912
216 Reynolds's Newspaper – Sunday 11 August 1912

the building. Mrs Neal's husband, Joseph, was a fireman at the Gas Works in Colnbrook. He tended the furnaces that burnt the coal to produce the gas. This meant uncomfortable working conditions shovelling coal whilst working in extreme heat.

Caroline Neal was still selling newspapers and confectionary at her shop, well into the Second World War. In 1941 she appeared in court when three boys who had run away from home and camped in an old van pleaded guilty to stealing a quantity of cigarettes, matches and other articles from her Bath Road store worth £3.6s.8d. The father of one of the boys told the court that he would pay Mrs Neal back for the stolen items and wished the Magistrate to send his boy to a residential training school, and he would do his best to find employment for the other boys. They were all placed on probation.[217] Mrs Neal died in 1954 aged eighty-four.

* * *

Walter Fewell had taken up William Wild's suggestion and bought the fruit farm opposite the Weekly House at Heath Gardens in 1892 for £1000. It is now a listed building. Walter Fewell came to Longford to live a quiet, healthy life in the country. He was attracted to Longford for its non-conformity and his friendship with the Wild family.

Heath Gardens

Grade II Listed by English Heritage in 1974. They dated it as mid-eighteenth century, with a mid-nineteenth century extension at the rear.

In 1911 it had a drawing room and a dining room, kitchen with a good hot water supply, pantry, scullery, five bedrooms with a luxury that most village houses didn't have – a bathroom with hot and cold water and a lavatory basin. It also had gas for lighting and cooking and an attic. Outside were small glass houses, a tall four-stall stable, chicken house and open cart shed, and other useful old buildings.

Walter's family, originally from Essex, had moved to Chelsea where young Walter had learned about horticulture from his uncle, John Mason, who had a nursery in Park Walk, Chelsea. When Walter and his brother Fred had saved enough money they opened a greengrocer's shop in Beaufort Street, Chelsea. As the business flourished they acquired shops at 349 and 384 Kings Road and became the leading greengrocer in the area from 1880-1897. The long hours and unhealthy air of London proved too much for Walter's health and the whole family welcomed the move to Longford.

217   Uxbridge & W. Drayton Gazette – Friday 21 February 1941

Heath Gardens 1909.

Two more children were born after their move – daughter, Netta in 1898 and their son, Victor, in 1900. Both children would grow up with William Wild's daughters, Margaret and Elizabeth. The eldest Fewell daughter, Winifred, was fifteen and away at Boarding school in Whitstable in 1901 with another pupil from Longford, Florence Heyward from Bays farm. Ten years later the younger daughter, Netta Fewell, was at the same school with neighbour, Margaret Wild. They were not to know then how these friendships would shape their futures. Margaret's sister would eventually marry Netta's brother, Victor, and after the war Netta would marry a friend of Fred Heyward's from Bays farm.

Walter Fewell, as well as being a shrewd business man, was philanthropic and described as 'a man of the most lovable disposition, while his character for firmness of conviction, integrity of purpose, and honesty of belief, made him widely respected and greatly beloved.'[218] The family were not Baptists or Quakers, but Congregationalists and Walter's main interest became the Congregational Church at Poyle a mile away. He became Deacon and continued his philanthropy. The Fewell's donation of a billiard table to the Colnbrook Men's Institute in 1908 was later rewarded by the gift of a silver teakettle to mark their silver wedding anniversary. Walter Fewell

218   Chelsea News and General Advertiser – Friday 12 April 1912

was interested in parish affairs and chaired a public meeting to elect parish councillors on 7 March 1904 where he proposed William Wild, who was duly elected. When Walter's health finally failed and he died, aged 55, in Longford on Easter Monday, 8 April 1912, the Wilds were there supporting his widow and family.

Walter Fewell was buried at Harmondsworth burial ground, after a funeral service at the Harmondsworth Baptist chapel. A memorial service was held at Poyle Congregational Church the following week. As a mark of the impact he had made on the village his funeral was attended by most of the leading citizens in the area, of every denomination. Not only was there a long report of his funeral in the local newspapers, but Chelsea News and General Advertiser gave him a glowing obituary.

Walter's shops in Chelsea were now in the possession of his brother-in-law, Kent Clisby, a fruit wholesaler. Kent Clisby attended the funeral alone. His wife, Eliza Fewell's sister, was unwell. When she died four months later it was another devastating shock for the family. The two eldest Clisby children were independent, but the youngest, 14-year-old Hartley, had barely left school and was just starting work in his father's business. Without hesitation the beneficent, Eliza Fewell, agreed that Hartley could stay with them at Longford. Later in life Hartley had such fond memories of Longford that he forgot he had been born in Chelsea and on official forms entered his birthplace as Longford. With Walter dead and his son Victor only 12, Hartley's help with the fruit farm was invaluable and was an opportunity to learn the basics of the fruiterers business. His father, Fred, who now had a large business to run at Covent Garden and Chelsea would spend weekends at Longford and attend the Congregational church with the family. He became so integrated in the area that he eventually took over Walter's position as Vice-President of the Poyle and Colnbrook Young Men's Institute.

* * *

The 1911 census, which had to be completed by every household, took place at the height of the women's suffrage campaign when campaigners were becoming militant and saw the census as a protest tool. Emmaline Pankhurst said, 'If women don't count, neither shall they be counted', and encouraged her followers to boycott it. Some used inventive methods to avoid being at home on the night of the census and others just scrawled their protest over the census form and risked a £5 fine. There are no obvious female abstentions from the census in Longford, although one person in Harmondsworth did enter their dog, called Spider, on the form.

A second national event in that decade also required property owners to complete copious forms. In 1910 the Liberal-led coalition government of Herbert Asquith decided that the land tax was unfair as it favoured the large landowners. The national land valuation was the brain-child of the Chancellor of the Exchequer, David Lloyd George, and it was enshrined in law with the passing of the Finance Act (1909-1910). The national valuation covered every type of property from homes and land to mining, ports and industrial complexes. Surveyors drew up maps labelling each property with a number, and then followed this with visits to measure and judge the quality of the land and buildings. The valuation was set at the rental value of property at the time the Act became law, even though it took several years to complete all the surveys. It seems ironic that the conscientious proprietor, who maintained his house and land in good condition, attracted a higher valuation than that of a neglected property and therefore had to pay more land tax.

In Longford these surveys took place intermittently from 1911 until 1914. There were various problems with the survey and many appeals against the final valuation. Eventually the government ended the legislation in 1920, but what the survey achieved was a detailed national record of each property owner, occupier, description, size and value of each landholding just before the First World War.

From this archive we learn about the Prince of Wales pub (which no longer exists). We now know it only had a beer licence, and that the front of the building was rebuilt in 1909. It had a taproom, a small 'jug and bottle', a saloon bar and a clubroom behind the bar. In the rear was a small kitchen, it had a cellar behind the bar and a scullery at the rear. Upstairs were three bedrooms, and a sitting room. Outside was a three-stall stable, and an open shed. It had well-water, gas, a cesspool, and a two-up, two-down cottage earning four shillings a week in rent. Unfortunately only poor images of this building exist. It was situated between the Kings Arms and the Kings Bridge and after it closed in 1920 it became a domestic house called 'Orchard View' with the land behind it being worked as a small-holding. It was later demolished and is now a row of semi-detached houses.

The western end of the village with the Kings Bridge, carts outside the stores and post office, and in the distance the Prince of Wales and the Kings Arms public houses.

There were two shops in the village, one at each end of the main street. Mrs Neal's sweetshop was opposite the Peggy Bedford, and a grocery shop and Post Office was near the Kings Bridge. The Post Office had been bought for £400 and occupied in 1903 by Charles Hedley Cowley.[219] On the 11 October 1911 the Government surveyor came to call on the postmaster. The shop and post office was the first in Longford to be valued under the new Finance Act. It was a substantial building of five bedrooms, which the surveyor described as 'poor condition, badly built' and a separate old bakehouse fitted with a single old fashioned oven, which was 'old premises'. It was valued at the same amount Cowley had paid for it eight years earlier. The surveyor did not visit Longford again until May 1912. The following year the Shops Act 1912 introduced the requirement for all shops to close for one half-day a week, and for Harmondsworth parish that day was Wednesday.[220]

* * *

219   Windsor and Eton Express – Saturday 26 September 1903.
220   Uxbridge & W. Drayton Gazette – Saturday 07 November 1914

Although the majority of people in Longford in 1911 worked in agriculture, the types of occupation were diversifying. At least six residents worked on the railways, and four were watermen employed to look after the River Colne and its tributaries. Out of 75 households only 38 head of household worked on the land. There was an assortment of self-employed salesmen in trades such as buttons, boots, bride-cakes, gloves and surgical instruments. There was one compositor in the print trade who worked in West Drayton, and two iron workers. Horses were still the main energy source on the farms and there were carters and horsemen living in the village. The village also saw street vendors selling door to door. A man selling fly-papers would visit occasionally in the summer with one wound round his hat to advertise his wares. One man sold crumpets from a big tray, which he balanced on his head as he rang a hand bell. A rag and bone man with an open handcart that he had pushed from Hounslow would buy rabbit skins and bones off the children who had found them in the fields.

The White Horse, and The Square 1915. In 1911 the Staines Rural District Council agreed that telegraph posts could be erected along the Bath Road by the General Post Office.

* * *

By 1911 Great Britain was on its third monarch of the century. The old Queen, Victoria, had died in 1901 and her long-time heir Edward VII came to the throne. After a lifetime of scandal and gossipy events surrounding his life he proved to be a good and effective Head of State but he only had nine years on the throne before he died.[221] His son, George V, was crowned at Westminster Abbey on Thursday 22 June 1911. Around the country, in celebration, bonfires were lit at 10pm on high points, but Harmondsworth, almost at sea-level, had no vantage points on which to build one. The day was declared a (national) Bank Holiday and Harmondsworth celebrated by organising a tea and sports day for the children which took place on the meadow behind the Great Barn on the Tuesday after the Coronation. The band of St Mary's School, Southall, played at the event and Messrs Beach's Old English Fair set up their amusements. There was a baby show, and then the sports commenced at 2.30pm. As each child returned to their home at the end of a memorable day they were presented with a souvenir Coronation mug.[222]

* * *

The army had a long-established presence on Hounslow Heath. Now in the early twentieth century, and with the growth of new inventions, strange things appeared in the sky over Longford. The Army was experimenting with the use of flight as a military resource and had formed an Air Battalion of Royal Engineers in Chatham, Kent, which later became the Royal Flying Corp. This Corp established Experimental Works at Feltham (South of Hounslow Heath) and a grass airfield on Hounslow Heath was used for experimental hot-air balloons, airships and early aircraft flights. At the beginning of 1910 a hanger was built for army officers to be given flying training which allowed the field-workers of Longford to be some of the first to witness these strange flying machines.[223] On one occasion whilst a military balloon was passing over the village at a low altitude, the trail rope caught in some trees and for a short while the occupants had a rather exciting time. However, help was forthcoming and they were freed to go on their journey in safety.[224]

* * *

The government surveyor was still working his way around the individual buildings in the village to produce valuations. On 4 May 1912 it was the

---

221   Ridley, Jane, *Bertie: A Life of Edward VII*, (London, 2012), p.476

222   Uxbridge & W. Drayton Gazette – Saturday 17 June 1911

223   Mills, Steve, *The Dawn of the Drone: From Back-Room Boys of World War One*, (2019); https://en.wikipedia.org/wiki/Hounslow_Heath_Aerodrome

224   Uxbridge and W. Drayton Gazette, Friday 1 January 1915.

Peggy Bedford's turn to receive a visit from the surveyor. Mr H. Hunt, the licensee opened the door to Mr Fleck and showed him around the premises. Mr Fleck valued the land (ornamental gardens) at £588 which included 290 feet of Bath Road frontage valued at thirty shillings per foot. Any land that had road frontage was valued higher because of its potential for housing, but other land was valued at £140 per acre. The house and stables were valued at £862, which was not a large amount for a building with seven bedrooms, three servant rooms, two staircases, two public bars, a private bar in a large room, a sitting room, kitchen, large scullery and damp cellar. The surveyor described the Peggy Bedford as a 'Very old inn on Bath Road formerly a posting inn. Large accommodation for horses and vehicles. Casual trade now very small and very little local trade. Tenant states [that] his rent has been reduced to £40. Good sized garden and orchard not well kept up. The trees are old and of no value. Trade stated by tenant to be: mild ale about two and a half barrels per week, Bitter eight barrels per annum, with sixty-five gallons of spirits sold last year.'[225] Harman & Co., who had a brewery in Uxbridge, now owned the Peggy Bedford. Mr H. Hunt had been licensee since 1 March 1909 and had originally been paying £55 per annum rent before it was reduced. Obviously, the lack of customers meant there was less money for care and maintenance of the building and grounds. It seemed the Peggy Bedford was past its glory days and even the cycling public had abandoned it. However its large function room was still a good place for large meetings.

On Tuesday evening 21 October 1913 the inaugural meeting of the Rural Workers Union, West Middlesex Branch, was formed at a gathering at the Peggy Bedford. The farmers' had begun their own National Farmers' Union in 1908 to fight for the rights of farmers and their industry, now the workers wanted to regulate relationships between them and their employers and to improve their social and welfare conditions. Mr Stephen Bird, a forty-year-old carter who lived with his wife, children, mother-in-law, and three boarders in a very old, poorly maintained labourers' cottage at the Moor in Harmondsworth was Chairman for the evening and at the meeting they elected their first officers.[226] Mr George T. Hicks, from Colnbrook, was elected secretary. Mr. H. W. Maskell, who had been very vocal at the meeting, was elected Chairman. He was a coal porter who lived

---

225   The National Archives, Harmondsworth Valuation Field Book, 101-200, IR/58/39633

226   A carman was a main who delivered goods in a horse and cart. Today the equivalent would be a "white van man".

at 10 Doghurst cottages next to the Three Magpies pub at Heathrow. John Frith, agricultural labourer, a twenty-nine year old widower who boarded at the Moor in Harmondsworth, was elected treasurer. Their headquarters was to be at the Peggy Bedford and the meeting closed with thanks to the host, Mr H. Hunt.[227]

Peggy Bedford early 20th Century.

Two months later the Rural Workers Union held a recruitment evening at the Peggy Bedford when Mr. E.P. Bennett, J.P. ex-MP for Mid-Oxon, gave an inspiring address to a crowded room.[228] He spoke of the wretched housing of the labourers, and stated it was time these skilled men should receive a living wage. He was very pleased the Union was going so strong, especially the Longford Branch, which was gathering new members every week. The meeting closed with a vote of thanks to Mr Bennett and to Mr Hunt, the host, for the splendid way the room was decorated. Afterwards a large number of men signed on to become members of the Union.

The Union meeting bought some much needed income to the pub, but not enough to make it prosper. It would need a new strategy and a change of landlord to return the inn to it former fame.

* * *

227   Uxbridge and W. Drayton Gazette – Saturday 25 October 1913
228   Uxbridge and W. Drayton Gazette – Saturday 6 December 1913.

Nearly a year after the Peggy Bedford had been surveyed the government surveyor turned up on the doorstep of a public house at the other end of the village, the Kings Arms, on the morning of 27 June 1913. It was to be the last property surveyed in Longford. The Kings Arms had been bought by the Brandons Putney Brewery on 19 December 1898 who had installed James Moreton and Alfred H. Palmer as the licensees. They were paying £30 a year in rent. The pub had a full licence and was described by the surveyor as 'Brick & Tile Building twenty-three foot high. Modern in good condition. Accommodation: Bar modern, saloon, public bar, Jug & Bottle, Small private room, kitchen, scullery, Large archway at side. Good cellar. Good sitting room, 5 bedrooms (1 a passage room). Outside was a 2-stall stable and a brick and tiled coach house with a loft over it. Water was obtained by a pump in the yard, and there was cesspool drainage.' The building was valued at £500.

Kings Arms 1908 with the Weekly House in the background.

Now that the dreaded valuation visits were complete the Longfordians tried to get back to the serious business of growing food, but by 1914 other worries were on the minds of Longford Residents. Events were happening in Germany and Austria, which caused the British Government to be drawn into a European conflict, and on 4 August Britain declared war on Germany.

Suddenly life changed for the young men. The call for army volunteers stirred the spirit of adventure in the farm labourers who had barely been further than the cinema in West Drayton. Some were living in poor accommodation and doing monotonous farm work. This was a chance to travel, have some excitement with pay and be back home for Christmas, they told themselves as they set off for the recruitment meeting at Uxbridge.

Chapter 22

From turnips to trenches (1914-1918)

The group of young lads could hear the Uxbridge Brass Band as soon as they got off the motor bus from Harmondsworth. Each beat of the drum, each throaty note of the trumpets, calling them towards the sound. On 4 August 1914 the King had declared that Britain was at war with Germany. Volunteer soldiers were called for. Some young men in the parish, had immediately gone to Hounslow Barracks to enlist. Now, on the last day of August, and fired by increasing patriotic fervour, this little group had heard there was going to be a recruitment rally in the Uxbridge Market Place.

As they followed the stirring sounds of the military music, the crowds got thicker. Military men and local councillors stood on a dais between the arches of the Georgian Market Hall ready to address the crowd. The Chairman of the Council, Mr W. J. Hutchings, asked everyone to sing the National Anthem and then spoke about the object of the meeting. Young men were required 'to save, not only England, not only Europe, but the world

---

Recruitment

After the initial response for army volunteers when war was declared on 4 August 1914, a month later is was soon obvious that more men were needed. Lord Kitchener set out to raise a second army by sending out recruiting teams to all areas to explain the reason for the war and to urge that the 'very existence of the British Empire is now at stake'. The Middlesex Regiment decided to form a Reserve Territorial Battalion of 800-900 men and allocated a recruitment target to each district. On Monday 31 August 1914 the Uxbridge and Hillingdon Band played rousing patriotic music to a big crowd in the Market Place in Uxbridge. The Uxbridge district's target was 200 men and so a rally was held that recruited 60 men in two days for the 8th Battalion. A total of 750,000 men had volunteered by the end of September.

Uxbridge & W. Drayton Gazette – Saturday 05 September 1914

itself from the tyranny of a despot. King and country needed their services to help crush the power of one of the most cruel and unprincipled foes this nation has ever had.' Then the crowd heard a stirring speech from the Commanding Officer of the 8th Battalion of the Middlesex regiment asking for recruits. They 'wanted the type of men of which the Uxbridge Company was now composed; real hard-workers and no slackers.' Applause broke out when he said, 'No Englishman under forty had a right to lift up his head if he did not enlist.' After three cheers for the King the recruitment officers were kept busy handing out application forms, and then the recruits were sworn in. Three doctors and a number of ladies moved around the crowd urging men to enlist whilst the Uxbridge band played martial music and the Salvation Army Band competed by playing the Marseillaise.

The group from Harmondsworth, enthused with the air of excitement and patriotism that pervaded the occasion, and sensing that, whatever their home circumstances, they would be branded a disgrace and cowardly if they did not enlist, all filled in their forms. Five of the young men in the group who enlisted were from Longford. Two were never to return. In other parts of Harmondsworth four men from the Sipson market garden firm of Wild and Robbins joined that day and when they returned to tell their boss what they had done were rewarded with £5 each – a month's wages.[229]

The following morning (Tuesday 1 September 1914) the recruits had a medical examination at the Uxbridge Drill Hall and out of the eighty-one men who had given their names, twenty-six were found to be medically unfit. Those that were accepted said goodbye to their wives and sweethearts in the afternoon. The Council Chairman gave them a rousing address praising their patriotic spirit, and wished them luck. Then they marched to Vine Street Station and boarded a train for Sittingbourne for initial training.

An account of the training at Sittingbourne in the local paper from the week before paints a picture of a tough regime of long days digging trenches in the rain and very little sleep. It reported that comradeship carried them through.[230]

Back at Longford, in the pervading zeal of patriotism, the news of the young men's enlistment was greeted with pride and congratulations, but behind the excitement there was a feeling of foreboding. For both the

---

229   Uxbridge & W. Drayton Gazette – Saturday 05 September 1914

230   Uxbridge & W. Drayton Gazette – Saturday 22 August 1914

families and the farmers it was a time of worry. The families had lost a wage-earner (the initial pay of one shilling and two pence a day left little for the soldier to send home to their families), but they feared for their loved one's safety. News of casualties at the Battle of Mons in which few of the 2000 British soldiers survived was beginning to trickle through. The local paper reported those that were in hospital, but glossed over the names of those who died. This war might not be over by Christmas after all.

The harvest was still in progress. Soon the apples in the orchards would ripen. This was a busy season for farmers and market gardeners who always required extra labour at this time. Now they were going to be even more short-handed.

At the start of the war, out of the 80 households in Longford there were 37 single men in the 18-35 volunteers age-group. Some households already had serving soldiers in the regular army. All young single men felt under pressure to enlist. Married men felt their duty lay with supporting their family. They were the wage-earners and for some, if a son had enlisted, there would already be a shortfall in the household income. Farmers with crops in the ground and animals in the fields knew their duty was to continue producing food. A Longford farmer, Mr Bateman, had a close encounter with the war machine in November 1914 when an Army biplane landed in his field when it became too dark for the pilot to continue flying. It remained in the field overnight. The next morning the pilot and his mechanic, accompanied by another biplane, took off to return to its base.[231]

The community rallied round. Longford, a Baptist village, already had an unofficial support system in their community but now their nation needed them. Those men too young or old to fight, and the women and girls left behind when their men went off to war, were not slow to form their own patriotic support groups. First aid classes and rifle clubs began and charities for distress-relief were formed. Women were doing jobs around the farm considered men's work a few weeks previously. However, some people in the Harmondsworth parish were not convinced that everyone was playing their part.

At the end of November 1914 residents of Harmondsworth village were astonished to read a note pinned to the Vicarage Hall door which read: 'The Jellyback Brigade. The Young Men of Harmondsworth [who are] too

---

231 Uxbridge & W. Drayton Gazette – Friday 13 November 1914

slack or cowardly to join the Colours. The Roll of Dishonour. Please add your name to the list below.' As soon as it was seen it was snatched from the door. A couple of days later another notice appeared with a sarcastic assumption that it had been removed by someone wishing to add his name to the list of 'jellybacks'.[232] Again it was torn down, and replaced with a note saying 'Mind your own business' and 'Send your sons'. These notices were written by the daughter of the vicar, Irene Strickland Taylor, and the reference to 'sons' was meant for her two brothers both of recruitment age and both clergymen. Her response was to inform the 'jellybacks' that the Archbishop of Canterbury had forbidden the clergy to enlist. The rejoinder to that was a broken window in the door and a daubing with mud and stones.

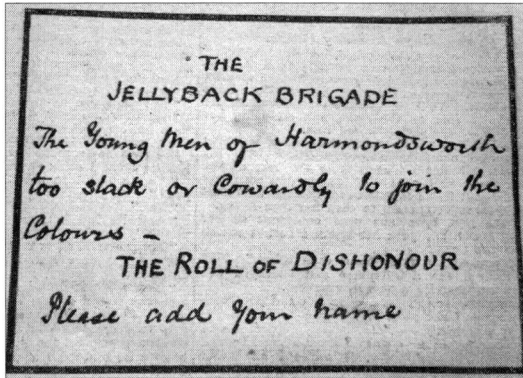

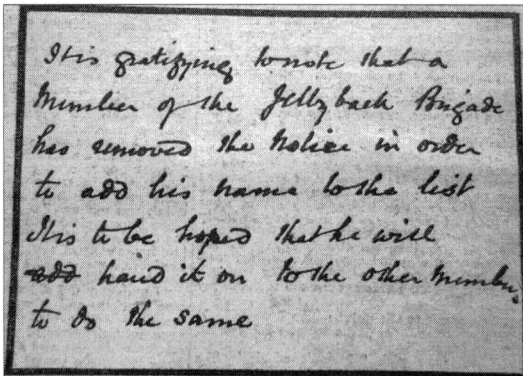

The Jellyback Brigade

Harmondsworth villagers were incensed. Not only was it the talk of the village, but the story made the national newspapers. One newspaper printed an article entitled 'How not to Recruit', and described the actions of the vicar and his daughter and their misguided attempt to add to the recruitment figures. The newspaper pointed out that in the first two months of the war 139 men had already enlisted from the parish, roughly one from every other household. The article went on to say 'Recruiting will not be stimulated by gratuitous insult, as people were not going to be badgered by foolish people'.[233]

As a consequence of all the adverse publicity the vicar, Rev. John C. Taylor, found it necessary to publish a letter in the *Daily Sketch* claiming that on 1 December ten of the 'deserters from the jellyback brigade' went to Hounslow barracks that morning and six were accepted for enlistment. He said that they, in the vicarage, rejoiced in what the newspaper called 'a comedy' so long as our purpose is accomplished. He and his daughter sent indignant letters to other newspapers that were too long for them to publish in full. It did not alter the general opinion of the newspapers that their intervention was inappropriate and the local newspaper even went as far as to conclude 'There are still

Vicar's Christmas card

a few of the over-zealous and fearsome persons about who, in their efforts to get young men to fight their battles for them, whilst they are snug at home themselves, manage to do more harm than good.'[234] With unfortunate timing, in the same edition in which this editorial appeared there was also a report of the death of the vicar's wife and mother of the perpetrator of the

233 Daily Citizen (Manchester) – Monday 30 November 1914
234 Uxbridge & W. Drayton Gazette – Friday 18 December 1914

controversy who died suddenly six days earlier and whose funeral took place that very day. The commotion was over and there was no further mention of jellybacks in the village.

As if to make amends for their lack of empathy, the Vicar and his congregation sent a Christmas card, the following year, to all serving Harmondsworth men.

* * *

For the farmers, in the middle of harvest, the reduced labour force was a problem. The young lads with their strength and energy were the ones on which the farmers relied to plough the fields, build the ricks and drive the produce to market. Women could do the lighter jobs but brawn was now in short supply. There was also a shortage of horses. To get their crops to market required horses, but horses were also needed for the war effort. Horses were being requisitioned so hastily that a carriage with two horses was stopped on the Bath Road on 10 August by the military, the horses commandeered and removed, leaving the carriage and its passengers stranded.[235]

As the farmers' wrestled with their labour problems they also wrestled with their consciences. Fred Heyward a single man of 33 was the tenant farmer of Bays Farm, Longford. The farm had nineteen acres and he had a separate piece of land of thirty-three acres which his father, and before that his maternal grandfather, Frederick Gray, made into a thriving market garden. Both the Gray and Heyward families were extensive Baptist families. Fred Heyward kept pigs and poultry but mainly grew market garden crops and fruit and walnuts. It was labour intensive especially in the strawberry-picking season.

As well as the unsettling war-time situation, the end of 1914 was also devastating for the Heyward family when Fred's mother, Maria S Heyward, died unexpectedly on 8 November 1914 aged 60 in the neighbouring parish of Harlington. She had been a pillar of the church community for 32 years. After the initial shock of losing his Mother, Fred began to think about where his duty lay. Baptists' beliefs and their adherence to the words of the bible did not cause them to be total pacifists, but members could decide for themselves how their conscience balanced patriotism and pacifism. Fred's sister Florence kept house for him at Longford and he was very grateful

---

235   Uxbridge & W. Drayton Gazette – Saturday 15 August 1914

for her help with domestic duties. However, she was courting Reginald Jenkinson, a fruit salesman from Harlington, and when they married on 16 October 1915 Fred was free of family obligations and could follow his conscience.

The farm was his main concern. Fred needed to keep it going for the sake of his workers, and to have something to return to. He knew of a family from his local Baptist chapel, who were now managing a Norfolk farm. He contacted them and Henry Du Rose agreed to return to Middlesex to be his manager at Bays Farm. In November 1915 Fred travelled to Norfolk handed over the keys to the Bays Farm to the family and immediately went into Norwich to enlist.

Fred joined up under his full name of Richard Frederick Heyward. He had a medical at Norwich on 26 November 1915, was pronounced physically fit and was sworn in to the Norfolk Yeomanry Territorial Force the same day. During his army training he injured his right ankle which kept him in hospital for 15 days. By August 1916 he was promoted to Lance Corporal.

Meanwhile the Du Rose family had settled in at Bays Farm, although settled was not the right word for Henry and Helena Du Rose as their once close family were separated by the war. Henry was managing the market garden with their two younger sons, and their two young daughters were helping Helena in the house and dairy. The two older sons were already at the front. For Helena it was a worrying time. She just wished the war to end so that the family could be re-united but it was not to be. Tragedy was about to strike.

* * *

Helena Du Rose sighed as the candle flickered once more and she momentarily lost sight of what she was writing. It was late and her eyes were tired but she wanted to get this letter off to Harry. He was on active service in Egypt and she knew how much the letter, and the little package containing the gifts of chocolate, peppermint, dried fruits and bootlaces, as recommended by the War Office, meant to him. He was just 17 when he joined up at the start of the war in August 1914. She knew he saw joining up as an adventure but he was so young and inexperienced in life. She worried about him, as she did about his brother, one year younger, who was now in France. She was so proud of them for serving their country but it was an anxious time. She did not know what horrors they were experiencing. The newspapers kept details of the war to a minimum and those at home had little idea of the progress of the battles or the mounting numbers of casualties. She remembered their young, shiny faces as they set off to volunteer for the army, and tried to hide her sorrow and anguish. All she could do was send them comfort in the form of a letter and hope the war was over before fifteen-year-old Jack was old enough to join up.

Jack was in the farmyard. She could hear him harnessing up the horse to the cart fully laden with produce with which he was about to make the fifteen-mile journey to the London market. London was getting desperate for food. In fact there were food shortages everywhere. It was nearly 2am – time for Jack to leave if he was to get to Covent Garden in time for the opening of the market. It was dark in the yard but he had a kerosene lamp burning in the stable. The cart had already been loaded and once the horse was secure he could leave. She heard him call to her.

'All right Jack. I will come out', she said, and she put down her pen put on her shawl and went into the yard.

The horse was standing quietly in the shafts, but Jack wanted her to hold on to him whilst he went back to the stable to turn out the lamp. Helena looked at the horse as she stood next to it holding the bridle, a gentle creature who knew his routine and that he was about to set off to market. He knew nothing about the war in France, or even that France existed. He did not know how lucky he was that he was still following his normal routine and had escaped requisitioning by the army. Helena looked towards the stable. Jack closed the stable door and returned to the cart. The horse, hearing him approach, suddenly swung its head round and hit Helena behind the shoulder. The unexpected jolt knocked her off balance and, as she stumbled, she cried out 'I'm falling'. As she fell she reached out to find something to steady herself and the first thing she grabbed was the rein, the horse responded and moved forward. Helena had not managed to stop her fall and lay sprawled on the ground just as the horse moved forward dragging the cart with its heavy load over her body.

Jack rushed indoors and awoke his sleeping father, 'Dad, come quick, mother's fallen under the wheel'. Henry hurried downstairs and saw his wife lying in the yard. He carried her indoors and sent for Dr Walker who was there in 40 minutes. She stayed all morning in the kitchen and in the afternoon seemed better. The doctor suggested she should go to bed and she was helped up the stairs. She died there the following day on Thursday 1 June 1916. She was just 54 years old.

Her devastated family were in shock, but arrangements had to be made. A funeral was arranged for Saturday but because it was a sudden death the Coroner had to be informed. On Saturday the bereaved family walked in the gloomy mist of the morning the few yards along the Bath Road to The Peggy Bedford pub for the inquest. The dismal weather, unusually cold for June, reflected the sadness felt by the mourning party. In the pub's large private parlour where Queen Victoria used to take tea the coroner had assembled a jury of local citizens to hear the evidence. The son and husband gave their accounts and the doctor the cause of death. Husband Henry estimated that the fully laden cart weighed about a ton and a half. The doctor said the cause of death was haemorrhage of the liver and spleen. The chairman of the jury, Mr Boniface, announced the inquest jury's verdict as Accidental Death.[236] The official proceedings over, and with the death certificate in his pocket, Henry Du Rose and his family returned to Bays Farm, now a sad empty farmhouse without the woman who held the family together.

The funeral was held later that afternoon at the Parish Church of Harmondsworth attended by many neighbours, mostly ladies as the men were away on active service or desperately trying to keep up with the work on the farms. Helena's eldest son, by her first husband, attended with his wife. Valentine Osborne Ralph Du Rose had joined the Grenadier Guards in 1905 and was home convalescing. A stepdaughter, Maud Caroline, from Henry's first marriage, was also there. Helena and Henry had both been widowed when they married in 1894 and already had a family of three children between them. They then added five children of their own. It was a blessing for Helena that she would not know that two of her sons would be killed in action and two more would survive the war but return damaged, physically and mentally.

Corporal Harry Arthur Du Rose did not hear of his Mother's death until some months later. Whether it was this news of her death, or the fatigue of two years of fighting, but something snapped and his misdemeanours caused him to be court martialled and reduced to the ranks. Seven weeks later he was badly injured and taken to the General Hospital in Alexandria

236   West Middlesex Gazette – Thursday 08 June 1916

Harry's Gravestone
Alexandria (Hadra) War Cemetery
Alexandria, El Eskenderiya, Egypt PLOT D.
72. MEMORIAL ID 56150182

WWI Memorial Plaque
(Photo: Bob Speel)

where he died of his wounds on 7 December 1916 aged nineteen.[237] The news of Harry's death may not have reached his father, Henry, in the eighteen days before Christmas that year, but he was still mourning Helena's death when he put on a brave face to attend his eldest daughter's wedding on Christmas Day 1916. Maud Caroline Du Rose, aged 26, was marrying a 52 year old widower Kent Fred Clisby, brother-in-law and frequent visitor to the Fewells at Heath Gardens, where his youngest son was living. Henry was pleased to see his daughter settled and financially secure. Kent Clisby was a well-respected businessman who did a lot of business with the market gardeners of West Middlesex.

Henry and Helena's other son, Herbert James had joined the 9th Norfolk Regiment as a Trumpeter. He later transferred to the 6th Northampton Regiment and was fighting in France at the time of his mother's death. He too never returned home. He was killed in action on 31 August 1918 aged 19 and is buried at Combles Cemetery, The Somme, France. Both men are commemorated on the WWI memorial inside Harmondsworth parish church.

---

237   https://www.findagrave.com/memorial/56150182/h-du_rose

Most memorials only record the men who died during the war but occasionally memorials also commemorate those who served and survived. The memorial at Beighton & Moulton St Mary in Norfolk where both the Du Rose boys were living when they enlisted includes survivors. Alongside the names of the two dead Du Rose boys is that of their half-brother Valentine who, although he survived the war, later died of his injuries in 1920.

Henry Du Rose, having lost two wives and two sons by 1919, was again to find happiness on 12 April 1919 when he married Emma Brown a friend of the family twenty years younger than him. Emma had often stayed with the family. She had stepped in to help Henry after Helena's death. She was there for him when he needed support and the friendship blossomed into romance. By then Jack, who witnessed his Mother's fatal accident, had joined the army. He survived the war and remained in the army but became restless. Without his mother and two older brothers, and with his father remarried, he no longer had strong ties to Britain and so, at the age of 26, he took up the government's offer of an assisted passage to Canada. Under the Empire Settlement Act, of 1922 The Government of Canada offered ex-servicemen inducements to emigrate to Canada which included reduced transportation fares, agricultural training and financial aid. Jack went to Halifax, Nova Scotia, and eventually became a carpenter, married and had two children. He died there in 1991.

* * *

Meanwhile, Fred Heyward, in 1916, was still finishing his military training in Norwich when he was devastated to receive a letter telling him of Helena Du Rose's death. Longford remained in his thoughts throughout his war service. Three months later he set sail from Devonport on a troop ship *Caledonia* for active duty to Salonika. Also on that ship was Frederick Cyril Walter Heugh from Snettisham, Norfolk, who had joined as an army cyclist. After two weeks they arrived to join the Allies fighting the Bulgarians. On arrival The Allies were successfully holding the enemy at bay but the troops were poorly equipped for the conditions and disease was rampant.[238] Within a month Fred was in hospital with an undiagnosed illness and during 1917 he was hospitalised three times with malaria. Also in hospital in June 1917 was Cyril Heugh who had a leg injury which caused chronic synovitis for the rest of his life. They became good friends.

---

238   www.iwm.org.uk/history/a-short-history-of-the-salonika-campaign

By February 1919 Fred Heyward was at last on a ship on his way home to be invalided out of the army on 31 March 1919 with a glowing reference praising his sobriety, his intelligence, his enthusiasm as a NCO and his tactful handling of his men. His friend Cyril Heugh returned in March 1919 and went straight to Napsbury hospital in St Albans, Hertfordshire, with his injured leg. He was finally demobbed with a disability pension in May 1919, and met up with Fred Heyward.

Fred returned to Bays Farm where his help was badly needed. Henry Du Rose was doing his best with the resources available but now with the loss of two sons, and the two younger sons in the army he was short-handed. Fred found farming had changed. With the shortage of man-power field crops could not be harvested. There was more emphasis on pigs and poultry, which required less labour. He still had crops in the field and in June placed his usual advert for ladies to pick strawberries, but now he was advertising a rate of 6 pence (2.5p) an hour. The amount he would have paid a man before the war. Women and young boys had traditionally been paid less than the men in agriculture, but now he had to offer competitive rates as women had more opportunities now to earn good money in factories.

Fred never fully regained his health and never married. After the war he invited Cyril Heugh to stay with him and help him with the farm. Cyril would later marry Netta the daughter of Walter Fewell from Heath Gardens in Longford.

THE BAYS FARM,
LONGFORD, MIDDLESEX.
Sale of Live and Dead MARKET GARDEN STOCK.
Messrs. ROBt. NEWMAN & SON
Are instructed by Mr. R. F. Heyward to Sell by Auction,
On MONDAY, SEPTEMBER 22nd, 1919,
At 12 for 1 o'clock,

FOUR young HORSES, 3 sows with pigs, Berkshire boar and 21 stores, poultry, 1-horse market van, 2 strawberry vans, 2 manure carts, 300 baskets, 150 boxes, 3 iron ploughs, 2 sets harrows, roll, 2 horse hoes, harness, rick of MEADOW HAY, about 10 acres of potatoes, cabbages, beet and onions and 10 trees of walnuts.

On view the Saturday previous and morning of Sale. Catalogues at the Farm; or of the Auctioneers, Harlington, Middlesex.

Bays Farm advert

In September 1919 the freehold of Bays Farm was sold to H.J. Jarvis, a Market Gardener from Stanwell.[239] Henry John Crowder Jarvis worked the Bays market garden for the rest of his life and died there in 1957. Fred moved back to Harlington where his brothers each had farms. He had a small market garden at the Dower House in the High Street before retiring and moving out to

---

239   Uxbridge & W. Drayton Gazette – Friday 19 September 1919

Oxfordshire to be closer to his sister Florence and her husband. He died there in 1938 aged 57. Fred had done 'his bit' for the war effort and survived but in doing so had to live with poor health for the rest of his life.

* * *

Three million men had enlisted in the first two weeks of the war, but because of heavy losses the government decided on compulsory conscription and The Military Service Act was introduced on 21 January 1916. Conscripts could apply for exemption, which required them to plead their case in front of a local appeal board. At this stage of the war the government had not woken up to the fact that with the loss of imported food due to U-boat action the country was becoming seriously deprived of food. Farm-work was not classed as an essential occupation.

Both local and central appeal tribunals were tough on the appellants. The first appeal before the Slough tribunal was from Fred's father, Richard Heyward, who owned Manor Farm in Harlington. He had 106 acres of Market Garden and before the war had a workforce of ten men, one boy and six women. By the time of conscription he had six men and two women and had to give up 24 acres of market garden to grow wheat and oats. Richard Heyward had three sons, Fred who had enlisted, Harold who was dying of a brain tumour and young Sidney. Richard had poor eyesight and he relied on his youngest son, Sidney, to be the farm foreman and to supervise the sales at Covent Garden which he attended six nights a week in the Summer and three in the Winter. Sidney was 17 at the start of the war and not eligible to be called up until he was eighteen. He attested at Staines (made himself available for military service) on 10 December 1915, just days after Fred had enlisted, although at the same time he also applied for an exemption. A temporary exemption was granted for six months and then extended. On 9 January 1917, Harold, lost his fight with the brain tumour and died aged 34. His father, Richard Heyward, still struggling to cope with failing eyesight, the loss of his wife and son, and the shortage of manpower on the farm, faced another major set-back when in February 1917 the Middlesex Tribunal dismissed a further appeal for Sidney to remain with him as farm foreman. They did allow him to make a further appeal to the Central Tribunal. Applying to yet another tribunal meant more form filling and more time away from the farm attending the tribunal with the anxiety of an uncertain result.

Ironically the chair of the local tribunal, County Counciller Rowland Richard Robbins, JP, was a Baptist farmer in Harmondsworth who knew all the local farmers and was well aware of their problems. He wore two hats at these appeals. As a Middlesex County Councillor he had the interests of the war effort to consider, but he was also on the Middlesex Agricultural Committee which later became known as the War Agricultural Committee, and as such tried to keep a balance between the need to grow the nation's food and the needs of the military. Robbins had been an early enthusiast of the embryonic National Farmers' Union, a lobby group started in December 1908, to urge the government for help when farming was going through a long and deep slump due to cheap imports. He became President of the National Farmers' Union in 1921, but had to give it up when he became seriously ill in August 1921. He continued as an important spokesman for agriculture until his death in 1960.

At the Central Tribunal hearing Richard Heyward's case for an appeal was that his son was needed for his experience and expertise. He said he had already lost 20 tons of potatoes due to lack of labour and 2 acres of Christmas cabbage was ploughed in for the same reason.

'I have had to take my son away from selling at Covent Garden to try and keep up with the work on the farm.'

He then listed the crops he intended to grow in the coming year: oats, wheat, potatoes, Brussels, Christmas cabbage, onions, beetroot, rhubarb, raspberries, grass and a fruit garden (orchard) of ten acres, spring cabbage, turnips and spinach. He said the County Council had found him two men to help on the farm, who were inexperienced and needed supervision, and with the nearby factories at Hayes paying better wages he was finding it very difficult to get labour. A further six month exemption was granted but at the next hearing, at the end of November 1917, the Central Tribunal had to hear the appeal in the absence of the appellant who was busy threshing. The appeal was dismissed.

So, after two years of fighting with the authorities, Sidney was called-up on 15 January 1918. He became a signaller in the Royal Garrison Artillery. He was demobbed a year later and married a farmer's daughter from Norfolk in a non-conformist ceremony in Westminster in August 1919. His brother Fred was a witness at the ceremony. They returned to Manor Farm, Harlington, to live.

* * *

At The Farm, in Longford, Henry James Wild, was in poor health and relying on his four sons to manage the farm. He died at the end of 1915 and his funeral on 2 October was held at the Harmondsworth Baptist Chapel, which was filled to capacity. There were hymns and scripture readings and then an address which described the deceased as a man of sterling integrity and capable in business. The organist was his son-in-law, Alfred Light. After further prayers the mourners made their way to the church yard for the burial in the grave 'which had not been opened since the great great grandfather of Mr Wild had been laid to rest in it in 1785'.[240]

Fred Heyward and most of the Baptist farmers from the area attended as well as his solicitor, Mr Lovibond, and Mr R.R. Robbins, JP, County Councillor. Henry James Wild had been the dominant farmer in Longford for fifty years. As the largest employer in Longford, he was highly respected by the whole village. He had not involved himself in village politics, but was a committee member for the Harmondsworth charities, a member of the Colnbrook Baptist chapel for 54 years, and a Deacon for 36 years. He and his wife Mary, had been married for 48 years and had nine children.[241] His four sons continued to run the farm, diversifying some of the farm into poultry breeding because of the shortage of labour.

Six months later two of the attendees at the funeral were to meet on opposite sides at a conscription appeal tribunal. When Mr R.R. Robbins presided at the tribunal on 1 July 1916 there were 91 appeal cases to be heard.[242] One appeal was for the middle two Wild brothers, John (39) and Henry Josiah (29). Their solicitor, Mr Lovibond, fought their case at the tribunal.[243] One brother, Charles (34) had attested (enrolled as ready for military service) and was not the subject of the appeal, and another, William, (48), was over age for conscription at

Men of Longford who died in WW1
G. Bryant
E.J. Cowdrey
H.A. Du Rose
H.J. Du Rose
W. Eggleton
H.E. Hawkett
W. Puzey
W.A. Cordell
A.J. Ruby
E. Sessions
H. White

240   West Middlesex Gazette, Friday 8 October 1915.
241   Uxbridge and W. Drayton Gazette, Friday 1 October 1915.
242   Uxbridge & W. Drayton Gazette – Friday 07 July 1916
243   Middlesex Chronicle – Saturday 25 August 1917

that time. The appeal resulted in conditional exemption for John, and three months for the younger brother.

By the end of the war, eleven Longford men had died for their country. The whole parish of Harmondsworth lost 94 men in the First World War – nearly ten percent of the pre-war male population. Far from being 'jellybacks' 417 men had left the parish and taken up arms. The men of Harmondsworth had played their part in the war but so had the women. While the men were away the women were not idle. They were breaking through the barrier that demarked the gender bias between 'mens' jobs and 'womens' jobs and demonstrating to employers that women were capable. An army of women descended on the farms of Harmondsworth and enabled the farms to keep productive at a time when the nation was facing starvation.

Chapter 23

Fighting On The Home Front (1917-1919)

As the sun rose across the orchard on an August morning the evaporating dew from the grass under the trees produced an ethereal mist rising up towards the branches. The cockerel had been the wake-up alarm call for the girls in the barn who were stirring from their beds in the loft. It was six in the morning but the kettle was already boiling on the stove in the makeshift kitchen. 'It's going to be a fine day', said Tilly Beasley to nobody in particular as she shook her straw mattress and climbed down from the loft to get her breakfast. The big barn doors were open and a gentle breeze blew through the huge ancient timbers as the twenty girls bustled about washing, dressing, eating breakfast and preparing sandwiches. 'Mrs Forster. Your turn to be 'Mother' today. What are we having?' called out Maureen Carr. 'Wait and see, said 'Mother', it will be your turn tomorrow – you and your sister.' The group took it in turns to prepare everyone's evening meal. Just then a burley older man in a tweed suit, waistcoat and flat cap with a smoking pipe in the corner of his mouth, stood, silhouetted, in the door way. 'Come on, come on, now, work to be done. Shake a leg,' he said to howls of mock protest from the assembly. He was an old soldier, a veteran of the Afghan wars, still wanting to do whatever he could for the war effort by volunteering to supervise the gang of volunteer fruit pickers. At 8am 'Sergeant' Morley blew his whistle and the women left the barn and the farmyard and walked to the vast orchards of Perry Oaks farm. As they walked a bi-plane flew overhead from the nearby Hounslow airfield drowning out the call of the skylarks, the sounds of the engine merging with that of the unfamiliar sound of a Fordson tractor working the soil in a nearby field. Horses were scarce now that the army had requisitioned so many but the government finally had a supply of tractors they could lend out to farmers for ploughing.

The 'Worcester' Brigade at Perry Oaks Farm with Mr Morley supervising.

As they reached the orchard they each took a ladder and basket and waited for 'The Sergeant' who told them where to pick. The ten-foot long wooden ladders with splayed bottoms were heavy, but the women were developing muscles they did not know they had. They were academics and professional women getting a holiday with pay in the country in the scholastic summer break of 1917 and patriotically doing 'their bit' for the war effort while the men were away fighting in the trenches. They called themselves the 'Worcester Brigade' after the apples they were picking. They soon set to work in the orchard.

At 10am the 'Sergeant' blew his whistle and the girls sat down under the trees to eat a snack. They could

National Land Council

The National Land Council was the gender-neutral name used by the National Political League which was founded in 1911. The National Land Council, realised. at the start of the first World War, that with labour-shortages food might become scarce. The organisation seized the opportunity to demonstrate that women had the ability to do the same work as men. They provided training in horticulture and farming skills for its members who were mainly middle-class educated women. These women did not have to commit to full-time working, but could volunteer on an occasional basis.

Citation: Broadhurst, Mary Adelaide. Oxford Dictionary of Biography

hear the busy buzz of bees on wild flowers in the long grass around them and watched as they headed for one of the many beehives dotted around the orchard. It was getting hot but the women were appropriately dressed. There was no uniform, but each wore a khaki armlet with a purple triangle on which were the letters 'N.L.C.' for National Land Council. Some wore hats or tied their hair in a scarf. Some chose to wear a loose overall over their clothes, but because they had to climb ladders their skirts were noticeable shorter than the ankle-length fashion at the start of the war, and thick stockings protected their legs from the tree branches as they climbed. It was still thought inappropriate for women to wear trousers, and an official Women's Land Army had not yet been established which would issue regulation hats and overalls. At 10.20am the whistle was heard again and they set to with the large wicker baskets over their arm as they climbed the ladders to reach the ripe apples destined to be on sale at Covent Garden market the following morning. At 1pm they trooped back to the barn where they had an hour to lunch on bread and cheese or jam, and a cup of tea. Sidney Whittington, the farmer, appeared at the barn door. 'How's it going?', he said, 'Everybody happy?'. There was a chorus of cheers. Sidney had been a little anxious a fortnight ago when the girls arrived. He had never employed women before to pick apples and was worried that they might not have the stamina to work such long hours but they had proved him wrong and he liked their cheery presence around the farm. Before they arrived he had had the barn cleaned out and erected a make-shift kitchen in a shelter next to it and also fixed up a copper boiler so that they could wash their clothes. He was very pleased with their work and wanted to give them every comfort. 'Coming in for a sing-song this evening?' he asked. He was happy for them to use the parlour and the piano in the evenings although it sometimes disturbed his four-year-old and one-year-old, but he would not have been able to harvest his crop without them and it was only for a month. There were some well-qualified musicians amongst the women and he enjoyed hearing them play and sing. 'Have you got enough food for supper?', 'Yes, thank you,' said Mrs Forster whose turn it was to cook, 'and a nice steamed pudding for afters.'

At two o'clock the whistle blew and they all returned to the fruit-picking in the orchard. As six o'clock got nearer the heat of the afternoon was beginning to tire them. Miss Greenfield got down from the ladder with her basket full. She wondered if the shift would end before she had time to start on another tree. She glanced towards the 'Sergeant' to see if he was about to blow his whistle, who nonchalantly turned away. Deciding to carry on picking, she moved the ladder, grabbed an empty basket, and climbed to the top of the tree only for a grinning Corporal Morley to blow his whistle glancing in her direction.

As they put away their ladders and left their full baskets for the carters to deal with they made their way back to the barn. A cup of tea awaited them and then they washed and changed, wrote letters, did some washing or just read until the supper was ready. Afterwards some went into Longford to do some shopping or made use of the piano in Mrs Whittington's farmhouse parlour for a musical evening. The long summer days in the open air, as well as the unaccustomed physical work, meant they were tired by nightfall when they were ready to climb the ladder into the barn loft to collapse onto their straw-stuffed mattresses for a sound sleep.

With the amount of creative talent amongst the assembly it was not long before someone suggested putting on a show at the end of their month's 'holiday'. In any spare time or breaks they worked on the words and music of a Gilbert and Sullivan-type comic opera. They called it 'Apples and Plums'. The action took place in the Merry Hoax Farm. The two main characters were the farmer who is adored by the pickers and who is flattered enough to flirt outrageously with them. The second main character is the gang-master, an old soldier with endless stories about his early love adventures. The plot culminates with the farmer, who is about to offer himself as a raffle prize to his adoring pickers, being embarrassed when his bride-to-be arrives on the scene.

On the last night of their stay people gathered for the eagerly anticipated concert. The farmer and his family, the farm workers, the lady from The National Land Council who organised the placement, and some of the fifty other women pickers who had been billeted around the village doing similar work in Harmondsworth's orchards, all crowded into the barn and perched on any available vantage point. A newspaper reporter was present to record the scene for his readers. Miss Kingham played the gang-master with 'delightful touches of realism' and Miss Greenfield was a 'most engaging' farmer. Four ladies performed the dance routines and the music was provided by an improvised orchestra using 'homely' instruments.[244] The concert was filmed and shown at a local cinema, but no trace of this film can now be found.

---

244   Middlesex Chronicle – Saturday 15 September 1917

The next morning, as the pickers packed up their belongings, there was time to reflect on the last month's work. The whole enterprise had been a success for all concerned. The farmer, after all his worries about managing his 300 acres with only one ploughman and general labour shortages, was pleased and relieved that he had his fruit crop harvested. The women, married and single, of all ages, had proved their ability. They went home feeling patriotic and fitter. After a month of complete contrast to their normal lives, they felt they could return feeling virtuous and to some extent smug that they had shown the nation that they were just as able as men. They vowed to return the following year.

A few months later, in January 1918, the same orchard had an unexpected visitor when a large bi-plane travelling south from the Midlands encountered a snowstorm. The pilot was attempting to land at Hounslow aerodrome when part of the fuselage became dislodge and caught in the propeller blades. He crash-landed in the orchard at Perry Oaks Farm where the girls had been picking three months earlier, and emerged from the wreckage unhurt.[245]

The barn at Perry Oaks that was used as accommodation for the apple pickers.
Now under Heathrow Terminal 5.

* * *

---

245   Uxbridge & W. Drayton Gazette – Friday 04 January 1918

The women working at Perry Oaks were breaking down barriers in all directions. They were proving to farmers that women were not afraid of hard work and were just as capable as men. They were showing other women that there was no shame in working in the open-air and that a suntan did not mark them out as lower class. The fruit pickers of Perry Oaks were showing people that farm work was respectable and classless – even patriotic. Society was changing.

Most women, in the early twentieth century, were full-time homemakers. Their role was to produce and nurture children, provide meals, and organise the home. Few married women in the 1911 census put an occupation next to their name. Daughters had to help their mother with the younger children in the house until they married or went into service. Upper class wives would do charity and church work as well as supervising the servants but could not do paid work. Culturally their husband's standing in society was diminished if he could not wholly provide for his family. Farmer's wives usually had help in the house and would also supervise the poultry and dairy work as well as manage the live-in farm servants. Women who had skills such as millinery or dress-making would work from home around their domestic duties. Single women and widows with no particular skills might work part-time in the fields picking and tending produce. At busy times of the year, i.e. harvest or strawberry time, all the available women and children were expected to help on the farm, but women were never paid the same as the men and they were only given jobs without responsibility. The 1914-18 war changed attitudes. Women could now prove their worth in areas beyond their domestic thresholds. It was patriotic to do something for the war effort, paid or unpaid, and for those with men away fighting in France it relieved their anxieties if they kept busy.

When war was declared it did not take long before various voluntary parish enterprises began. Within a month of the war starting, and in a plentiful fruit season, ladies began bottling and making extra preserves to donate to hospitals and convalescent homes. This was the start of groups of women passing on their household knowledge and skills to help others. In essence this was the start of the Women's Institute. At the same time the women of the whole parish of Harmondsworth, who wanted to make a positive difference to the lives of the men who had joined-up, came together to form a branch of the Queen Mary's Guild of Needlework. They knitted numerous socks and made items of clothing which were then forwarded to the front or to military hospitals.[246] Between August and the end of December 1914 they made a total of 904 garments which were sent, not only to the military, but to the Red Cross Society and to Belgian refugees.[247]

On the land there were manpower shortages. Before the war women earned less than half what a man was paid. The month before the war started there were 80000 women in permanent employment in agriculture in Great Britain. For unskilled girls and women, who did not go into service, their only chance of earning money was from working in all weathers and uncomfortable conditions doing poorly paid field work. Women were not thought capable, or willing, to do 'men's jobs' like carting or looking after the horses on the farm. By the end of the war more than three times the number of women were working nationally in agriculture thanks to a government recruitment drive. Some of these women were earning twenty shillings a week – more than a man earned before the war.[248]

Wages had to rise not only to attract women workers to the land but because the farms were competing with a new alternative occupation. In March 1917 adverts appeared requesting 100 girls to do 'light and clean' work in munitions at the Universal Music Co. Ltd., Hayes, Middlesex (later called EMI).[249] Although it was four miles away from Longford some women saw it as a better alternative than working all weathers on the land.

The farmers were losing their workforce in both directions but the prevailing attitude that women could only do light jobs was still present in employers' minds. It took a food crisis before there was a change in perception of women's abilities.

The Middlesex County Council created Emergency Committees in District Council areas. The Committee that covered the Harmondsworth area was chaired by county councillor, R.R. Robbins. At their first meeting they decided to expand their committee by adding five members and all the new additions were women. This was a departure from the culture of male-dominated parish governance.

246   Uxbridge & W. Drayton Gazette – Friday 15 November 1918

247   Uxbridge & W. Drayton Gazette – Friday 01 January 1915

248   Report of the Food Production Department for the year 1918. The National Archives MAF 42/8

249   Ealing Gazette and West Middlesex Observer – Saturday 01 December 1917

In the Autumn of 1915, as well as the Emergency Committees each County was asked by the Government to set up War Agricultural Committees. It had taken them over a year to realise that the pre-war reliance on imported food, plus crop failures abroad, were now leaving Britain with a potential food shortage. The 'War Ags', as most farmers called them, were charged with making land use more efficient and increasing food production. The following year each County established a Women's Agricultural Committee to work alongside the 'War Ag' to help with the recruitment and training of women. By May 1917 the 'War Ag' had established district sub-committees. The representatives for Longford were William Wild in the Weekly House and H.J. Jarvis from The Island, Longford (who later bought Bays Farm). The job of the district sub-committee was to identify spare pasture land that local farmers were willing to plough and sow using their own resources and to suggest other land that could be ploughed if the labour and equipment was available. As the fight to produce more food continued the Board of Agriculture spent more money on staff and equipment. The Middlesex War Agricultural Committee now had a Tractor Ploughing Department with eight full-time staff and four honorary staff. They had command of 20 American-built tractors in total (which was less than half the number requested) and they also had 79 horses to use on land not suitable for tractor ploughing. With the help of soldiers on agricultural furlough and prisoners of war they now had 1000 men working on the land.[250] Middlesex now had the quantity of men required but not necessarily the skills.

* * *

The people of Longford had always grown their own food in their cottage gardens, but for some people in urban areas it was a new experience. The government was now urging people to grow their own vegetables, keep a few chickens, goats, and rabbits (for eating), and town-dwellers were given allotments in parks and on waste land. They also supplied seed, livestock and advice. The 'War Ags' bought surplus crops from the householders and organised the supply of bottles for the local bottling of fruit and vegetables. September 1917 saw a total of fifty tons of sugar distributed in Middlesex to 3000 applicants who would make their fruit into jam to supply the troops.

---

250   Middlesex War Agricultural Committee Mtg held at Guildhall 11 March 1918 at
      4.30pm. London Metropolitan Archives. MCC/Min/43 /1

At the end of 1917 the Food Production Department of the Board of Agriculture was enlisting the help of the 137 Women's Institutes in England and Wales. A year later the Institution had grown to 744 branches. Today they are still the largest women's voluntary group in the United Kingdom. Harmondsworth formally inaugurated a Women's Institute at a well-attended meeting on 8 March 1919 with Lady Hillingdon and Lady Strafford as patrons.[251]

The Middlesex Women's War Agricultural Committee began the work of recruiting and training women to work on the land early in 1917. The aim was to organise women's labour to plough, milk, look after stock, as well as do valuable field work. Some women with previous experience were already working on the land and others formed into gangs for potato planting, hoeing, haymaking, potato spraying and general field or market garden work. To begin with many farmers, farm labourers and village women were hostile to the influx of women to work on the land and appalled at their mode of dress.[252] It was still unusual for a rural community like Longford to see a woman wearing trousers. Women's groups such as the Women's Farm and Garden Association and the Women's Legion were already recruiting and training girls to work on the land. Eventually, late in the war, the Board of Agriculture adopted these groups and their methods and the Women's Land Army was formed. Their uniform was a hat, an armband, and an overall.

WW1 land girls. Ada Finch (centre back) worked with poultry at The Farm, Longford.

Some of the Longford farms were allocated Land Girls and the Radio Times printed a picture of one group.[253] The girl at the centre back of the cart is Ada Gertrude Finch. She worked for the Wild's at The Farm as a poultry girl during the war. Before the war Ada Finch had been

251   Uxbridge & W. Drayton Gazette – Friday 11 July 1919
252   Howkings, Alun, *Death of Rural England*, (Routledge, 2003), p.32
253   Radio Times, Issue 820. BBC Radio, "Women on the Land" 21.30 21 June 1939.

working in her Father's draper's shop in Wood Green, London. She was 31 and had spent all her life in London when she volunteered with the land army and was sent to rural Middlesex. After the war she stayed in Longford and in 1925 married a market gardener, widower Edward Smith, who lived at Riverside farm. They had a son, Dennis, two years later and she remained in Harmondsworth until her death in 1954.

By the end of the war the value of the Women's Land Army was just beginning to be recognised when it was thought their jobs were needed for the demobilised men. However, with so many war casualties the numbers of men returning to the land was much lower than the workforce before the war. Those that survived the fighting had had enough of mud and deprivation. They wanted a cleaner, better paid, job in a factory. The Government, who now had increased acreage under cultivation, calculated that the agricultural workforce was short by 100,000 employees.[254] More women were needed so recruitment continued into 1919 when the basic weekly wage for trained women was raised to 25 shillings a week. [255]

By June 1919 the army was still demobilising and farm hands were being prioritised. Any farmer could apply for the demobilisation of a man on compassionate grounds and would "receive every consideration".[256] Meanwhile, to the south of Harmondsworth in the neighbouring parish of Feltham farm workers had started an unofficial strike over pay and hours. The men were demanding £3 for a 44-hour week and the women £2. After negotiations with the Executive committee of the Middlesex branch of the National Farmer's Union, (Chairman R.R. Robbins) the strikers settled for tenpence ha'penny an hour for a 54 hour week (£2 7s 3d a week) and the women seven pence an hour.

Another effect of the war on British farming was the increase in vermin. With men and horses all taking part in the war effort fox hunting had all but ceased, and the fox population exploded. Moles became another problem for the farmers and some Women's Land Army volunteers were trained as mole-catchers. Rabbits were also abundant due to a shortage of ferrets. The rabbits had bred rapidly after many ferrets were unofficially taken to France to get rid of the rats in the trenches. In fact to this day The Yorkshire Regiment has two ferrets as Regimental Mascots, a tradition started during

254   *Times* [London, England] 19 Mar. 1919: 14. *The Times Digital Archive*. Web. 27 Jan. 2018.

255   *The Times* (London, England), Saturday, Mar 15, 1919; pg. 7; Issue 42049.

256   Uxbridge and W.Drayton Gazette, Friday 13 June 1919.

WWI when soldiers used them in the trenches for the hunting of rabbits to feed themselves.[257] It seems believable that the ferrets also relieved the scourge of the rat-infested trenches. At home, schoolboys were encouraged to scavenge for vermin.

In March 1918 Mr Whittington, at Perry Oaks farm, started a club he called 'The Harmondsworth and Harlington Sparrow, Starling and Rat Club.' It was a way of reducing the number of grain-eating pests that fed on the growing crops. The young lads of the village would go hunting for vermin and get a reward for doing so. Between 1 March and 1 September the number of dead vermin delivered to 'headquarters' (Perry Oaks Farm) was 655 rats at two shillings per dozen, 586 sparrows at threepence a dozen, 308 sparrow eggs at tuppences a dozen, 33 starlings at four shillings per dozen, 15 starlings eggs at threepence a dozen.[258] The new season started on Saturday 5 October 1918 when mice were added to the pest list for which they were paid threepence a dozen.

The Board of Agriculture urged people to distinguish between house sparrows and hedge sparrows. Hedge sparrows fed on insect pests and were therefore useful and should not be destroyed whereas house sparrows were regarded as pests and could devastate the corn harvest.[259]

Not only were children helping with pest destruction, but in agricultural areas the Board of Education allowed children over 12 to forsake their schooling to help with the harvest.[260]

* * *

After the war the people of Harmondsworth subscribed to a memorial to those who had died. Although a large sum was raised the village decided against a large stone memorial deciding instead that a brass plaque in the church, listing the names of the dead, would be sufficient. The rest of the money, as befits a Baptist community where their way of life was governed by the words of the bible, was spent on giving every child a well-bound copy of the bible with an inscription inside the cover.

257   https://holisticferretforum.com/about-ferrets/ferret-tales/famous-ferrets/

258   Uxbridge & W. Drayton Gazette – Friday 04 October 1918

259   Middlesex Chronicle – Saturday 19 May 1917

260   Middlesex Chronicle – Saturday 25 August 1917

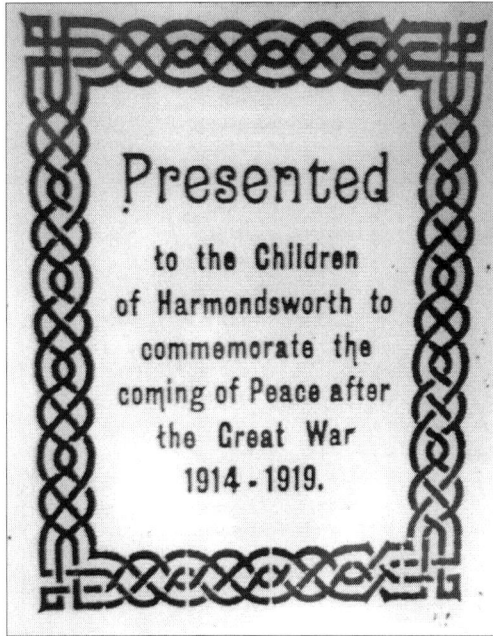

Presented to the Children of Harmondsworth to commemorate the coming of Peace after the Great War 1914 - 1919.

* * *

William Woodward lived at 4, The Square, Longford. His cottage was just yards from the river Colne. As a riverman he always wore thick rubber boots to work. In summer his job was to cut the weeds from the banks using a flexible scythe blade with a handle at each end. In winter the large mud boat was used to dredge the stream. When the boat was full of sludge he pulled up to mud landing, a shallow bank near Accommodation Lane, and shovelled it out. By ancient right anyone whose land bordered the river could have the rich black alluvial mud full of humus to put on the land, but they had to be aware that it also contained many weed seeds.

William, one of four rivermen living in Longford, was a big muscular man and was a popular choice to be anchorman for the tug-of-war team at the Peace Day celebrations. After a cold start to the month, Peace Day on 19th July 1919 was warm and dry when Harmondsworth celebrated with a sports day. It was a public holiday and there were races for people of all ages and a tug-of-war between the Harmondsworth villages. In spite of William's efforts and the encouragement of all the Longfordians the Longford team were beaten.

The farming community of Harmondsworth was changed by the war. The loss of ten percent of the young men on the battlefield, and the desire of the returning soldiers to have cleaner, better paid jobs in factories, had a large impact on the farmers and their ability to keep the land viable. Longford life changed; farming methods changed; and families changed. No longer did families perpetuate in the village through generations, and no longer was farming the main occupation. A new era had begun.

Chapter 24

A Village in Transition (1922-1937)

After the Great War motor cars were no longer a novelty in Longford although few villagers owned one. Occasionally one would stop at the Peggy Bedford whilst their occupants took refreshments before continuing their journey, but on 18 May 1922 there was a string of cars parked outside the old inn as well as a number of motorbikes. The press pack was in the village.

The editor of the Uxbridge and West Drayton Gazette gave his reporter a change from the routine reporting of weddings and funerals. He instructed him to 'Go to Longford and see the heavyweight boxer of Great Britain in training.' The reporter did not hesitate. He was on his way immediately; after all there was also a free meal in the offing.

He arrived to find that his chance of an exclusive report was unlikely. Another twenty reporters had arrived from London. Boxing was an exciting spectator sport with millions of fans eagerly anticipating every title fight. Frank Goddard had won the heavyweight title in 1919 and lost it a month later. He was to regain it again in 1923 but in the meantime he was training for a contest with another ex-heavyweight champion, Bombardier Billy Wells. They had both agreed to a 20-round match at £100 a side.[261]

Frank Goddard, nicknamed 'The fighting farmer', was a mountain of a man with a punch described as like a kick from a Clydesdale stallion. He had trained for his previous contests at the Ostrich in Colnbrook, but Mr Walter Shubrook, the publican of the Peggy Bedford, sensed a marketing opportunity and invited him to train at his hotel for his current fight.

---

261   Boxing World and Mirror of Life – Saturday 06 May 1922

Peggy Bedford Hotel 1922.

Frank Goddard

Goddard lived and trained at the hotel for all his subsequent boxing bouts. [262] Mr Shubrook had fitted out one of his large outbuildings, no longer required as stables, as a gym and with the open countryside around it was a perfect place for road training.

It suited both parties to publicise the training sessions. By generating interest in the fight the promoters increased their ticket sales and for the hotel the publicity increased its prestige and attracted more customers. An invitation went out to all the newspapers to send their representatives. They stood around the gym as Goddard went through his workout. He moved from punch ball, skipping rope, bag punching, sparring

262   Daily Herald – Friday 19 May 1922.

and then floor exercises. He was demonstrating his fitness and trying to demoralise his opponent with his confidence. His right-hand hit the punch bag, suspended from the roof, like a 'veritable mule-kick' and after a few such hard punches the bag collapsed and had to be rehung.[263] His expected sparring partner got lost on his way to the gym and another boxer, Sailor Tom Jones, although lighter, took his place, and suffered at the hands of a stronger man. After posing for photographs Goddard and the gentlemen from the press adjourned for lunch. Mr Shubrook supplied the lunch which was paid for by the National Boxing Syndicate.

Goddard's match with Bombardier Billy Wells took place at Crystal Palace on 27 May 1922 and Goddard won with a knockout in the sixth round. Billy Wells had been British and British Empire heavyweight boxing champion from 1911 to 1919. He was also the man seen hitting the gong at the start of J. Arthur Rank cinema films from the 1930s until 1948.

The training facilities at the Peggy Bedford became popular with boxers. The following year Dave Magill was living and training at the hotel. He was giving boxing 'demonstrations' every afternoon at 2.30pm which were open to the public.[264] He lost his fight with Jack Bloomfield on 17 May 1923 at Olympia, Kensington, London, and with it his Commonwealth Light Heavyweight title. The fame of the Peggy Bedford, and its association with so many events, attracted visitors nationally and internationally helped by Longford now being easier to reach by public transport.

Since 1902 several attempts had been made to extend a trolley-bus line along the Bath Road which would have involved overhead lines and rails in the road surface. Although there were objections the idea received the support of the licensee of the Peggy Bedford and local councillors, but Great Western Region Railway, who had a station at Colnbrook, objected to it. No one seem to consider the hazardous effect the sunken trolley-bus rails would have been to both bicycles and motor cars. Eventually the motorised bus brought regular public transport to Longford. The 81 bus route from Hounslow to Slough began in the 1920s and still runs this route today.

* * *

263   Uxbridge & W. Drayton Gazette – Friday 26 May 1922
264   Uxbridge & W. Drayton Gazette – Friday 11 May 1923

Number 81 bus outside the Peggy Bedford 1920.

People adapted and survived through catastrophic events but for Longford the Great War was the beginning of a major transition. For centuries life had continued unaltered for generations of village labouring families but now they no longer needed to be rooted to the village. Transport changes led to greater mobility. People no longer had to work where they lived and they had a greater choice of occupation. Large headquarter buildings for companies such as Technicolor, Black & Decker and Penguin Books were built on the edge of Longford, along the Bath Road.

On the farms mechanisation reduced the reliance on horses although they were still used right up to the Second World War. Some farms never went back to labour intensive market gardening but instead enlarged their orchards and increased their poultry and pig farming.

The type of resident in Longford was also changing and the bond of religious and family ties was loosening. Where once there were farmhouses and labourers cottages the dwellings were becoming homes for outsiders attracted by the rural setting and the proximity to London. Ancient farmsteads that had been in a poor state of repair for years were being demolished and new homes built in their place, which after 1924, had the luxury of mains electricity. Once the same family names were known in Longford for generations, but now new families were moving into the village. A few had show-business connections.

Riverside House was a large bungalow of eleven rooms next to the Duke of Northumberland's river. It was owned by William John Large in 1926. He was born in Birmingham, had emigrated to the United States in 1905, married and produced two daughters in rapid succession, Dorothy and Barbara. While living in New York William Large was doing whatever he could to make money. As his two pretty little girls grew up he and his wife dressed them in showy clothes and encouraged them to entertain the neighbours. The family moved to Grand Rapids, Michigan, where William Large found a job as a tyre salesman but a vaudeville theatre, called the Pastime Vaudette, had been built in the town in 1911 and the girls began performing there in their own comedic singing and dancing act. The talented girls were a hit with the public and their father was eager to promote them. In 1919 at the age of ten and eleven he took them out of school, gave up his job, and in August the whole family were on the American Line ship *Haverford* sailing from Philadelphia to Liverpool. Now known as Dollie and Billie they were soon performing in variety shows around Great Britain and were very successful. Their father was not slow to invest their earnings and bought an estate in Ayrshire as well as Riverside House in Longford.

Longford was a base for the family when they were not touring. Still teenagers, on 21 May 1926 the girls were appearing at the Tivoli in Melbourne, Australia, where they had a seventeen minute slot in a variety show. Their mother was with them but William Large was in Shoreham, Sussex, and a resident housekeeper, Mrs Lawrence, was at their Longford home. She was awakened by a dog barking at around 1am and found the house on fire. She just had time to grab a few clothes and save herself and the pet dog before the flames destroyed the house.[265] The Slough Fire Brigade did not receive a call until 2.45am and were there within 15 minutes. The Harmondsworth Brigade were already in attendance but no other brigade was called and the house was a mass of flames that did not subdue until around 5am. All that remained was a piece of wall and the remains of a glass veranda, and the only contents visible were the bath, cistern and gas stove. The cause of the fire, which started at the rear of the premises, was unknown. The site of this house is now a car space for a nursery school.

For Dollie and Billie their life as performers was short-lived. After touring Australia, the US, and South Africa they were mainly based in Paris

---

265   Daily Mirror – Saturday 22 May 1926: Uxbridge & W. Drayton Gazette – Friday 28 May 1926

by the end of the 1920s. It was here in 1930 that Barbara became pregnant and on 19 December her son, Marcel Large Taggart was born. It was not until the following March that she married his father in Berlin and they returned to his native Philadelphia later that year. Still touring, the sisters were in Tennessee with the baby when he was found dead one morning in his cot. He was two years one month and ten days old. The marriage ended in divorce. By this time vaudeville theatres were being converted to cinemas and the glory days for the sisters were almost over. Their parents returned to California and although the sisters continued to perform they no longer topped bills or played at the best theatres. One of their last performances was in a second-rate variety show at Worthing in 1932. Dorothy married a French Perfume salesman in 1934 and they lived in Santa Clara, California where she was a saleslady, but the marriage was short-lived. In the meantime their father had invested their earnings in a hotel and restaurant in San Mateo, California, and by 1940 the sisters, now 32 and 31, were helping their parents in the business. With only elementary education and their careers and marriages at an end they could do little else.

* * *

In the early twentieth century, when motorised vehicles were now mixing with horse-drawn transport, the traffic congestion on the Old Bath Road through Longford and the narrow bendy streets of Colnbrook was becoming a problem. The Middlesex County Council decided on a solution although not a new solution. As far back as 1799 a new road had been suggested 'by which the Colnbrook-Pavement could be avoided', and the distance between London and Windsor reduced by two miles.[266] The proposed new road 'would be very elegant' and part of the Windsor Park wall would be removed to make an entrance into Windsor by Frogmore. The plans were shown to King George III who approved them and the new road was awaiting the Treasury's approval, but the building of this new road never happened. It was proposed at a time when Britain was fighting Napoleon Bonaparte, and there were uprisings in Ireland. The Treasury funds were stretched. The proposal was aired again in October 1910 after the death of King Edward VII. A correspondent of the Times suggested that a new 'Royal Route' be built from London to Windsor to connect the Monarch's two main residences in a processional road built as a memorial to the

266   Bath Chronicle and Weekly Gazette – Thursday 28 November 1799

King. It would also be of permanent benefit to the people of London and would relieve congestion in the streets. The route should follow the Bath Road until a point near Longford where a new road would be built across country to avoid Longford and Colnbrook.[267] It was a good suggestion but nothing would be done for another fifteen years.

It was not until 1925 that the Middlesex County Council took action to start building the Colnbrook Bypass. The County Council's surveyors, however, had been at work prior to the plans being finalised. David Wild, grandson of H.J. Wild, was planting blackcurrant bushes with Alf Flaxman in a field next to Accommodation Lane, a lane that takes a semi-circular route alongside the rivers on the western boundary of Harmondsworth and Longford, when two men appeared who were driving pegs into the ground. The four men got into conversation and the strangers said they were surveying for a future Colnbrook Bypass. Alf Flaxman said to David Wild, 'These chaps don't know what they are up against making a road on this 'ere bungum.' (the local name for the London Clay soil in that part of the parish.)

The surveyor said, 'We shall soon get over a little difficulty like that.' They did, but the contractor, John Brook, went bankrupt because of it.

The Council set out the schedule for the compulsory purchase of land for the new road. Longford would effectively be marooned in a side road and its hostelries would lose the reliable passing trade. Bays Farm, then owned by Henry Jarvis lost two sections of land between the Dukes River and the River Colne. The Peggy Bedford had its four acres of ornamental gardens practically cut in half and William Wild and other landowners also lost land. The amount of land compulsorily purchased was minimal, but the inconvenience of having fields split by the new road and each section needing to be approached separately made cultivating inefficient and added to the farmers' difficulties.

The Peggy Bedford continued as a popular hotel and pub but when the bypass was being built in 1927 the owner, Harmon's brewery, built a new pub just 300 meters away at the apex between the new bypass and the old Bath Road. This was officially called The Peggy Bedford, in honour of the hostess of the historic King's Head. As well as transferring the licence in 1928, the landlord since 1921, Walter Edward Shubrook, also transferred

---

267   Windsor and Eton Express – Saturday 15 October 1910.

New Peggy Bedford when the Colnbrook bypass was still under construction. 1927.

with his family, to the new premises. He was there for less than two years when he died aged 58 but his wife and daughter then took over the licence and continued to manage the pub for another twenty years. The new building also had a hotel and off-licence.

When the old building was delicenced it was put up for sale. With its walls steeped in the tales of highwaymen and royalty it was sold to Mr A.C. White of London who leased it to Mrs Williams to run as a guest house. By then the once admired gardens still had a tennis court, summer house and walled kitchen gardens but they were only a quarter of their original size. The house itself was still substantial and there were cart-sheds, stables and pig-stys outside but the amenities were poor. It had gas, but no mains water and no main drainage. Water still had to be pumped from a well.

Some of the fixtures and fittings were transferred from the old building to the new Peggy Bedford to add an ambiance of nostalgia. The old pewter tankards were now rehung around the top of the bar, but the portrait of Peggy Bedford which had hung in the old inn until the beginning of the

20th century had been taken by a former landlord and its whereabouts is unknown.[268]

The new Colnbrook Bypass, which ran from Longford to Brands Hill, Buckinghamshire was opened for traffic on 19 June 1928, the first day of the Ascot Race Meeting.[269] Opening on this date was a relief for the residents of Longford and Colnbrook. In previous years vast numbers of motor buses and cars would clog the streets of the villages during Ascot Week making it dangerous for villagers to go about their business. This kept the local constabulary busy all day long directing traffic.[270]

Now that the bypass had removed the noise of passing traffic through Longford a different sound attracted the residents' attention. As well as motor vehicles becoming commonplace on the roads, aircraft were frequently seen overhead and neighbouring Heathrow was the source. In 1929 Fairey Aviation, who were making aeroplanes in nearby Hayes, were looking for a large flat area to use as an airfield to test fly their aircraft. About 150 acres of land, allocated to the Vicar of Harmondsworth in lieu of tithes in the 1819 Enclosure Act, came on the market at Heathrow and Richard Fairey, Chairman of Fairey Aviation Ltd, paid £15000 for it. He called the airfield The Great West Aerodrome. It was a grass airfield perfect for his biplanes to use for take-off and landing. On the side of the airfield he built a large aircraft hanger to store the planes.[271] It was an incongruous place to have an airfield being surrounded by the very productive orchards and fields of the Heathrow farms. To reach the airfield from either the Bath Road (A4) or the old Roman South West Road (A30) the visitor had to travel down a lane barely wide enough for two vehicles to pass, and the traffic competed with produce-laden horse-drawn farm carts and milkcarts, horses and tractors.

Flt-Lt C. S. Staniland was the chief test pilot for Fairey Aviation and on 11 September 1933 he was testing a new design of aircraft when, after taking off from the Fairey airfield, the plane went into a spin and dived towards the ground. He was unable to regain control and he made the decision to bail out at 1400ft.[272] As he jumped the downward velocity knocked him

---

268   Uxbridge and W. Drayton Gazette – Friday 19 October 1928.

269   The Times, Saturday, June 9, 1928, p.16.

270   Windsor and Eton Express – Saturday 5 July 1913.

271   Sherwood, P.T,.*Heathrow & District in Times Past.*, 1979 p.11

272   Larne Times – Saturday 16 September 1933

Fairey grass airfield and hanger 1930 surrounded by orchards and farmland at Heathrow.

back into the rear seat. Struggling to free himself he finally jumped clear of the plane at 700ft and opened his parachute. He landed safely in a field in Longford. The unmanned plane continued to zig-zag and then made a pancake landing, right way up, in a gravel pit near the new Peggy Bedford Hotel.[273] A witness described the incident as, 'A wonderful landing for a plane without a pilot'. The Fairey factory in Hayes sent out engineers to dismantle the plane before returning it to the factory.

More changes were to take place at Heathrow. The vast orchards at Perry Oaks, where the army of apple pickers had come to the rescue of Sidney Whittington during the war, was compulsorily requisitioned by the Middlesex County Council. In June 1933 the council bought the land for £33,000 and built a modern sewage sludge works. It processed human waste to be made into agricultural manure which was a boon for the farmers of Harmondsworth now unable to obtain the quantities of horse manure that once helped boost the productivity of the fertile soil. At the time of the requisition no one foresaw the growth of air transport. The sludge works

273   Northern Whig – Tuesday 12 September 1933

inhibited the layout of the future Heathrow airport with the two runways straddling the site, but it was a haven for rare birds for decades. It was not until 2002 that the works were removed and Heathrow Airport's Terminal Five built in its place.

Progress was not the only reason for change at Longford. In January 1934 there was a destructive fire at the former Peggy Bedford public house. No one was in the building at the time, but a neighbour, Mr Hunter, had been looking after the house for the owner. He was woken by the sound of crackling noises and found the house alight. The size and intensity of the fire caused the flames to be seen from miles away.[274] After sending someone for the fire brigade at Harmondsworth he did manage to drag some of his furniture out of his cottage as he feared that would be consumed too but the fire brigade fought to prevent that happening. The Harmondsworth fire brigade arrived five minutes after they received the call but the roof had already fallen in and the crew were hampered by the severe frost that made the roads slippery and reduced their supply of water. In the aftermath of the fire The New Peggy Bedford opened its doors at 2am to serve hot tea to the fireman. The tea had to be served by candlelight because the fire had knocked out the electricity supply to the village and, after falling beams damaged the gas main, the gas company had to be called at 3am to turn off the supply. The fireman did not leave the smouldering ruins until 7am the following morning by which time some of their hosepipes were frozen solid. However they were able to save the very oldest portion of the house at the rear of the main building which remains today as a Grade II listed building.

The fame of the old coaching inn prompted the disastrous fire to be reported in newspapers all over the United Kingdom. The reporters commiserated at the loss of the ancient building, its massive oak beams, great fireplaces and its skittle alley, and expanded on the legends associated with it.[275] The reports claimed that the inn was the headquarters of highwayman Dick Turpin; had been used as a meeting place for Charles II and Nell Gwynne; and had been used by Oliver Cromwell, but none of these stories can be substantiated. Charles II was fond of Windsor Castle and built a house called Burford House on the edge of Home Park at Windsor. He and

---

274   Uxbridge and W. Drayton Gazette – Friday 26 January 1934

275   "A Famous Inn of Former Times." *The Times*, 24 January 1934, p.7. *The Times Digital Archive*, http://tinyurl.galegroup.com/tinyurl/BYufx4. Accessed 20 August 2019.

Nell Gwynne used to meet there and it is possible they travelled through Longford together, and might have changed horses at the Peggy Bedford. Dick Turpin's connection is more tenuous. His 'hunting ground' had been the Great North Road and Enfield Chase so West Middlesex would have been an unlikely place for his headquarters.[276]

The original King's Head (Peggy Bedford) after the fire January 1934

The two great elm trees which stood in front of the hotel survived. Legend suggests Queen Elizabeth I planted them. One was hollow with age and people threw coins in it for luck, from which it gained the nickname 'Peggy's moneybox'. Later some of the materials from the burnt out building were used to construct a house alongside the ruin. It was called Phoenix Cottage and built in the Elizabethan style to match the surviving older part of the inn. The Tudor part of the old inn continued as a dwelling and between 1944 to 1947 the resident was Major-General Harry Foster and his wife.

The old Peggy Bedford frontage had now gone and with it the Queen Anne extension which had seen many royal visitors before the age of the train, but this was not the last visit Longford had from Royalty. On the Silver Jubilee of King George V's reign, on May 6 1935, at 3.45pm precisely

---

276   Coventry Evening Telegraph – Tuesday 23 January 1934; Wikipedia "Nell Gwynne"

the village excitedly greeted the appearance of a closed car flying the Royal Standard as it followed the old route to Windsor through Longford and Colnbrook. Within the car were Queen Mary and her son the Duke of Gloucester. Schoolchildren had gathered outside the new Peggy Bedford, each with a Union flag to wave and the car slowed to walking pace as it passed through the crowds of cheering villagers with the Queen waving and smiling in their direction.[277] King George V was due to visit Longford as part of his Jubilee celebrations but was unwell. Queen Mary, not wanting to disappoint the villagers of Longford, where every house was 'emblazoned with colour', fulfilled the engagement on his behalf.[278] The procession went on to Eton were the royal party alighted and got into horse-drawn carriages for the ceremonial entry into Windsor with military escort.

Four days later, as part of the Jubilee celebrations, a motorcade of fourteen buses and five ambulances brought 700 men from the St Margaret's Association for limbless men. The men had attended a service in St George's chapel, Windsor, after which they were transported to the new Peggy Bedford for tea.[279] The garden, which they 'greatly admired', was the only place large enough for a gathering of that size.

This was not the last of the royal visits. Two years later Longfordians had the chance to again decorate their houses and cheer their monarch. After the Coronation of George VI and Queen Elizabeth in May 1937, Mrs Shubrook, the licensee of the New Peggy Bedford, heard that the newly crowned Monarchs were to journey by car for a formal state entry to Windsor. She wrote to Buckingham Palace to request the royal car to slow down as it passed the Peggy Bedford in order that the school children of Harmondsworth could see the King and Queen. She received a favourable reply.

When the royal car containing the King and Queen and Princesses Elizabeth and Margaret got to Longford they found not only a thousand cheering children, but that the streets were lined with Scout and Guide troops from the surrounding district. Instead of taking the direct route along the bypass the royal car drove slowly past the pub and then through Longford village.[280] Every window of the Peggy Bedford was packed with

277   Sunderland Daily Echo and Shipping Gazette – Saturday 15 June 1935

278   The Uxbridge and West Drayton Gazette – Friday 21 June 1935.

279   Uxbridge & W. Drayton Gazette – Friday 10 May 1935

280   FROM OUR CORRESPONDENT. "Royal Visit To Windsor." *Times*, 7 June 1937, p. 11. *The Times Digital Archive*, link.gale.com/apps/doc/CS186462407/TTDA?u=bou_ttda&sid=TTDA&xid=bcf9292b. Accessed 19 Dec. 2020.

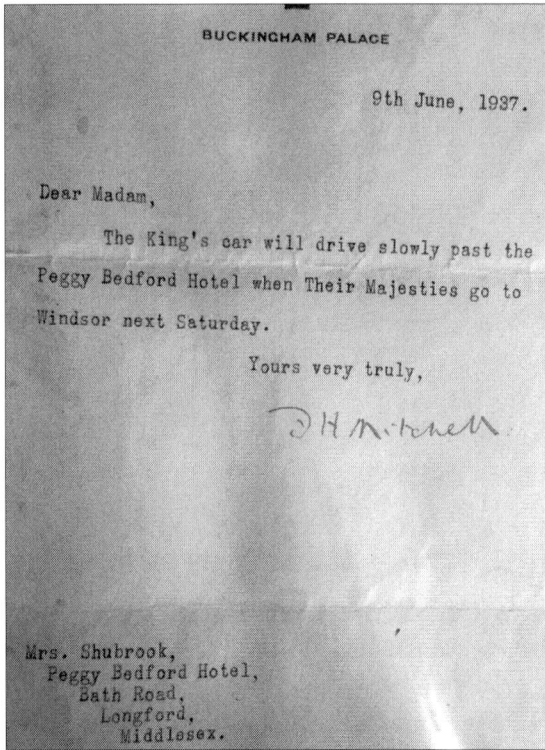

BUCKINGHAM PALACE

9th June, 1937.

Dear Madam,

The King's car will drive slowly past the Peggy Bedford Hotel when Their Majesties go to Windsor next Saturday.

Yours very truly,

D H Mitchell.

Mrs. Shubrook,
  Peggy Bedford Hotel,
    Bath Road,
      Longford,
        Middlesex.

Letter from Buckingham Palace to acknowledge Mrs Shubrook's request.

people and the Bath Road was thronged with spectators which the police struggled to keep on the pavements. There were so many cars looking for somewhere to park that Joseph Philp opened up his farmyard to allow more parking spaces.[281] The joy and excitement of seeing the monarch pass through Longford had not been experienced since Queen Victoria's day.

Less than a month later Longford was to experience another dramatic event when on the night of 6 July 1937, a passing lorry driver saw flames through the windows of the Peggy Bedford hotel. There were six people asleep upstairs who did not know about the fire until the lorry driver, Thomas Mills of Datchet, aroused them by banging on the door shortly after 2am. Mrs Shubrook the licensee and one of the men staying at the hotel made their escape down the main staircase but the others, assisted by lorry drivers who threw ropes up to the top windows, made their escape through the windows using hastily knotted sheets and piles of chairs. Harmondsworth

281   Uxbridge Gazette, June 18, 1937.

Brigade arrived on the scene promptly but soon after their arrival the roof collapsed. The fire appeared to have been burning in an unoccupied bedroom for some time before being spotted. The Harmondsworth and Staines Brigades stayed until midday but were unable to save the upper storey that was completely gutted. The ground floor was not damaged except for the torrents of water that had doused the flames. The following day it was business as usual for Mrs Shubrook and her daughter who opened the public bar, even though they were still a little shocked and bruised by their

Knotted sheets.

frightening experience the night before. They put their lucky escape down to Mr Mills, and the brewery that owned the Hotel praised the fire service.[282]

Peggy Bedford after the fire.

282   Uxbridge and W. Drayton Gazette – Friday 9 July 1937.

The affection in which 'Peggy' was held was reflected in the coverage by the newspapers who gave regular updates on the rebuilding after the fire. By November 1937 they reported on 'Peggy's New Hat' as the roof was completed, and in December 'Peggy's Coming Out Party' at which the vicar of Harmondsworth Rev. R. Ross made presentations to the two lorry drivers who rescued the residents during the fire. Also present were the members of the fire brigade. The afternoon tea party went on into the evening with the brigade and their engines sounding their bells as they left, bringing all the neighbours running to their doors.

* * *

At the Wild's farm, next to the Weekly House, farming continued although the crops were changing. Flowers were an increasing part of the Covent Garden market and the Wilds responded. David Wild, son of one of the four brothers managing the farm described the sight of huge clumps of Crown Imperial lilies being transported to Covent Garden 'standing majestically in bushel market baskets and tied on top of a cart load of produce with binder twine'. Crown Imperial lilies grew well in the rich fertile loam of the Longford farm where they were left undisturbed for many years. His grandfather, H.J. Wild, had originally brought the bulbs from his mother's garden at Langley in 1867 and planted them out at Longford. H.J. Wild also grew several acres of old double Van Sion daffodils on the land reclaimed from Hounslow Heath. Every second year the bulbs were ploughed out and the largest of them sold to a seed and bulb merchant, Watkins and Simpson of Feltham. This very old daffodil variety had been known since the seventeenth century and is still available today. Another flower H.J. Wild grew was Mrs Sinkins Pinks, which he was given by the lady herself who was the wife of the Master of Slough Workhouse, and who grew the pinks in her garden.

David's father, John Gregory Wild, had been living at Springbank but in 1927 he moved his family to land owned by the Wilds at Heathrow where he built a house, raised his two sons and grew vegetables, flowers and greenhouse fruit. No amount of foresight would have prepared them for what was to happen seventeen years later.

The Royal visits and two large fires were major events in the life of early twentieth century Longford and after the drama the community settled back into normal village life, but it wasn't to last. There were events going on in Europe over which they had no control. The politics of the rise of Nazism seemed a long way from rural Middlesex but the repercussions were to have a devastating effect on Longford and one Harmondsworth man found himself in the wrong place at the wrong time.

Chapter 25

Catalyst for Change (1939-1944)

George Mossman from Harmondsworth stepped off his train from London onto the chilly platform of Nuremberg station. He had visited this busy neo-baroque station many times and made his way to the platform where the train to Prague was waiting. It was March 1939 and although German politics were changing under the Nazi party George felt he could safely travel through the country whilst protected by his British passport.

The cold noisy station was bustling with travellers and the sound of hissing and belching steam trains was no different to George's previous visits but on this occasion there was a sombreness to the scene that chilled him more than the weather. Were there more people in uniform or was it his imagination?

As he boarded the Prague train he heard English voices and followed the sound to their compartment. He was on his way to the Prague Trade Fair and knew there would be other British people making the same journey. He settled into his seat next to the three Englishmen and joined their conversation.

'We drove to Nuremberg by car,' they told him.

'For the last twenty miles we passed nothing but German troops on the move' [283]

'Where are they going?'

'We have no idea. They must be relocating within Germany'.

---

283   Uxbridge & W. Drayton Gazette – Friday 07 April 1939

Had George known their destination he would have turned back, but he did not worry as he knew he would soon be safely over the border into Czechoslovakia.

When he arrived in Prague there was a lot of excitement in the streets. The people had heard that the Czech President had been summoned to Berlin. Loudspeakers in the streets were urging people to stay calm. The next morning, 15 March 1939, George Mossman, woke in his hotel bedroom and phoned the porter at 7am to ask for some tea.

The porter said, 'I don't know about the tea but I have just heard some terrible news.'

'What is it?'

'The State has been handed over to the Germans and the troops will arrive by 11am.'

George was now seriously alarmed. A year before he had been in Vienna when the Germans marched into the capital to annexe Austria. The reunification of Austria with Germany had been expected as part of Hitler's plan for a Greater Germany and many Austrians had welcomed it so there was no concern among people on the street. Neither was there much alarm among heads of other European countries, but now the Germans had invaded another sovereign country. This went against the Munich agreement.

George contacted a member of his export company, who was also in Prague for the trade fair, and they decided to leave together immediately. His colleague had arrived in Prague by a different route and did not have the normal visa to travel through Germany. Snow was falling quite heavily as they made their way to the German Consulate to get the visa but by the time the permit was issued they were too late to catch the train. On the way back to their hotel they turned the corner into Wenceslas Square and were met with an alarming sight. They came face to face with the first German troops driving into the City. The long line of military vehicles slowly paraded along the main road through hostile crowds of Czech people throwing snowballs, catcalling, whistling and shaking clenched fists whilst they sung the Czech National Anthem. Everywhere the devastated people were on the streets with ashen, worried faces showing their dismay and tears streaming down the faces of men, women and children. The people were walking about the streets in utter dejection, despair written on their faces, and almost everyone's eyes were red from weeping.

George and his colleague were relieved when they left Prague the next morning by train but became anxious when the train stopped at the border town of Pilsen. Here the passengers were turned off the train and told they had to make their own way back to Prague. The border was closed. They tried to talk to the German military staff at Pilsen but they were ignored. Then they met an American who had intended to travel by road to Zurich until he had been turned back. He offered to drive them back to Prague. He drove furiously and did not slow when he encountered German troops. Instead he sounded his car horn urgently and they, thinking the car was German High Command, moved aside. It had been snowing and the American deliberately drove in the puddles spraying slush and water over the troops as he passed them. Several times he was told to stop but he ignored the instruction and just kept going. In Prague there was a curfew at 8pm and rumours that Hitler had taken up residence in Prague Castle, the President's Palace, where he proclaimed that Czechoslovakia was now the German Protectorate of Bohemia and Moravia. George Mossman realised that with the closing of the borders, it was not enough to have a visa to cross Germany, they now needed a military permit to travel. The following day they went to the German headquarters to try to get a permit, but without success. They waited for hours but the German commander was too busy to see them. Eventually, with the help of the British Embassy, they and others with the same request got an interview with the German commander. There was little courtesy. They were told to line up in twos with Aryans on one side and non-Aryans on the other. The non-Aryan British were commanded to report to the police in their area. The commander said he did not have time to give them permits to travel and they should come back the next day. Eventually five British men, all in the export trade, who had been in Prague for the trade fair received military passes to travel over Germany to England. It seems the word 'export' was enough to impress the commander. They left Prague on the Saturday, five days after they arrived and four days since the invasion. On the way to the train station George encountered many people begging him to take their valuables out of the country for them. The Czechoslovakians, especially the Jewish community, knew their freedom and way of life was to change dramatically and were so desperate they were willing to trust a stranger to preserve some of their treasured possessions. It broke George's heart to refuse them. He was a kindly Christian man; a churchwarden at

St Marys Church in Harmondsworth; a scout leader; and a family man. He was always ready to help anyone, but he knew he would put himself in jeopardy if he gave any assistance.

Once on the train, however, he did voice his opinions to a lonely-looking German Air Force officer. George has been a pilot in the Royal Naval Air Service in WW1.[284] He loved to talk 'flying' with another pilot, but his 'interesting' conversation with the German made George's travelling companions nervous that they would all end up in a concentration camp.

When the British men finally crossed the border into Switzerland they were all very relieved and emotional after the terror of the last few days. It had been a frightening experience to find their British passports, a symbolic talisman that offered protection to its citizens, were regarded as worthless by German authorities.

George Charles Mossman returned home safely to his family in Harmondsworth. He had witnessed history in Prague, He had seen the effect oppression had on the people of an invaded nation and how the Nazi Regime could become unstoppable if Britain did not help defend countries against such aggression. For George, his experiences that week would stay with him for the rest of his life.

Now that Germany had broken the terms of the Munich agreement, the British Government realised Hitler's invasion plans could escalate. Poland looked likely to be his next target and Britain promised to support the Poles to prevent that happening. The United Kingdom prepared for war. Germany invaded Poland on 1 September 1939 and two days later Britain declared war on Germany. Everyone in Britain was galvanised into the war effort by the fear of invasion and a determination to prevent it. From the start of the war the government had learned from the mistakes made in the Great War and prioritised the land for food production. The County War Ags and the district sub-committees sprang into action in the same format as twenty-four years earlier. The Woman's Land Army was re-established at the commencement of hostilities, headed by Lady Denman who was also President of the Women's Institute.

The farms of Longford and Heathrow continued in full production at the start of the war, with the market gardens keeping London fed. Those villagers left behind after conscription were doing war work. This war was

---

284   Royal Naval Air Service became the Royal Air Force April 1 1918

Government poster.

different to the last one. This war was not one where the civil community's only role was to make socks for the soldiers and nurse the wounded on their return from distant fighting. This was a war in the air and the civilian population were all in danger. Longford held special attractions for the enemy bombers who dropped many types of bombs on, and around the Fairey airfield and the sewage works at Perry Oaks, and as a result the whole district suffered, particularly during the blitz of 1940.

Because of the fear of invasion sentries were posted at strategic points, such as the railway at Colnbrook and the Fairey airfield at Heathrow, and labourers going between fields were often asked to identify themselves. The distant thud of falling bombs and the sound of anti-aircraft guns now permeated the peace of the countryside. Air raid sirens sounded frequently but it was not until the night of 29/30 August 1940 that a bomb was dropped on the parish. A time bomb, dropped on the sewage works at Perry Oaks, exploded at 8.15am the following morning. A second bomb failed to explode. On 5 September about 80 heavy explosive incendiaries fell in a line along the Bath Road aimed at the large factories of Technicolor and Penguin Books on the northern side of the road but most fell on the farmland to the south. One fell in the garden of the Peggy Bedford and caused a crater 12 feet deep x 30 feet x 14 feet wide, which destroyed their ornamental garden.

The farmers worked the land by day and watched the skies by night; some became Air Raid (ARP) Wardens, and some joined the Home Guard. There was a certain amount of rivalry between the ARP wardens, and the Home Guard, but in February 1941 another group of volunteers joined the war effort. These were the firewatchers who had the job of watching for the dropping of incendiary bombs and trying to extinguish them before they could be destructive, sometimes just with the aid of a stirrup pump and a bucket of water. On the night of 26 February the fire watchers reported for duty at the ARP warden's post, signed on, and then stayed there nearly all night which inconvenienced the wardens who put in a complaint to the authorities. Another problem for the wardens was that soldiers on patrol or sentry duty in the district were using the posts to sleep in, and that off-duty wardens were making unauthorised phone calls. Each ARP post had a telephone, which few householders had at that time, and in this time of emergency it was the only way people could be contacted. The ARP warden's job was voluntary but they were given a uniform and an allowance for refreshments whilst on duty. This was one shilling and sixpence if they were on duty from 4-8 hours, and three shillings if they did 8-12 hours. If the air raid warning siren sounded during the day the wardens would help escort the children home from school.

Driving in the blackout was hazardous. On 21 February 1941 at 1.40am eight bombs were dropped on the sewage farm at Perry Oaks. They did little damage apart from one that landed on the road. A small car that was driving in the blackout along Tithe Barn Lane that leads from Perry Oaks to the Bath Road suddenly found itself in a bomb crater.

In the fields one of the new hazards for the workers was finding unexploded bombs or pieces of shrapnel where they were working, but on 7 June 1943 a large piece of an aeroplane's tail landed next to David Wild's field workers when a spitfire crashed in the allotments on Bath Road by the Police Station. The pilot had bailed out and landed a mile away. He survived but others were not so lucky.

Three months later, on 16 September 1943 a Halifax bomber, obviously in distress, flew low over Harmondsworth. As it flew over farmland alongside the Bath Road at Heathrow it jettisoned a bomb which blasted out the windows of a wide area. It then flew over Longford and Harmondsworth and blew up in a fireball as it crashed on the scrubby heathland of Harmondsworth Moor.[285] The petrol tanks exploded and all the joint British/Canadian crew lost their lives. Eight-year-old twins, Douglas and George Rust, witnessed this accident. To this day the boys are convinced the crew jeopardised their own lives to avoid landing on Harmondsworth village. Two days later three hundred people attended the combined church service held at the spot where the plane

Halifax memorial box

HALIFAX MEMORIAL

16 September 1943, a RCAF Halifax bomber crashed on Harmondsworth Moor whilst returning from a mission, with the loss of all seven crew.

F/O B. Begbie RCAF

F/O F.V. Webb RCAF

Flt/Sgt. A. Chibanoff RCAF

Sgt D.R. Coe RAF

Sgt H.W. Frost RCAF

Sgt A.R. Gaiger RAF

Sgt E.T. Potts RAF

crashed. As the years went by few remembered the sacrifice of these gallant airmen, but George and Douglas did not forget. In 1999 they persuaded British Airways, who now owns the land at the crash site, to erect a memorial on the spot where the plane crashed.

* * *

One week after the D-Day allied invasion of Normandy the Nazi's launched a fresh offensive on Britain.[286] A new unmanned flying bomb (V1) began targeting London. These bombs were first seen in London on 13 June 1944

285 A full account of this aircraft and the crew can be found at http://kenscott.com/memorial/halifax/
286 D-Day 6 June 1944

and two days later one reached Longford. It landed 200 yards along a track near the Weekly House. Although it left a relatively small crater (4 feet deep and 10 feet wide), the blast effect caused damage over the whole of Longford including making a large hole in the roof of the Weekly House. One person was injured by flying glass. It was not until March 1945 that the last V1 bomb raid alert was recorded in the Harmondsworth ARP warden's log book.

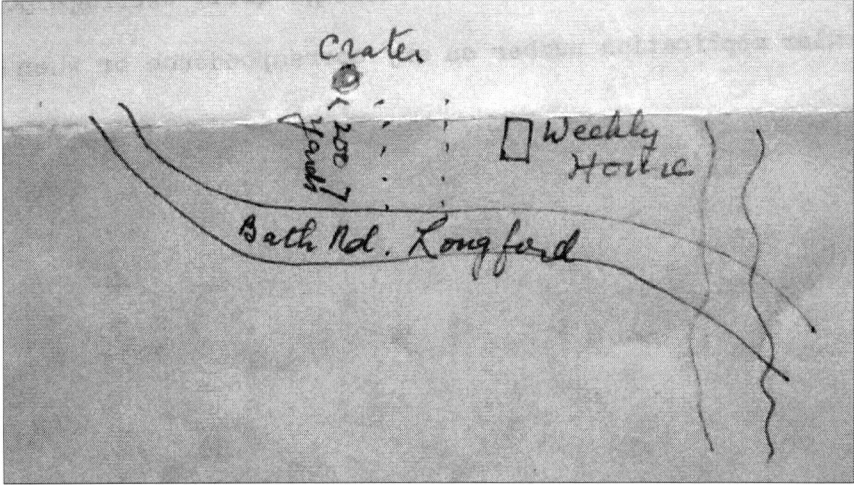

ARP warden's log book 13 June 1944. Diagram of where the flying bomb landed.

* * *

At the new Peggy Bedford Mrs Shubrook, after serving a customer with his requested drink, asked, 'Do you knit, sir?'

'Do I what?'

'Do you – er knit, sir?'

'Well ...."

'Here are two knitting needles and some wool. Would you be good enough to knit as much as possible, sir, while you drink.'

This request greeted most customers entering the public house. Locals, travellers, military personnel, all were working away knitting six-inch squares which would be joined together to make blankets. Mrs Peggy Shubrook, the landlady, got the idea when she was sitting behind the bar and a customer asked her what she was knitting. She explained she was knitting blankets for evacuated children. The customer remarked that it would take a long time to complete one blanket, so Mrs Shubrook asked if he wanted to help, to which he good-humouredly agreed. After this, Mrs Shubrook bought many needles and more wool and started asking the customers to join in. Not only were customers ready to help out, but Mrs Shubrook also extended the knitting to local people who for one afternoon a week would be served tea at the pub whilst they had a community knitting session.[287] This became popular and the knitting more ambitious; socks and scarves for Servicemen joined the output. Many newspapers around the country reported on Mrs Shubrook's enterprise and people began sending anonymous gifts of wool.[288]

Mrs Shubrook and customers at the bar of the Peggy Bedford

Fund-raising events were held in the village to raise money for more wool. At one Whist Drive, too many people arrived and some had to be turned away. Various people donated prizes at the event such as eggs, cake and groceries – a boon when food was rationed. A total of £5 was raised.[289]

287   Uxbridge & W. Drayton Gazette – Friday 27 October 1939
288   Uxbridge & W. Drayton Gazette – Friday 08 December 1939
289   Uxbridge & W. Drayton Gazette – Friday 10 May 1940

Other fund-raisers also took place to ensure there was a plentiful supply of wool. When the knitted items were completed they were parcelled up with a sprig of White Heather for luck, and sent to suitable military recipients. A parcel arrived at a Fighter Squadron who returned their thanks to the Peggy Bedford with a signed photograph.

Mark Whatmore, 73, knitting 'Socks for Soldiers' at the Peggy Bedford[290]

* * *

There were 1,965 residents in the whole parish of Harmondworth in 1939, but these numbers increased as bombed-out London families were billeted in the parish.[291] In September 1940 the Harvest Festival in the Parish church had the usual donations of flowers and produce around the altar and at the end of the service they were distributed among the local refugees.

Then in 1944 suddenly, and with little notice, the majority of the farmland at Heathrow and Longford was requisitioned under The Emergency Powers

---

290   The Illustrated, 18 November, 1939.
291   1939 Register.

(Defence) Act, 1939, which gave sweeping powers to the government to take 'possession or control, on behalf of His Majesty, of any property or undertaking'. Whereas land for other airfields had been commandeered at the start of the war Heathrow already had the Fairey airfield and the rest of the area was more valuable to the nation as a food source. However, secret government discussions had taken place, even before the war, about where to site Britain's first major civil aerodrome and the flatlands of Heathrow was one of those areas under discussion. This site was controversial and it was thought there could be major objections from various government departments and from Sir Richard Fairey, who wanted to retain his airfield. Now, with the war on, the Secretary of State for Air saw his chance to avoid getting entangled in public enquiries and planning legislation by using the wartime Emergency Powers Act to requisition the land. He made a case for building a big airport with concrete runways as a necessity for handling heavy aircraft to fight the war in the Far East.

This proposal was put before Cabinet in 1944 at a time when all the government efforts were being channelled into Operation Overlord and the D-Day landings. Prime Minister Winston Churchill did not want to be distracted by thinking about the location of a civil airport, and the 3000 men it would take to build it, and proposed deferring the decision for six months. This worried the Secretary of State for Air because if the D-Day landings were successful the war would soon be over and they would not be able to use the Emergency Powers. A revised, less ambitious, plan for the airport was submitted and the Cabinet yielded.[292] The eviction notices were issued.

Just a month before the 6 June D-Day invasion, the Air Ministry sent out letters to requisition seven farms, a beer house, and the Fairey airfield at Heathrow. John Wild from Longford, who had settled his family at Heathrow in 1927 and built not only a house and greenhouses, but a thriving market garden, received a letter from the Air Ministry. It was originally dated February 1944, but because of the delay caused by Churchill's reservations the date had been crossed out and amended to 2 May 1944. They were required to vacate their farm by 24 July. They had just two months to dismantle what they could of their glasshouses and outbuildings, harvest as many crops as they could whilst leaving many growing crops in the ground still to reach maturity, and to find somewhere

---

292   Sherwood, Philip, *Heathrow: 2000 years of History,* (Stroud, 1999), p.70

else to live. For most people losing their home would have been difficult enough but the Wilds were also losing their business and source of income. The final paragraph of the eviction letter warned them that under the Defence Regulations they were forbidden from making any sketch, plan, or other representation (photograph) of a prohibited place and so now few photographs remain of the farms of Heathrow.

As the bulldozers moved in and construction of the runways began it was clear that this high-quality fertile soil would soon be buried under tons of concrete and the growing of crops that supplied eager Londoners at Covent Garden would be no more. What wasn't clear, at first, was the impact the airport would have on the neighbouring village of Longford but it soon became apparent.

Chapter 26

The Demise of Farming (1946-2013)

Almost as soon as the civil airport was opened in 1946 more space was needed. Another compulsory purchase was made by the Government, in 1948, for the expansion of London Airport. This time it included many of the Longford farms. The land owned by the executors of H.J. Wild, i.e. his sons, at The Farm, was reduced by 60 acres which included the loss of two houses, five cottages and farm-buildings. Mr H.J.C. Jarvis of Bays Farm lost 33 acres. A total of 754 acres of land, 4 farmhouses, 28 cottages, 2 bungalows, many farm buildings and a public house were compulsorily purchased. The peripheral parishes also lost land.

It was the end of farming in Longford. The whole of the eastern side of the village was lost to the airport. To the west a few fruit farms with orchards and compact market gardens existed for a while, but they were too small to be viable. Land was sold off and houses and apartment blocks, industrial buildings and carparks grew up along the Bath Road and gradually covered the farmland. The original plans for the runway layout for the 1944 airport would have erased the whole of the parish of Harmondsworth from the map but time, money and man-power was scarce and a compromise was made to just build half the original plan on the land south of the Bath Road with further expansion left for the future. As the airport evolved, especially as aircraft became larger and air traffic busier, the airport needed more space. There were many attempts to expand the airport over the whole parish which left it blighted and with an uncertain future.

Farming and labouring families alike moved to new farming areas, and with them went what remained of the Baptist 'glue' that held them together, The remaining four Wild farmers, sons of Henry James Wild

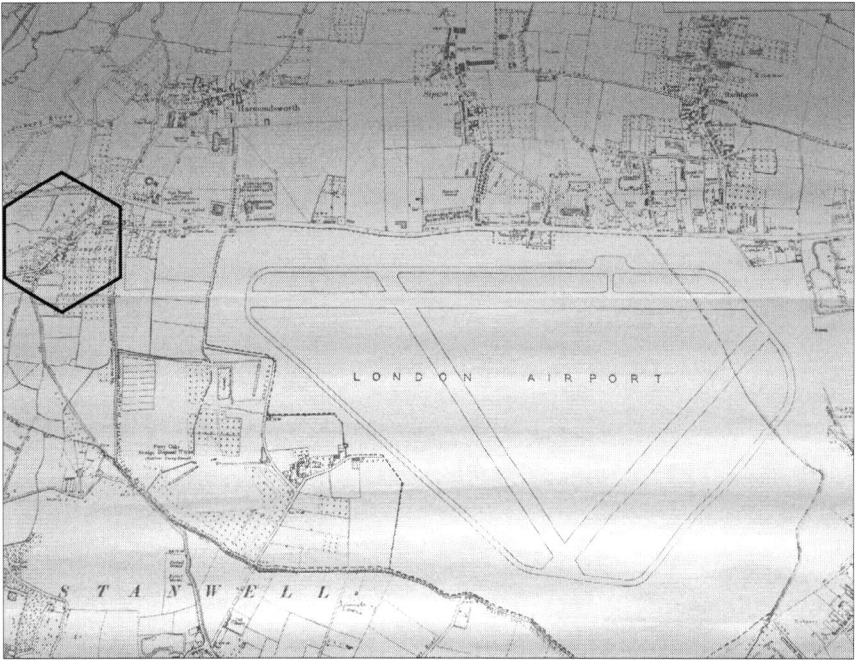

The modified runway layout plan. Longford highlighted. 1946.

gradually left farming, William Henry Wild, who was the eldest son, died leaving no son to carry on the farm. From an early age he had devoted much of his time to community affairs. Not only did he take on his father's responsibilities at the farm and played his part in the farm's prosperity, but he helped with the administration of the Harmondsworth local charities. He was a member of the Staines Rural Council for 30 years, a volunteer with the Colnbrook Volunteer Fire Brigade for forty years, a trustee on the Staines Board of Guardians, and a member of the Harmondsworth Parish Council. In his younger days he was also a well-known cricketer. He had lived at the Weekly house for 40 years, but three years before his death he had a bungalow built which he called Wildhurst where he lived for his remaining days. He died there on 3 April 1943 aged 74. He is buried in the family grave in Harmondsworth.[293]

At The Farm was his brother Charles and wife, Esther, who lived there with a farmhand lodger. They had managed the farm throughout the war with the help of the Women's Land Army. Five years after William Wild's death Charles also died aged 66. He and his wife, Esther had no children.

293   Obituary. Uxbridge & W. Drayton Gazette, Friday 9 April 1943.

Another brother, John, who had been farming with his two sons at Heathrow until his land was requisitioned, moved his family to Essex to continue farming. They were the last of the Longford Wilds in farming and even after moving away still thought of Harmondsworth as home and would make annual nostalgic visits. The fourth and youngest brother, Henry Josiah Wild, who was not in the best of health emigrated to Canada to be with his son, where he died in 1974. He had been standing in the farmyard in the morning of 1 October 1956 when a severe thunderstorm with strong winds and lightning suddenly blew up and he saw coming out of the low clouds the triangular shape of an RAF Avro Vulcan. The new prestigious British bomber, capable of carrying nuclear weapons, was the first Vulcan to be delivered to the Royal Air Force. So proud were they of this new acquisition that they immediately took it on a 26,000 mile goodwill tour of the Commonwealth. On this October morning in poor weather it was landing at Heathrow from Australia at the end of its tour.[294] A large crowd of dignitaries, press and onlookers were waiting at the terminal for its arrival. Because of the atrocious weather conditions the pilot had been advised to divert to another airfield but the senior officer on board, Air Marshal Sir Harry Broadhurst, not wanting to disappoint the waiting welcoming party, decided to attempt a landing.[295] Its approach to the runway was initially too high, but then the glide path was over-corrected and the aircraft become dangerously low.

At Longford, short of the runway, the wheels hit the ground in a Brussels sprout field belonging to the Wilds, severing the undercarriage. The aircraft then bounced onto the runway and burst into flames.[296] The pilot and the Air Marshal ejected from the plane and were unhurt, but four other passengers had no means of escape. It was a sad and disastrous end to the Vulcan's goodwill journey.

The 1950s marked the end of an era for the Weeklys and Wilds who for nearly three hundred years had dominated the farmland and village of Longford. The last member of H.J. Wilds family to live in Longford was his daughter, Marian Light, who with her husband, the Baptist preacher Alfred Light, lived at Walnut Tree Cottage, 551 Bath Road, Longford. Alfred died in 1954, and Marian died five years later. They had no children.

---

294   Birmingham Daily Post – Wednesday 03 October 1956

295   https://en.wikipedia.org/wiki/1956_London_Heathrow_Avro_Vulcan_crash

296   https://web.archive.org/web/20080418062038/http://www.thisislongford.com/heathrow.htm. Wikipedia: https://en.wikipedia.org/wiki/1956_London_Heathrow_Avro_Vulcan_crash

Walnut Tree Cottage, 551 Bath Road, Longford. 2018.

Longford, stripped of its farming and non-conformist heritage now became home to a different type of resident and many of them were connected with the new airport. The first Commandant of the Civil Airport at Heathrow, which opened in 1946, was Air Marshall Sir John D'Albiac.[297] He and his family moved into what was then called The Stables which is now the Grade II listed remains of the original Peggy Bedford. He lived there from 1947 until at least 1955. It was under his command that the airport developed the two east/west parallel runways rather than the triangular runway system originally built.[298]

Later, his successor moved his family into the village. Mr George John Warcup was appointed deputy general manager in charge of Heathrow operations by the new British Airports Authority when it began in 1966. He had been commandant of the airport since 1960. He was living with his wife and two children at 501 Bath Road, a large house that is now a nursery school, when he died suddenly in 1970 at the age of 58.

The Warcup's next door neighbour, in Longford Cottage, the current name for the former Quaker Meeting house (493 Bath Road) was the grandly

297 For a Ministry of Information Film about the building of the airport see https://archive.org/details/london_airport_TNA/london_airport_TNA.mpg

298 http://news.bbc.co.uk/1/shared/spl/hi/programmes/the_day_britain_stopped/timelines/heathrow/html/1940s.stm

named Alexandrina Georgina Lexlie Maclaren. She had been living there with her husband since before WWI and when her husband, Ian Maclaren, died she continued to live there in an eccentric fashion. Her neighbours believed she was nocturnal, sleeping by day and awake at night. She was very old, wizened and with wild hair. A large horse-chestnut tree in her garden produced huge conkers but the children of the village were too frightened to venture into her garden to collect them. If she saw the children she would come out of her front door looking like the witch from a fairy tale shouting and threatening them. She died there in June 1986 aged 82.

Some of the Longford residents still had family connections in other parts of the parish. George Charles Mossman, who had witnessed the invasion of Prague, lived with his family at the Sun House, the former pub next to the church in Harmondsworth village. He and his family played a full part in the community. As well as being a Church Warden and a Scoutmaster, he was also President of the Tennis Club and two of the long-term members of the club were Betty and Victor Newell who lived at Heath Gardens, Longford. They lived opposite the Weekly House now empty and forlorn. After William Wild moved out in 1940 it had been used as an ARP post and Home Guard HQ during the war. It was now in need of serious renovation to prevent it going the way of several ancient properties in Longford which were demolished and replaced with modern residential housing. In 1948 George Mossman's son-in-law, Christopher Challis, the renowned cinematographer, bought it. He had the dedication to restore the house and preserve the building for future generations to enjoy.

Restoring the Weekly House was not an easy or quick job with the post-war shortages of building materials but Christopher Challis with the help of the well-respected local blacksmith, Tom Adams, renovated the house, bit by bit. The roof was repaired with appropriate tiles, not the modern ones used for a quick patch after the V1 bomb damage, and two new dormer windows were added to give the attics rooms more light. On the northern side of the ground floor was a cool store room with hooks for storing hams and next to that a white washed dairy. On the eastern wall of the house was a large single-storey kitchen with a huge fireplace matching the one on the other side of the wall in the morning room, where a century earlier the lightning bolt had struck Richard Weekly. As well as the kitchen there was a boot room, log store and an outside privy. The two main rooms had huge beamed fireplaces large enough to stand-up in, with recesses in the chimney for smoking hams. These fireplaces and those of the bedrooms all connected to the central chimney. Christopher Challis turned one of the bedrooms into a bathroom on the first floor where there were two large square bedrooms and a smaller one. The beautiful staircase with wooden banisters continued up to the attic on the second floor where there were two large rooms and a box room. Behind the panelling in the southern attic room was a secret cupboard that at one time had a hidden passageway that led, via irons set in the brickwork of the central chimney, to the hallway. The derivation of this 'priest-hole' is still a mystery to be unravelled. Christopher Challis and his wife Peggy brought up their three children in the Weekly House and once more it became a family home.

Outside the Weekly House there was an ancient granary on staddle stones and a large late seventeenth century weatherboarded barn with a tiled roof and queen post truss construction built in the traditional way with wooden pegs and no nails.

The interior of the Weekly House barn.

In the garden were still remnants of the once productive orchard. There was a peach tree on a wall and pear, apple, walnut and fig trees as well as a huge mulberry. Other trees produced plums, greengages and apricots all carefully bottled by Mrs Challis for the winter. The Weekly House was given a Grade II listing in 1974 by English Heritage and after three centuries of being a family home is now in regular use as office space.

Although farming as the main source of work and income died out in Longford mid-twentieth century it did not diminish the value of the village. After the little Baptist chapel, built by Richard Weekly, closed to worshippers in 1971 the village became secular and residential, but it was no less loved by its inhabitants. The Hillingdon council recognised its uniqueness by making it a conservation area in 1988 and after Terminal Five was built on the remains of the Perry Oaks sewage works in 2008 Heathrow Airport Limited commissioned an 'Assessment of Potential Effects to the Historic Environment Resource' specifically as it related to Longford. The report was published in August 2011 and as well as listing all the historic buildings in Longford recognised that the village was 'an historic settlement of possible Saxon origins'.[299] Heathrow Airport Limited proposed to erect a five metre high noise barrier at Longford along the edge of the realigned Duke of Northumberland's river in August 2013. However, The London Borough of Hillingdon referred the matter to the Mayor of London who refused the planning application.

Present day Longford, still with two working public houses, continues to be a place for the travelling public to rest and refresh and is still a place of contrasts – a rural, tranquil, residential village sat next to a behemoth of modern transport technology. It seems Longford's glorious history is forgotten and unappreciated but while its buildings remain they are a reminder of the part Longford played in the panoply of history.

---

299   https://planning.hillingdon.gov.uk/OcellaWeb/iewDocument?file=dv_pl_
      files%5C41573_APP_2013_1288%5CAppendix+O+Assessment+of+Potential+Ef-
      fects+to+the+Historic+Environment+Resource.pdf&module=pl

Chapter 27

Longford in Limbo

Longford today has about a hundred dwellings as well as a guesthouse, two pubs, several small apartment blocks, a children's nursery and some business premises. Where once the villagers had a choice of food retailers to satisfy their needs now the nearest shop is at the Petrol Filling Station on the Colnbrook bypass. Many twentieth century houses have been added on former farmland but the introduction of the conservation order in 1988 ensured subsequent planning applications complied with the integrity of the historic centre of the village meaning that many of today's features would still be recognizable to its Tudor residents.

Walking through the village today there is an ambiance of tranquillity and serenity despite the aircraft noise. It is nostalgia exemplified. There is no litter, no untidy grass verges, and every garden is neat and floriferous. Some of the ancient buildings are currently unoccupied and neglected because of the uncertainty over their future. The village has a children's playground and a relaxing biodiversity area with seating between the trees.

We will take a walk through Longford and remind ourselves of the history of its Grade II listed buildings, ignoring the twentieth century buildings. Just as you enter Longford today, hardly noticeable against a carpark fence, is the stone that announces that it is 15 miles from Hyde Park Corner in London.

The milestone marks the point where the main Bath Road (now the A4) separates from the original Old Bath Road which enters Longford village. On this junction once stood the new Peggy Bedford, a local landmark which was demolished in 1993 amid protests. In its place is now a McDonalds and a petrol filling station.

The Milestone.

The Turnpike Pump.

A little further on from the milestone, preserved as a relic of bygone days, is one of the original wayside water pumps installed by the Colnbrook Turnpike Trust to damp down the dusty baked-earth road in the summer months, and used up until the first world war.

Beyond the Thistle Hotel (itself built on Fairview Farm, a large prosperous enterprise until 1968 when the last of its land was bought to build the airport perimeter road) only buses and bicycles are allowed to drive into the village from the easterly direction so we must proceed on foot to find the history around us.

Mature trees frame the road as it welcome us into the village. On the right, behind an impressive brick wall, is a detached neo-Elizabethan house with fake leaded-light windows that was built out of the remains of the old Peggy Bedford when it burnt down in 1934.

Beside that and set further back, just visible through the trees, is the original Tudor building of the old Peggy Bedford (King's Head) that welcomed monarchs and highwaymen, bigamists and prize fighters. Next to this building is a separate ancient stable block with an early diamond mullioned window, aligned with the road and as old as the house.

The original Peggy Bedford 2018.

Old Peggy Bedford stable block 2018.

Both buildings are Grade II listed and on Historic England's Heritage at Risk Register 2020. These structures have been witness to the evolution of travel throughout the centuries, and were known for so long, nationally and internationally, by the name of its former landlady that its original name has long been forgotten.

Almost opposite the former inn behind tall trees is a building, set at right-angles to the road, which was originally a Meeting House of the Society of Friends (Quakers) visited by the Society's founder, George Fox in 1681, and where 120 devout followers of the Society are now buried and forgotten under the car parking area of this now Grade II listed residential house.

The Friends Meeting House 2018.

A few metres further along the Bath Road we encounter the first of four bridges. This one is called Longford Bridge and is barely noticeable until one looks over the brick wall. The river that flows under the bridge is the Duke of Northumberland's river, a man-made tributary from the Colne river originally built during Henry VIII's reign to boost the supply of water to the Mills at Isleworth and Twickenham. The mills were owned by Syon Abbey until 1594 when it became the property of the Duke of Northumberland and now still flows into the gardens at Syon Park.[300]

As a private river it caused problems with the authorities as no bridges could be built or utility pipes allowed to cross the river in case it interrupted the flow of water. The inconvenience of having to ask permission to do any work near the river encouraged the Middlesex County Council to buy the freehold in 1930.[301] The river once flowed in a straight line south but it was diverted around the airport perimeter during the building of the airport. It continues to flow through Stanwell and East Bedfont and onwards to join up with the River Crane before reaching Syon Park.

Duke of Northumberland's river 2018.

As we walk across the bridge, we see some discreet factory buildings and then a large three-story block of flats called Bays Farm Court. This was where Frederick Heyward farmed before he went to war in 1915 and where Helena Du Rose lost her life in a carting accident.

On the left is a white cottage with a front door opening onto the pavement called Orchard Cottage. Externally it looks like an early to mid-19th century

300   https://www.syonpark.co.uk/explore/our-history/arrival-of-the-percy-family
301   Radcliffe, C.W., *Middlesex*, (London, 1939), p.170

building but internally it is a timber-framed building dating from the 16th century. It is Grade II listed and was once a farm and the house was part of a larger group of buildings.[302] The farm came into the possession of the Wilds and various members of the family lived there at one time. It is now a private residence.

Orchard Cottage 2018.

It might be worth mentioning here, that if you are following this walk on Google Street View Orchard Cottage is the last listed building visible. The street view cameras have not venture into the centre of the Conservation Area of Longford.

The earliest buildings in the village are timber framed, some with later additions. In the centre of the village, about 100 metres from Orchard Cottage, is an area called The Square which used to be the village green until a former landowner built two cottages on it (Maywin Cottages). Opposite this is a house called Yeomans whose original timber framing is exposed. Yeomans, which is now divided into three apartments, dates from

---

302   British Listed Buildings. https://britishlistedbuildings.co.uk/england/heathrow-villages-ward-hillingdon accessed 11/7/2019

the 16th century. This Grade II listed building was once owned by Thomas Streating, and inherited by the Weekly family in 1773 who divided it into three to house their labouring families.

Yeomans. 16th Century Grade II listed building. 2018.

Opposite Yeomans is the White Horse, a Grade II listed building which has an internal timber frame dating from the sixteenth century and an outer cladding of brickwork dating from the 18th century. It is still in use today, as it has been since the 16th century, as a hostelry selling food and drink. The inn serviced locals and travellers alike, although it did not have the capacity for the volume of coach trade that was enjoyed by the Peggy Bedford, but it is a survivor and today it remains a destination for a good meal in a rural setting.

Next door to the White Horse is a quintessentially old-world thatched cottage. It is locally listed by the London Borough of Hillingdon because of its contribution to the street scene. Internally it is of a similar age to the inn next door. It is beautifully thatched, with a thatched well-cover, but it did not always look like this. Until it was sold in 1976 it was called White's Farm and had a conventional tiled roof. The sale of White's farm ended a long line of members of the White family growing market garden

The White Horse 2018.

produce. From a large packing shed they sold vegetables, fruit and nuts, chickens and eggs, with Mrs White supplementing these provisions with home-grown flowers, jam and pies. It was renamed Ash Tree Cottage after it was sold but is known to everyone as 'Thatched Cottage'. Until 1976 it had no bathroom and an outside toilet. In the early twentieth century it was the venue for the village's annual Guy Fawkes night when a large bonfire would be built on the field at the back where the farm borders the river.[303]

On the other side of the White Horse facing onto The Square is a building now divided into two dwellings called Queen River Cottage, (526 Bath Road) and Willow Tree Cottage (528 Bath Road). Both are Grade II listed because of their 1739 origins. They are known locally as 'The Barracks' as they were originally built to house the militia who patrolled the Bath Road and Hounslow Heath to protect the travelling public from highwaymen. Between the two buildings used to be an archway which led to the stables for the militia's horses.

Walking past these cottages, away from the Old Bath Road, brings us to the bank of the Colne river and a four-acre island in between two tributaries. The Island House, where Thomas Willing ended his days and T.J. Toovey enjoyed his retirement, was replaced in the 1960s by a block of four apartments. There was a water mill on this island mentioned in the Domesday Book. The mill had variously has been used for flour, paper,

303   Middlemiss, Rosemary Padgett, *Memories of Longford and Harmondsworth,* (2015)

Thatched cottage 2018.

"The Barracks" 2018.

calico and silk manufacture. The building that replaced the Mill in late-Victorian times is Colne Cottage listed by the Borough of Hillingdon because of its architectural interest and there is another building on the Island of a similar age and interest. Today the Colne flows peacefully on its way to the Thames at Staines in a tranquil rural setting as it has done for millennia.

After leaving the island and returning to the Bath Road we see a square house almost opposite the Thatched Cottage, called Springbank, once a market garden of nineteen acres lived in by various members of the Wild family.

Colne Cottage 2018. Built on the site of the old water mill.

The Colne river at Longford 2018.

Springbank 2018.

Next, we see the long low building beside the pavement that was the Forge, behind which are the apartment blocks of Blacksmith's Court, built where the wheelwright's house, barn and three cottages once stood. It was here that kind, gentle, God-fearing William Passingham lived with his ill-chosen bride who brought such shame and loss of reputation to him that he emigrated to South Africa. The Forge is not listed but has existed since at least 1740 when bell-maker Thomas Swain lived and worked there.

A little further on from the Forge is a group of modern office premises. This is where the dominant farm of the Weeklys and Wilds was situated.

The farmstead, barns, granary and stables have all gone but the house that Thomas Weekly moved into in 1679, and where Richard Weekly was struck by lightning, is still there. This Grade II listed house whose bomb-damaged roof was repaired by Christopher Challis and who was also responsible for its restoration is now magnificently preserved. The

The Forge 2018.

The Weekly House 2018.

adjoining ancient long black weather-boarded barn, also Grade II listed, has not been so lucky and is badly overgrown with ivy and nettles. This is on Historic England's Heritage at Risk Register for 2020.

The Weekly Barn, July 2018.

Beside this barn, is the Kings Arms, not listed, but at least 200 years old. It was the place where Joseph Reynolds was robbed by two women in 1839. It had many landlords through the centuries, and despite all the changes in Longford it continues as a public house and is a welcome addition to village life.

Opposite the barn is the little side road called Heathrow Close, with a Guest House on one corner and a large square red-brick building on the other. This house is Heath Gardens, a listed building, built late eighteenth century, which once had five acres of orchards, under planted with soft fruit bushes, and with pigs snuffling between the trees. This was where retired greengrocer Walter Fewell lived at the beginning of the twentieth century and before that the house had belonged to the Heath family, an extensive Baptist family that had farmed in Longford for centuries.

Heath Gardens. 550 Bath Road, Longford 2018.

The Kings Arms 2018.

As we approach the end of the houses at Longford there are some post-war properties on the left where once the Prince of Wales public house stood. The last building on the right hand-side, a single storey building attached to two two-storey cottages, is the Baptist Chapel, built by Richard Weekly in 1859 after his survival from a lightning strike at the Weekly House. The wonky chimney no longer exists, but a plaque on the outer wall denotes that it was the Zion chapel. After the last Sunday School was held there in 1971 it became a private house.

The Baptist Chapel. Now a private house. 2018.

The final listed structure in Longford is at the end of the village where the road crosses the King's river. It is the cast iron bridge that William IV had erected in 1834 to replace a broken down wooden one. The artificial river is still Crown property and still feeds the water gardens of Hampton Court.

William IV made the journey frequently, with his wife Queen Adelaide, across this bridge when travelling to and from Windsor Castle as did every monarch until the advent of the railways. He knew the replacement of the bridge was his responsibility, but instead of a perfunctory standard structure, he gave the village a bridge to be proud of.

The Kings Bridge 2018,

The 16-mile milestone on the Bath Road
between Longford and Colnbrook.
Situated next to a bridge that goes
over the M25. 2018.

The farms of Longford extended beyond the village and across two more rivers and the low-lying flood plains between Longford and Colnbrook where the rickety bridges and swirling mists encouraged highwaymen to lurk. Longford is the western-most village of Middlesex and lies just half a mile from the London Orbital Motorway (M25), which is regarded as the de facto extent of Greater London. At the side of the Bath Road next to the bridge that carries the road over the M25 is the 16th milestone from Hyde Park Corner placed there by the Colnbrook Turnpike Trust in 1741 for the benefit of the coach traveller, but now unseen and unused by present day travellers. It is a remnant of the past glories of an ancient road.

We are now at the end of our walk through Longford. It has been a pleasant stroll past leafy gardens, tranquil waters, and ancient buildings. It is hard to imagine that one day, if the airport is expanded, this might not exist and instead of the rural setting there will be the roar of jet engines and the screech of rubber on tarmac.

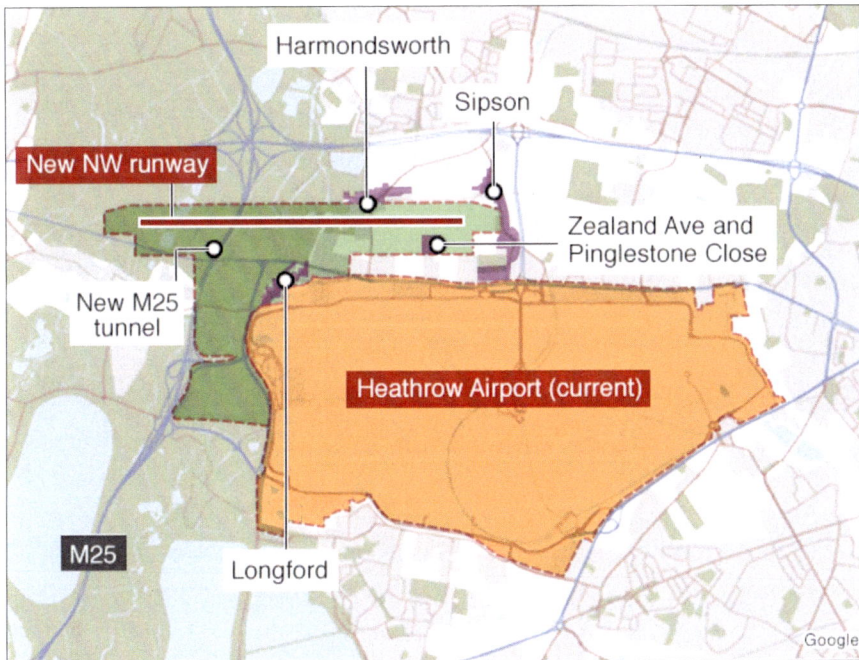

Government plans for the expansion of Heathrow airport.

It is a part of being human that we desire diversity in our environment. It is vital for our well-being that we need to maintain a variety of habitats for humans and nature to survive and enjoy. This is why Conservation Areas, Green Belt land, and the preservation of natural river courses exist, but change is inevitable. Nature, customs, language, and culture are in a constant state of flux but so slowly that we hardly notice. It is sudden change that creates discontent, especially when it is forced upon us. It is this fact that prompts protest and resistance. Since the 1950s the residents of Longford and Harmondsworth have fought off attempts to see their villages destroyed by progress. They are still fighting. Residents, Councils, environmentalists and other interested parties took the government to court on 27 February 2020 and the Court of Appeal ruled that the airport expansion application was unlawful because it did not consider climate change commitments. The judges added that future plans for a third runway could go ahead if the plans fitted with the UK's climate policy. A further appeal was made to the Supreme Court on 16 December 2020, which overturned the previous ruling as the plans met the climate change targets in place at the time. This left the way open for the expected submission of formal planning applications at the end of 2021. The Covid Pandemic has delayed these formal applications, but when they are submitted it is likely to lead to more petitions to the Courts as many diverse groups make their formal arguments regarding the building of the third runway at Heathrow. In the meantime Longford village remains in limbo. The jeopardy continues for the villagers and the structures.

Each generation builds on the achievements of its predecessor and therefore progress is unstoppable, but it is important that we should be able to look back and see what brought us to where we are now. This is what heritage and conservation is all about. It is not just nostalgia, but a way of learning from the past by finding out how human society evolved. By looking at the past through the eyes of the Longford inhabitants we are able to visualise and understand their humanity. This village is living history. History might be the study of the past, but events pervade the present and remain captured forever in the ambiance and fabric of a village. The story of Longford safeguards the history of the community for future generations – whatever its ultimate destiny.

Appendix 1

The Weekly Family Tree

The Weekly Family of Longford

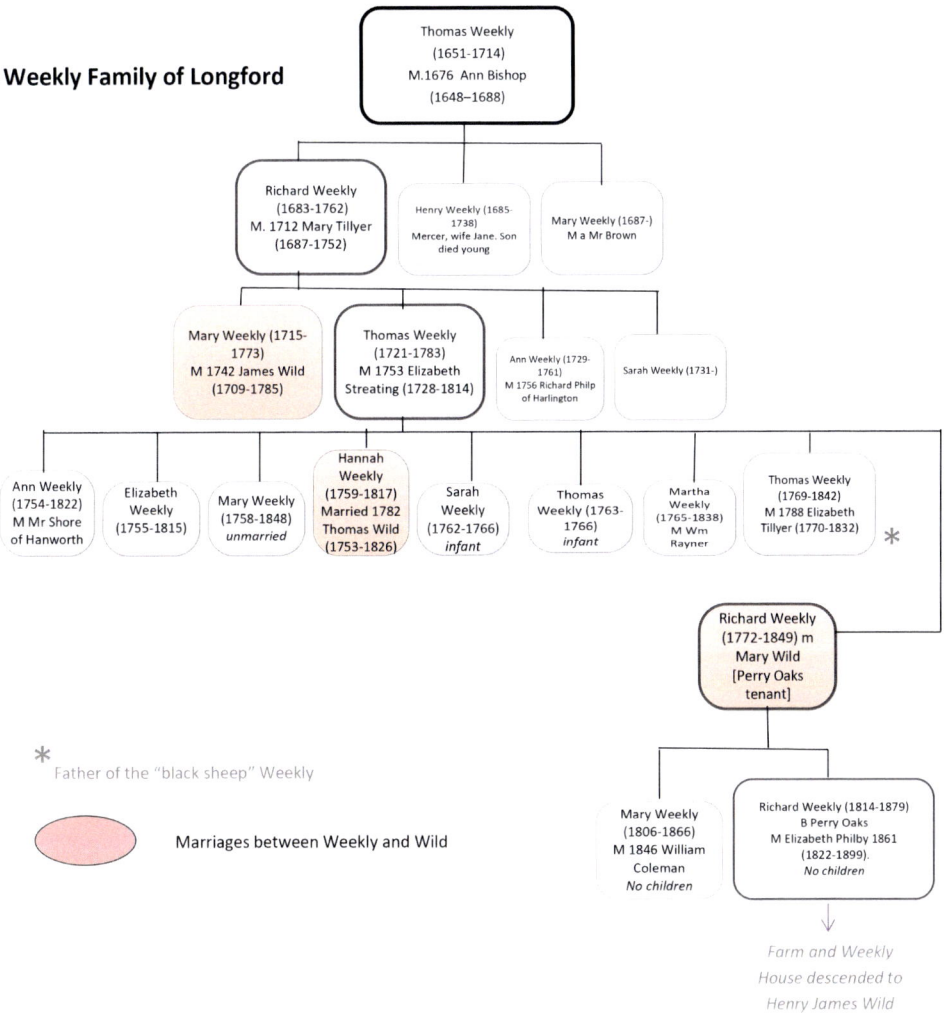

Thomas Weekly
(1651-1714)
M.1676 Ann Bishop
(1648–1688)

Richard Weekly
(1683-1762)
M. 1712 Mary Tillyer
(1687-1752)

Henry Weekly (1685-1738)
Mercer, wife Jane. Son died young

Mary Weekly (1687-)
M a Mr Brown

Mary Weekly (1715-1773)
M 1742 James Wild
(1709-1785)

Thomas Weekly
(1721-1783)
M 1753 Elizabeth
Streating (1728-1814)

Ann Weekly (1729-1761)
M 1756 Richard Philp
of Harlington

Sarah Weekly (1731-)

Ann Weekly
(1754-1822)
M Mr Shore
of Hanworth

Elizabeth
Weekly
(1755-1815)

Mary Weekly
(1758-1848)
unmarried

Hannah
Weekly
(1759-1817)
Married 1782
Thomas Wild
(1753-1826)

Sarah
Weekly
(1762-1766)
infant

Thomas
Weekly (1763-1766)
infant

Martha
Weekly
(1765-1838)
M Wm
Rayner

Thomas Weekly
(1769-1842)
M 1788 Elizabeth
Tillyer (1770-1832)
*

Richard Weekly
(1772-1849) m
Mary Wild
[Perry Oaks
tenant]

* Father of the "black sheep" Weekly

Marriages between Weekly and Wild

Mary Weekly
(1806-1866)
M 1846 William
Coleman
No children

Richard Weekly (1814-1879)
B Perry Oaks
M Elizabeth Philby 1861
(1822-1899).
No children

*Farm and Weekly
House descended to
Henry James Wild*

Appendix 2

The Wild Family Tree

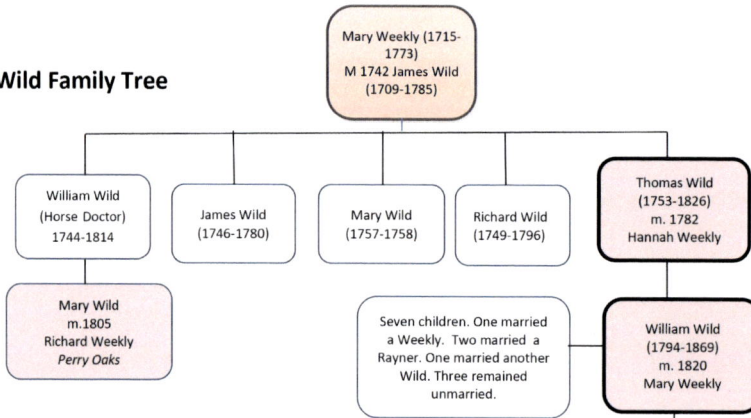

The Wild Family Tree

Mary Weekly (1715-1773)
M 1742 James Wild (1709-1785)

- William Wild (Horse Doctor) 1744-1814
  - Mary Wild m.1805 Richard Weekly *Perry Oaks*
- James Wild (1746-1780)
- Mary Wild (1757-1758)
- Richard Wild (1749-1796)
- Thomas Wild (1753-1826) m. 1782 Hannah Weekly
  - Seven children. One married a Weekly. Two married a Rayner. One married another Wild. Three remained unmarried.
  - William Wild (1794-1869) m. 1820 Mary Weekly

The Longford Wilds

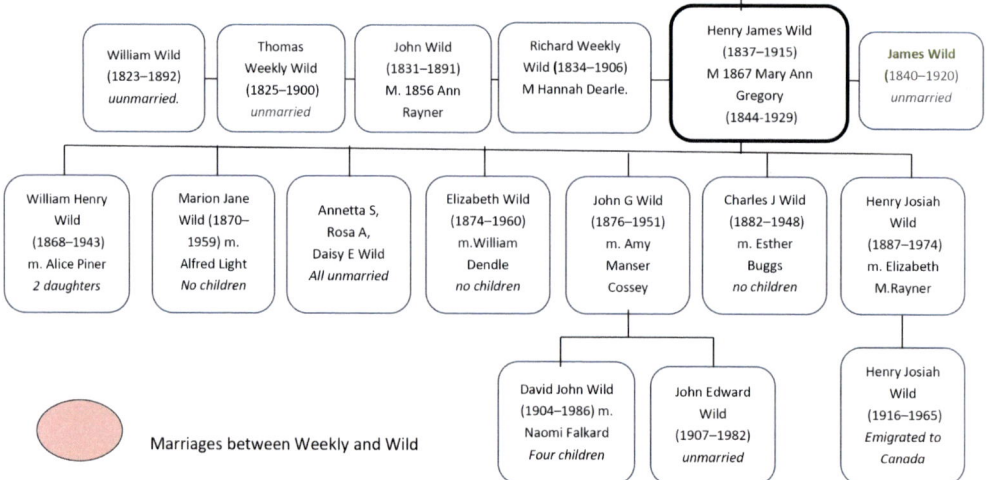

- William Wild (1823–1892) *uunmarried.*
- Thomas Weekly Wild (1825–1900) *unmarried*
- John Wild (1831–1891) M. 1856 Ann Rayner
- Richard Weekly Wild (1834–1906) M Hannah Dearle.
- Henry James Wild (1837–1915) M 1867 Mary Ann Gregory (1844-1929)
- James Wild (1840–1920) *unmarried*

Children of Henry James Wild:
- William Henry Wild (1868–1943) m. Alice Piner *2 daughters*
- Marion Jane Wild (1870–1959) m. Alfred Light *No children*
- Annetta S, Rosa A, Daisy E Wild *All unmarried*
- Elizabeth Wild (1874–1960) m. William Dendle *no children*
- John G Wild (1876–1951) m. Amy Manser Cossey
  - David John Wild (1904–1986) m. Naomi Falkard *Four children*
  - John Edward Wild (1907–1982) *unmarried*
- Charles J Wild (1882–1948) m. Esther Buggs *no children*
- Henry Josiah Wild (1887–1974) m. Elizabeth M.Rayner
  - Henry Josiah Wild (1916–1965) *Emigrated to Canada*

Marriages between Weekly and Wild

Farmed in Colchester after their Heathrow farm was requisitioned

Acknowledgements

This book is a tribute to the people of Longford and Harmondsworth and their tenacity in trying to fight for the preservation of their villages. I am indebted to former Harmondsworth residents who have helped me with my research. I would particularly like to thank Douglas Rust, whose childhood home in Harmondsworth is under threat of demolition, and who shared his memories, and a lifetime's collection of photos and memorabilia with me. His memories of his childhood, the church, and the people, and his wonderful collection of documents have been invaluable in my researches.

I also have to thank Sarah Kwiatkowski whose father, Christopher Challis, was responsible for restoring and preserving the Weekly House into the fine building it is today. Sarah, who spent her early childhood in the Weekly House, has furnished me with a detailed description of the interior at that time, and her memories of the village.

My gratitude goes to friends and family who were brave enough to be the readers of my first drafts and who gave me valuable feedback, especially Margaret Parrish and Anne Bartle. I am grateful for the editorship and encouragement of Stuart Walton and for the support and encouragement of my children, Susan, Peter and Simon. Most of all I have not enough adjectives to describe my wonderful husband, Brian, who has spent many hours reading and re-reading my manuscript and assisting with the photo-editing.

My heart-felt thanks to you all.

The author

Wendy Tibbitts is a historian with a MSc in English Local History from the University of Oxford. Born in West Middlesex she has spent many years researching the area in national and local archives, contemporary newspapers and personal interviews. She regularly blogs about her research at www.wendytibbitts.info. Any comments are always welcome.